The Palace Of Darkened Windows

By

Mary Hastings Bradley

The Palace Of Darkened Windows
by Mary Hastings Bradley

Copyright © 2023

All Rights reserved.

No part of this publication may be reproduced, stored in a retrieval system, or transmitted in any form or by any means, electronic, mechanical, photocopying or Otherwise, without the written permission of the publisher.
The author/editor asserts the moral right to be identified as the author/editor of this work.

ISBN: 978-93-59959-52-8

Published by

DOUBLE 9 BOOKS
2/13-B, Ansari Road
Daryaganj, New Delhi – 110002
info@double9books.com
www.double9books.com
Tel. 011-40042856

This book is under public domain

ABOUT THE AUTHOR

Mary Hastings Bradley was a traveler and author who lived in Chicago from April 19, 1882 to October 25, 1976. Alice Sheldon ("James Tiptree, Jr." author) was her mother. Mary Wilhelmina Hastings was born in Chicago, Illinois, USA in 1882. She earned her bachelor's degree in English from Smith College in 1905. She traveled to Egypt with a cousin after graduation and was inspired to write "The Palace of Darkened Windows" and "The Fortieth Door," which chronicle the lives of Egypt's veiled and secluded women. Both of these stories were later adapted into films, bringing Bradley's work to a wider audience. She met her husband Herbert Edwin Bradley in Oxford while undertaking research for her book The Favor of Kings. Herbert Bradley was a lawyer, large game hunter, adventurer, and explorer who later assisted in the establishment of the Brookfield Zoo. They married in 1910 and had a daughter, Alice, five years later. Mary, Herbert, and Alice journeyed to the Belgian Congo in 1921 and 1922 with her uncle, Carl E. Akeley of the American Museum of Natural History, in search of mountain gorilla specimens for the museum. Her books On the Gorilla Trail, Alice in Jungleland, and Alice in Elephantland detailed these adventures.

CONTENTS

CHAPTER I
　　THE EAVESDROPPER..7

CHAPTER II
　　THE CAPTAIN CALLS..21

CHAPTER III
　　AT THE PALACE 26

CHAPTER IV
　　A SORRY GUEST 35

CHAPTER V
　　WITHIN THE WALLS...46

CHAPTER VI
　　A GIRL IN THE BAZAARS 59

CHAPTER VII
　　BILLY HAS HIS DOUBTS...67

CHAPTER VIII
　　THE MIDNIGHT VISITOR..75

CHAPTER IX
　　A DESPERATE GAME...86

CHAPTER X
　　A MAID AND A MESSAGE..98

CHAPTER XI
　　OVER THE GARDEN WALL...107

CHAPTER XII
　　THE GIRL FROM THE HAREM....................................111

CHAPTER XIII
　　TAKING CHANCES..120

CHAPTER XIV
　　IN THE ROSE ROOM...130

CHAPTER XV
ON THE TRAIL 138

CHAPTER XVI
THE HIDDEN GIRL 146

CHAPTER XVII
AT BAY...151

CHAPTER XVIII
DESERT MAGIC 161

CHAPTER XIX
THE PURSUIT 171

CHAPTER XX
A FRIEND IN NEED 178

CHAPTER XXI
CROSS PURPOSES 189

CHAPTER XXII
UPON THE PYLON 197

CHAPTER XXIII
THE BETTER MAN 207

CHAPTER I
THE EAVESDROPPER

A one-eyed man with a stuffed crocodile upon his head paused before the steps of Cairo's gayest hotel and his expectant gaze ranged hopefully over the thronged verandas. It was afternoon tea time; the band was playing and the crowd was at its thickest and brightest. The little tables were surrounded by travelers of all nations, some in tourist tweeds and hats with the inevitable green veils; others, those of more leisurely sojourns, in white serges and diaphanous frocks and flighty hats fresh from the Rue de la Paix.

It was the tweed-clad groups that the crocodile vender scanned for a purchaser of his wares and harshly and unintelligibly exhorted to buy, but no answering gaze betokened the least desire to bring back a crocodile to the loved ones at home. Only Billy B. Hill grinned delightedly at him, as Billy grinned at every merry sight of the spectacular East, and Billy shook his head with cheerful convincingosity, so the crocodile merchant moved reluctantly on before the importunities of the Oriental rug peddler at his heels.

Then he stopped. His turbaned head, topped by the grotesque, glassy-eyed, glistening-toothed monster, revolved slowly as the Arab's single eye steadily followed a couple who passed by him up the hotel steps. Billy, struck by the man's intense interest, craned forward and saw that one of the couple, now exchanging farewells at the top of the steps, was a girl, a pretty girl, and an American, and the other was an officer in a uniform of considerable green and gold, and obviously a foreigner.

He might be any kind of a foreigner, according to Billy's lax distinctions, that was olive of complexion and very black of hair and eyes. Slender and of medium height, he carried himself with an assurance that bordered upon effrontery, and as he bowed himself down the steps he flashed upon his former companion a smile of triumph that included and seemed to challenge the verandaful of observers.

The girl turned and glanced casually about at the crowded groups that were like little samples of all the nations of the earth, and with no more than a faint awareness of the battery of eyes upon her she passed toward the tables by the railing. She was a slim little fairy of a girl, as fresh as a peach blossom, with a cloud of pale gold hair fluttering round her pretty face, which lent her a most alluring and deceptive appearance of ethereal mildness. She had a soft, satiny, rose-leaf skin which was merely flushed by the heat of the Egyptian day, and her eyes were big and very, very blue. There were touches of that blue here and there upon her creamy linen suit, and a knot of blue upon her parasol and a twist of blue about her Panama hat, so that she could not be held unconscious of the flagrantly bewitching effect. Altogether she was as upsettingly pretty a young person as could be seen in a year's journey, and the glances of the beholders brightened vividly at her approach.

There was one conspicuous exception. This exception was sitting alone at the large table which backed Billy's tiny table into a corner by the railing, and as the girl arrived at that large table the exception arose and greeted her with an air of glacial chill.

"Oh! Am I so terribly late?" said the girl with great pleasantness, and arched brows of surprise at the two other places at the table before which used tea things were standing.

"My sister and Lady Claire had an appointment, so they were obliged to have their tea and leave," stated the young man, with an air of politely endeavoring to conceal his feelings, and failing conspicuously in the endeavor. "They were most sorry."

"Oh, so am I!" declared the girl, in clear and contrite tones which carried perfectly to Billy B. Hill's enchanted ears. "I never dreamed they would have to hurry away."

"They did not hurry, as you call it," and the young man glanced at his watch, "for nearly an hour. It was a disappointment to them."

"Pin-pate!" thought Billy, with intense disgust. "Is he kicking at a two-some?"

"And have you had your tea, too?" inquired the girl, with an air of tantalizing unconcern.

"I waited, naturally, for my guest."

"Oh, not *naturally*!" she laughed. "It must be very unnatural for you to wait for anything. And you must be starving. So am I—do you think there are enough cakes left for the two of us?"

Without directly replying, the young man gave the order to the red-fezzed Arab in a red-girdled white robe who was removing the soiled tea things, and he assisted the girl into a chair and sat down facing her.

Their profiles were given to the shameless Billy, and he continued his rapt observations.

He had immediately recognized the girl as a vision he had seen fluttering around the hotel with an incongruously dismal couple of unyouthful ladies, and he had mentally affixed a magnate's-only-daughter-globe-trotting-with-elderly-friends label to her.

The young man he could not place so definitely. There were a good many tall, aristocratic young Englishmen about, with slight stoops and incipient moustaches. This particular Englishman had hair that was pronouncedly sandy, and Billy suddenly recollected that in lunching at the Savoy the other day he had noticed that young Englishman in company with a sandy-haired lady, not so young, and a decidedly pretty dark-haired girl—it was the girl, of course, who had fixed the group in Billy's crowded impressions. He decided that these ladies were the sister and Lady Claire—and Lady Claire, he judiciously concluded, certainly had nothing on young America.

Young America was speaking. "Don't look so thunderous!" she complained to her irate host. "How do you know I didn't plan to be late so as to have you all to myself?"

This was too derisive for endurance. A dull red burned through the tan on the young Englishman's cheeks and crept up to meet the corresponding warmth of his hair. A leash within him snapped.

"It is simply inconceivable!" burst from him, and then he shut his jaw hard, as if only one last remnant of will power kept a seething volcano, from explosion.

"What is?"

"How any girl—in Cairo, of all places!" he continued to explode in little snorts.

"You are speaking of—?" she suggested.

"Of your walking with that fellow—in broad daylight!"

"Would it have been better in the gloaming?"

The sweet restraint in the young thing's manner was supernatural. It was uncanny. It should have warned the red-headed young man, but oblivious of danger signals, he was plunging on, full steam ahead.

"It isn't as if you didn't know—hadn't been warned."

"You have been so kind," the girl murmured, and poured a cup of tea the Arab had placed at her elbow.

The young man ignored his. The color burned hotter and hotter in his face. Even his hair looked redder.

"The look he gave up here was simply outrageous—a grin of insolent triumph. I'd like to have laid my cane across him!"

The girl's cup clicked against the saucer. "You are horrid!" she declared. "When we were on shipboard Captain Kerissen was very popular among the passengers and I talked with him whenever I cared to. Everyone did. Now that I am in his native city I see no reason to stalk past him when we happen to be going in the same direction. He is a gentleman of rank, a relative of the Khedive who is ruling this country—under your English advice—and he is——"

"A Turk!" gritted out the young man.

"A Turk and proud of it! His mother was French, however, and he was educated at Oxford and he is as cosmopolitan as any man I ever met. It's unusual to meet anyone so close to the reigning family, and it gives one a wonderful insight into things off the beaten track——"

"The beaten—damn!" said the young man, and Billy's heart went out to him. "Oh, I beg pardon, but you—he—I—" So many things occurred to him to say at one and the same time that he emitted a snort of warring and incoherent syllables. Finally, with supreme control, "Do you know that your 'gentleman of rank' couldn't set foot in a gentleman's club in this country?"

"I think it's *mean*!" retorted the girl, her blue eyes very bright and indignant. "You English come here and look down on even the highest members of the country you are pretending to assist. Why do you? When he was at Oxford he went into your English homes."

"English madhouses—for admitting him."

A brief silence ensued.

The girl ate a cake. It was a nice cake, powdered with almonds, but she ate it obliviously. The angry red shone rosily in her cheeks.

The young man took a hasty drink of his tea, which had grown cold in its cup, and pushed it away. Obstinately he rushed on in his mad career.

"I simply cannot understand you!" he declared.

"Does it matter?" said she, and bit an almond's head off.

"It would be bad enough, in any city, but in Cairo—! To permit him to insult you with his company, alone, upon the streets!"

"When you have said insult you have said a little too much," she returned in a small, cold voice of war. "Is there anything against Captain Kerissen personally?"

"Who knows anything about any of those fellows? They are all alike—with half a dozen wives locked up behind their barred windows."

"He isn't married."

"How do you know?"

"I—inferred it."

The Englishman snorted: "According to his custom, you know, it isn't the proper thing to mention his ladies in public."

"You are frightfully unjust. Captain Kerissen's customs are the customs of the civilized world, and he is very anxious to have his country become modernized."

"Then let him send his sisters out walking with fellow officers.... For *him* to walk beside *you*——"

"He was following the custom of my country," said the girl, with maddening superiority. "Since I am an *American* girl——"

The young Englishman said a horrible thing. He said it with immense feeling.

"American goose!" he uttered, then stopped short. Precipitately he floundered into explanation:

"I beg your pardon, but, you know, when you say such bally nonsense as that—! An American girl has no more business to be imprudent than a Patagonian girl. You have no idea how these people regard——"

"Oh, don't apologize," murmured the girl, with charming sweetness. "I don't mind what you say—not in the least."

The outraged man was not so befuddled but what he saw those danger signals now. They glimmered scarlet upon his vision, but his blood was up and he plunged on to destruction with the extraordinary remark, "But isn't there a reason why you should?"

She gazed at him in mock reflection, as if mulling this striking thought presented for her consideration, but her eyes were too sparkly and her cheeks too poppy-pink to substantiate the reflective pose.

"N-no," she said at last, with an impertinent little drawl. "I can't seem to think of any."

He did not pause for innuendo. "You mean you don't give a *piastre* what I think?"

"Not half a *piastre*," she confirmed, in flat defiance.

The young man looked at her. He was over the brink of ruin now; nothing remained of the interesting little affair of the past three weeks but a mangled and lamentable wreck at the bottom of a deep abyss.

Perhaps a shaft of compunction touched her flinty soul at the sight of his aghast and speechless face, for she had the grace to look away. Her gaze encountered the absorbed and excited countenance of Billy B. Hill, and the poppy-pink of her cheeks became poppy-red and she turned her head sharply away. She rose, catching up her gloves and parasol.

"Thank you so much for your tea," she said in a lowered tone to her unfortunate host. "I've had a delicious time.... I'm sorry if I disappointed you by not cowering before your disapproval. Oh, don't bother to come in with me—I know my way to the lift and the band is going to play God Save the King and they need you to stand up and make a showing."

Billy B. Hill stared across at the abandoned young man with supreme sympathy and intimate understanding. He was a nice and right-minded young man and she was an utter minx. She was the daughter of unreason and the granddaughter of folly. She needed, emphatically needed, to be shown. But this Englishman, with his harsh and violently antagonizing way of putting things, was clearly not the man for the need. It took a lighter touch—the hand of iron in the velvet glove, as it were. It took a keener spirit, a softer humor.

Billy threw out his chest and drew himself up to his full five feet eleven and one-half inches, as he passed indoors and sought the hotel register, for he felt within himself the true equipment for that delicate mission. He fairly panted to be at it.

Fate was amiable. The hotel clerk, coerced with a couple of gold-banded ones with the real fragrance, permitted Billy to learn that the blue-eyed one's name was Beecher, Arlee Beecher, and that she was in the company of two ladies entitled Mrs. and Miss Eversham. The Miss Eversham was quite old enough to be entitled otherwise. They were occupied, the clerk reported, with nerves and dissatisfaction. Miss Beecher appeared occupied in part— with a correspondence that would swamp a foreign office.

Now it is always a question whether being at the same hotel does or does not constitute an introduction. Sometimes it does; sometimes it does not. When the hotel is a small and inexpensive arrangement in Switzerland, where the advertised view of the Alpenglühen is obtained by placing the chairs in a sociable circle on the sidewalk, then usually it does. When the hotel is a large and expensive affair in gayest Cairo, where the sunny and shady side rub elbows, and gamesters and débutantes and touts and school teachers and vivid ladies of conspicuous pasts and stout gentlemen of exhilarated presents abound, in fact where innocent sightseers and initiated traffickers in human frailties are often indistinguishable, then decidedly it does not.

But fate, still smiling, dropped a silver shawl in Billy's path as he was trailing his prey through the lounge after dinner. The shawl belonged, most palpably, to a German lady three feet ahead of him, but gripping it triumphantly, he bounded over the six feet which separated him from the Eversham-Beecher triangle and with marvelous self-restraint he touched Miss Eversham on the arm.

"You dropped this?" he inquired.

Miss Eversham looked surprisedly at Billy and uncertainly at the shawl, which she mechanically accepted. "Why I—I didn't remember having it with me," she hesitated.

"I noticed you were wearing one other evenings," said Billy, the Artful, "so I thought——"

"You know whether this is yours or not, don't you, Clara?" interposed the mother.

"They all look alike," murmured Clara Eversham, eying helplessly the silver border.

Billy permitted himself to look at Miss Beecher. That young person was looking at him and there was a disconcerting gaiety in her expression, but at sight of him she turned her head, faintly coloring. He judged she recalled his unmannerly eavesdropping that afternoon.

"Pardon—excuse me—but that is to me belonging," panted an agitated but firm voice behind them, and two stout and beringed hands seized upon the glittering shawl in Miss Eversham's lax grasp. "It but just now off me falls," and the German lady looked belligerent accusation upon the defrauding Billy.

There was a round of apologetic murmurs, unacknowledged by the recipient, who plunged away with her shawl, as if fearing further designs upon it. Billy laughed down at the Evershams.

"I feel like a porch climber making off with her belongings. But I had seen you with——"

"I do think I had mine this evening, after all," murmured Clara, with a questioning glance after the departing one.

"An uncultured person!" stated Mrs. Eversham.

Miss Beecher said nothing at all. Her faint smile was mockingly derisive.

"Anyway you must let me get you some coffee," Billy most inconsequentially suggested, beckoning to the red-girdled Mohammed with his laden tray, and because he was young and nice looking and evidently a gentleman from their part of the world and his evening clothes fitted perfectly and had just the right amount of braid, Mrs. Eversham made no objection to the circle of chairs he hastily collected about a taborette, and let him hand them their coffee and send Mohammed for the cream which Miss Eversham declared was indispensable for her health.

"If I take it clear I find it keeps me awake," she confided, and Billy deplored that startling and lamentable circumstance, and passed Mrs. Eversham the sugar and wondered if they could be the Philadelphia Evershams of whom he had heard his mother speak, and regretted that they were not, for then they would know who he was—William B. Hill of Alatoona, New York. He found it rather stupid traveling alone. Of course one met many Americans, but——

Mrs. Eversham took up that "but" most eagerly, and recounted multiple and deplorable instances of nasal countrywomen doing the East and monopolizing the window seats in compartments, and Miss Eversham supplied details and corrections.

Still Miss Beecher said nothing. She had a dreamy air of not belonging to the conversationalists. But from an inscrutable something in her appearance, Billy judged she was not unentertained by his sufferings.

At the first pause he addressed her directly. "And how do you like Cairo?" was his simple question. That ought, he reflected, to be an entering wedge.

The young lady did not trouble to raise her eyes. "Oh, very much," said she negligently, sipping her coffee.

"Oh, very well!" said Billy haughtily to himself. If being her fellow countryman in a strange land, and obviously a young and cultivated countryman whom it would be a profit and pleasure for any girl to know, wasn't enough for her—what was the use? He ought to get up and go away. He intended to get up and go away—immediately.

But he didn't. Perhaps it was the shimmery gold hair, perhaps it was the flickering mischief of the downcast lashes, perhaps it was the loveliness of the soft, white throat and slenderly rounded arms. Anyway he stayed. And when the strain of waltz music sounded through the chatter of voices about them and young couples began to stroll to the long parlors, Billy jumped to his feet with a devastating desire that totally ignored the interminable wanderings of Clara Eversham's complaints.

"Will you dance this with me?" he besought of Miss Arlee Beecher, with a direct gaze more boyishly eager than he knew.

For an agonizing moment she hesitated. Then, "I think I will," she concluded, with sudden roguery in her smile.

Stammering a farewell to the Evershams, he bore her off.

It would be useless to describe that waltz. It was one of the ecstatic moments which Young Joy sometimes tosses from her garlanded arms. It was one of the sudden, vivid, unforgettable delights which makes youth a fever and a desire. For Billy it was the wildest stab the sex had ever dealt him. For though this was perhaps the nine thousand nine hundred and ninety-ninth girl with whom he had danced, it was as if he had discovered music and motion and girls for the first time.

The music left them by the windows.

"Thank you," said Billy under his breath.

"You didn't deserve it," said the girl, with a faint smile playing about the corners of her lips. "You know you stared—scandalously."

Grateful that she mentioned only the lesser sin, "Could I help it?" he stammered, by way of a finished retort.

The smile deepened, "And I'm afraid you listened!"

He stared down at her anxiously. "Will you like me better if I didn't?" he inquired.

"I shan't like you at all if you did."

"Then I didn't hear a word.... Besides," he basely uttered, "you were entirely in the right!"

"I should think I was!" said Arlee Beecher very indignantly. "The very notion—! Captain Kerissen is a very nice young man. He is going to get me an invitation to the Khedive's ball."

"Is that a very crumby affair?"

"Crumby? It's simply gorgeous! Everyone is mad over it. Most tourists simply read about it, and it is too perfect luck to be invited! Only the English who have been presented at court are invited and there's a girl at the Savoy

Hotel I've met—Lady Claire Montfort—who wasn't presented because she was in mourning for her grandmother last year, and she is simply furious about it. An old dowager here said that there ought to be similar distinctions among the Americans—that only those who had been presented at the White House ought to be recognized. Fancy making the White House a social distinction!" laughed the daughter of the Great Republic.

"I wonder," said Billy, "if I met a nice Turkish lady, whether she would get me an invitation? Then we could have another waltz— —"

"There aren't any Turkish ladies there," uttered Miss Beecher rebukingly. "Don't you know that? When they are on the Continent—those that are ever taken there—they may go to dances and things, but here they can't, although some of them are just as modern as you or I, I've heard, and lots more educated."

"You speak," he protested, "from a superficial acquaintance with my academic accomplishments."

"Are you so very—proficient?"

"I was—I am Phi Beta Kappa," he sadly confessed.

Her laugh rippled out. "You don't look it," she cheered.

"Oh, no, I don't look it," he complacently agreed. "That's the lamp in the gloom. But I am. I couldn't help it. I was curious about things and I studied about them and faculties pressed honors upon me. I am even here upon a semi-learned errand. I wanted to have a look at the diggings a friend of mine is making at Thebes and several looks at the dam at Assouan, for I am by way of being an engineer myself—a beginning engineer."

"You have been up the Nile, then?"

"Yes, I'm just back. Now I'm going to see something of Cairo before I leave."

"We start up the Nile day after to-morrow," said she.

"The day after—" he stopped.

'Twas ever thus. Fate never did one good turn but she sneaked back and jabbed him unawares. She was a tricksy jade.

"That's—that's gloomy luck," said Billy, and felt outraged. "Why, how about that Khedive ball thing?"

"Oh, that's when we come back."

She was coming back, then. Hope lifted her head.

"When will that be?"

"In three weeks. It takes about three weeks to go up to the first cataract and back, doesn't it?"

"Yes, by boat," he said, adding hopefully, "but lots of people like the express trains better. They—they don't keep you so long on the way."

"Oh, I hate trains," said she cheerfully.

Three weeks ... Ruefully he surveyed the desolation. "I ought to be gone by then," he muttered.

A trifle startled, the girl looked up at him. As he was not looking at her, but staring moodily into what was then black vacancy, her look lingered and deepened. She saw a most bronzed and hardy looking young man, tall and broad-shouldered, with gray eyes, wide apart under straight black brows, and black hair brushed straight back from a wide forehead. She saw a rugged nose, a likeable mouth, and an abrupt and aggressive chin, saved somehow from grimness by a deep cleft in the blunt end of it.... She thought he was a very *stirring* looking young man. Undoubtedly he was a very sudden young man—if he meant one bit of what he intimated.

Feminine-wise, she mocked.

"What a calamity!"

"Yes, for me," said Billy squarely. "You know it's—it's awfully jolly to meet a girl from home out here!"

"A girl from *home*——!"

"Well, all America seems home from this place. And I shouldn't be surprised if we knew a lot of the same people ... You can get a good line on me that way, you know," he laughed. "Now I went to Williams and then to Boston Tech., and there must be acquaintances——"

"Don't!" said Arlee, with a laughing gesture of prohibition. "We probably have thousands of the same acquaintances, and you would turn out to be some one I knew everything about—perhaps the first fiancé of my roommate whose letters I used to help her answer."

"Where did you go to school?"

"At Elm Court School, near New York. For just a year."

He shook his head with an air of relief. "Never was engaged to anybody's roommate there.... But if you'd rather not have my background painted——"

"*Much* rather not," said the girl gaily. "Why, half the romance, I mean the fun, of meeting people abroad is *not* knowing anything about them beforehand."

The music was beginning again. Unwillingly the remembrance of the outer world beat back into Billy's mind. Unhappily he became aware that the room appeared blackened with young men in evening clothes, staring ominously his way.

Squarely he stood in front of the girl. "I think this is the encore to our dance," he told her with a little smile.

She shook her pretty head laughingly at him—and then yielded to his clasping hands. "But we must dance back to the Evershams," she demurred. "It is time for us to go to our concert."

But Billy had no intention of relinquishing her before the music ceased. It was a one step, and it carried them with it in a gaiety of rhythm to which the girl gave herself with the light-hearted abandon of a romping child. Her light feet seemed scarcely to brush the floor; the delicate flush of her cheeks deepened with the stirring blood; her lips parted breathlessly over white little teeth, and when her eyes, intensely blue, met Billy's, the smile in them quickened in sparkling radiance. She was the very spirit of the dance; she was Youth and Joy incarnate. And the heart behind the white shirt bosom near which her fairy hair was floating began to pitch and toss like a laboring ship in the very devil of a sea.

"I think I'll go up the Nile again," said Billy irrelevantly.

She laughed elfishly at him, her head swaying faintly with the rhythm.

"Three weeks," said Billy under his breath, "that's twenty-one days—at ten dollars a day. Now I wonder how many hours—or moments—that rash outlay would assure?"

"You miser! You calculating— —"

"You have to calculate—when you're an engineer."

"But to be sure spoils the charm! Now I—I do things on impulse."

"If you will only have the impulse to dance with me—on the Nile— —"

"Why not risk it?" she challenged lightly, arrant mischief in her eyes. She added, in mocking tone, "There's a moon."

"That's a clincher," said he, with an air of decision. A faint question dwelt in the look she gave him. It was ridiculous to think he meant anything he was saying, but—she felt suddenly a little confused and shy under that light-hearted young gaiety which took every man's friendly admiration happily for granted.

In silence they finished the dance, and this time the music failed them when they were near the wide entrance to the room where the Evershams, beckoning specters, were standing.

"I'm keeping them waiting," said the girl, with a note of concern which she had not shown over her performance in that line earlier in the day. But Billy had no time for humorous comparisons.

"When can I see you again?" he demanded bluntly. "Can I see you to-morrow?"

"To-morrow is a very busy day," she parried.

"But the evening——?"

"I shall be here," she admitted.

"And could I—could I take you—and the Evershams, of course—somewhere, anywhere, you'd like to go? If there's any other concert——"

She shook her head. "We leave bright and early the next morning, and I know Mrs. Eversham will want her rest. I think they would rather stay here in the hotel after dinner."

"But you will keep a little time for me?" Billy urged. "Of course, staying in the same hotel, I can't take my hat and go and make a formal call on you—but that's the result I'm after."

They had paused, to finish this colloquy, a few feet away from the ladies, who were regarding with dark suspicion this interchange of lowered tones.

Suddenly Arlee raised her eyes and gave Billy a quick look, questioning, shyly serious.

"I shall be here—and you can call on me," she promised, and bade him farewell.

She left him deliriously, inexplicably, foolishly in spirits. He plunged his hands in his pockets and squared his shoulders; he wanted to whistle, he wanted to sing, he wanted to do anything to vent the singular hilarity which possessed him.

Then he saw, across the room, a sandy-haired young man regarding him with dour intentness, and the spectacle, instead of feeding his joy, sent conjecturing chills down his spine. His bubble was pricked. Suppose, ran the horrid thought, suppose she was simply paying off the Englishman? Girls, even blue-eyed, angel-haired girls of cherubic aspect, have not been unknown to perform such deeds of darkness! And this particular girl had mischief in her eyes.... The thought was unpleasantly likely. What had he, Billy B. Hill, of New York—State—to offer to casual view worthy of competition with the presumable advantages of a young Englishman whose sister was staying with a Lady Claire? Perhaps the fellow himself had a title....

Considerably dashed, he went out to consult the register upon that point.

CHAPTER II
THE CAPTAIN CALLS

Now, when the card of Captain Kerissen was handed to Miss Arlee Beecher the next afternoon, when she sauntered in from the sunny out-of-doors and paused at the desk for the voluminous harvest of letters the last mail had brought, and furthermore the information was added that the Captain was waiting, little Miss Beecher's first thought was the resentful appreciation that the Captain was overdoing it.

She hesitated, then, with her hands full of letters and parasol, she crossed the hall into the reception room. She intended to let her caller see his mistake, so with her burdened hands avoiding a handclasp, she greeted him and stood waiting, with eyes of inquiry upon him.

The young man smiled secretly to himself. He was a young man not without experience in ladies' moods and he had a very shrewd idea that somebody had been making remarks, but he did not permit a hint of any perception of the coolness of her manner to impair the impeccable suavity of his.

"Will you accord me two moments of your time that I may give you two messages?" he inquired, and Arlee felt suddenly ill-bred before his gentle courtesy and she sat down abruptly upon the edge of the nearest chair.

The Captain placed one near her and seated himself, with a clank of his dangling scabbard. He was really a very handsome young man, though his features were too finely finished to please a robust taste, and there was a hint of insolence and cruelty about the nose and mouth—though this an inexperienced and light-hearted young tourist of one and twenty did not more than vaguely perceive.

"They are, the both, of the ball of the Khedive," he continued in his English, which was, though amazingly fluent and ready, a literal sounding translation of the French, which was in reality his mother tongue. "My sister thinks she can arrange that invitation. You are sure that you will be returned at Cairo, then?"

"Oh, dear, yes! I would come back by train," Arlee declared eagerly, "rather than miss that wonderful ball!"

She thought how astonished a certain red-headed young Englishman would be to see her at that ball, and how fortunate she was compared to his haughty and disappointed friend, the Lady Claire, and the chill of her resentment against the Captain's intrusion vanished like snow in the warmth of her gratitude.

"Good!" He smiled at her with a flash of white teeth. "Then my sister herself will see one of the household of the Khedive and request the invitation for you and for your chaperon, the Madame——"

"Eversham."

"Eversham. She will be included for you, but not the daughter—no?"

"Is that asking too much?" said Arlee hesitantly. "Miss Eversham would feel badly to be left out.... But, anyway, I'm not sure that I shall be with them then," she reflected.

"Not with them?" The young man leaned forward, his eyes curiously intent upon her.

"No, I may be with some other friends. You see, it's this way—I didn't come abroad with the Evershams in the first place. I came in the fall with a school friend and her mother to see Italy. The Evershams were friends of theirs and were stopping at the same hotel, and since my friends were called back very suddenly, the Evershams asked me to go on to Egypt with them. It was very nice of them, for I'm a dreadful bother," said Arlee, dimpling.

"But you speak of leaving them?" he said.

"Oh, yes, I may do that as soon as some other friends of mine, the Maynards, reach here. They are coming here on their way to the Holy Land and I want to take that trip with them. And then I'll probably go back to America with them."

The Turkish captain stared at her, his dark eyes rather inscrutable, though a certain wonder was permitted to be felt in them.

"You American girls—your ways are absolute like the decrees of Allah!" he laughed softly. "But tell me—what will your father and your mother say to this so rapidly changing from the one chaperon to the other?"

"I haven't any father or mother," said the girl. "I have a big, grown-up, married brother, and he knows I wouldn't change from one party unless it was all right." She laughed amusedly at the young man's comic gesture of bewilderment. "You think we American girls are terribly independent."

"I do, indeed," he avowed, "but," and he inclined his dark head in graceful gallantry, "it is the independence of the princess of the blood royal."

A really nice way of putting it, Arlee thought, contrasting the chivalrous homage of this Oriental with the dreadful "American goose!" of the Anglo-Saxon.

"But tell me," he went on, studying her face with an oddly intent look, "do these friends now, the Evershams, know these others, the — the — —"

"Maynards," she supplied. "Oh, no, they have never met each other. The Maynards are friends I made at school. And Brother has never met them either," she added, enjoying his humorous mystification.

"The decrees of Allah!" he murmured again. "But I will promise you an invitation for your chaperon and arrange for the name of the lady later — *n'est-ce-pas?*"

"Yes, I will know as soon as I return from the Nile. You are going to a lot of bother, you and your sister," declared Arlee gratefully.

"I go to ask you to take a little trouble, then, for that sister," said the Captain slowly. "She is a widow and alone. Her life is — is *triste* — melancholy is your English word. Not much of brightness, of new things, of what you call pleasure, enters into that life, and she enjoys to meet foreign ladies who are not — what shall I say? — seekers after curiosities, who think our ladies are strange sights behind the bars. You know that the Europeans come uninvited to our wedding receptions and make the strange questions!"

Arlee had the grace to blush, remembering her own avid desire to make her way into one of those receptions, where the doors of the Moslem harem are thrown open to the feminine world in widespread hospitality.

The Captain went on, slowly, his eyes upon her, "But she knows that you are not one of those others and has requested that you do her the grace to call upon her. I assured her that you would, for I know that you are kind, and also," with an air of naïve pride which Arlee found admirable in him, "it is not all the world who is invited to the home of our — our *haut-monde*, you understand?... And then it will interest you to see how our ladies live in that seclusion which is so droll to you. Confess you have heard strange stories," and he smiled in quizzical raillery upon her.

The girl's flush deepened with the memory of the confusing stories her head was stuffed with; tales of the bloomers, the veils, the cushions, the sweetmeats, the *nargueils*, the rose baths of the old *régime* were jostled by the stories of the French nurses and English governesses and the Paris fashions of the new era. She had listened breathlessly, with her eager young zest in life, to the amazing and contradictory narrations of the tourists who were every whit as ignorant as she was, and her curiosity was on fire to see for herself. She felt that a chance in a thousand had come her lucky way.

"I shall be very glad to call," she told him, "just as soon as I return from the Nile."

His face showed his disappointment—and a certain surprise. "But not before?"

"Why, I go to-morrow morning, you know," said Arlee. "And——"

"It would be better—because of the invitation," he said slowly, hesitantly, with the air of one who does not wish to importune. "My sister would like to ask for one who is known personally to herself. She thought you could render her a few minutes this afternoon."

"This afternoon?" Arlee thought quickly. "I ought to be packing," she murmured, "my things aren't all ready.... And Mrs. Eversham is at the bazaars again and dear knows when she will be back."

Just for an instant a spark burned in the black eyes watching the girl, and then was gone, and when she raised her own eyes, perplexed and considering, to him, she saw only the same courteously attentive, but faintly indolent regard as before. Then the young man smiled, with an air of frank amusement.

"That would seem to be a dispensation!" he laughed. "My sister and the Madame Eversham—no, they would not be sympathetic!... But if you can come," he went on quickly, leaning forward and speaking in a hurried, lowered tone, "it can be arranged in an instant. I am to telephone to my sister and she will send her car for you. It is not far and it does not need but a few minutes for the visit—unless you desire. I cannot escort you in the car—it is not *en règle*—but I will come to the house and present you and then depart, that you ladies may exchange the confidences.... Does that programme please you?"

"I—I don't know your sister's name," said Arlee.

He smiled. "Nechedil Azade Seniha—she is the widow of Tewfik Pasha. But say Madame simply to her—that will suffice. Shall I, then, telephone her?"

Just an instant Arlee hesitated, while her imagination fluttered about the thought like humming-birds about sweets. Already she was thinking of the story she could have to tell to her fellow travelers here and to the people at home. It was a chance, she repeated to herself, in a thousand, and the familiar details of phones and motors seemed to rob its suddenness of all strangeness.... Besides, there was that matter of the Khedive's ball. It would be very ungracious to refuse a few minutes' visit to a lady who was going to so much trouble for her.

"I will be ready in ten minutes," she promised, springing to her feet.

The forgotten letters scattered like a fall of snow and the Captain stooped quickly for them, hiding the flash of exultation in his face. He thrust the letters rather hurriedly upon her.

"Good!... But need you wait for a *toilette* when you are so—so *ravissante* now?"

He gazed with frank appreciation at the linen suit she was wearing, but she shook her head laughingly at him. "To be interesting to a foreign lady I must have interesting clothes," she avowed. "I shan't be ten minutes—really."

"Then the car will be in waiting. I will give your name to the chauffeur and he will approach you." He thought a minute, and then said, quickly, "And I will leave a note for Madame Eversham at the desk to inform her of your destination and to express my regret that she is not here to accept the invitation." His voice was flavored with droll irony. "In ten minutes—*bien sûr?*"

She confirmed it most positively, and it really was not quite eighteen when she stepped out on the veranda, a vision, a positively devastating vision in soft and filmy white, with a soft and filmy hat all white lace and a pink rose. It is to be hoped that she did not know how she looked. Otherwise there would have been no excuse for her and she should have been summarily haled to the nearest justice, with all other breakers of the peace, and condemned to good conduct and Shaker bonnets for the rest of her life. The rose on the hat, with such a rose of a face beneath the hat, was sheer wanton cruelty to mankind.

It brought the heart into the throat of one young man who was reading his paper beneath the striped awning, when he was not watching, cat-like, the streets and the hotel door. He dropped the paper with an agitated rustle and half rose to his feet; his eyes, alert and humorous gray-blue eyes, lighted with eagerness. His hand flew up to his hat.

He did not need to take it off. She did not even see him. She was hurrying forward to the steps, following a long, lean Arab, some dragoman, apparently, in resplendent pongee robes, who opened the door of a limousine for her. The next instant he slammed the door upon her, mounted the front seat, and the car rolled away.

CHAPTER III
AT THE PALACE

That limousine utterly routed the tiny little qualm which had been furtively worming into Arlee's thrill of adventure. Nothing very strange or out-of-the-way, she thought, could be connected with such a modern car; it presented every symptom of effete civilization. Against the upholstery of delicate gray flamed the scarlet poinsettias hanging in wall vases of crystal overlaid with silver tracery; the mirror which confronted her was framed in silver, and beneath it a tiny cabinet revealed a frivolous store of powders and pins and scents. Decidedly the Oriental widow of said sequestration had a car very much up to times. The only difference which it presented from the cars of any modern city or of any modern lady was in the smallness of the window panes, whose contracted size confirmed the stories of the restrictions which Arlee had been told were imposed upon Moslem ladies by even those emancipated masculine relatives who conceded cars.

She peered out of the diminutive windows at the throng of life in the unquiet streets as they halted for the passing of a camel laden with bricks and stones from a demolished building; the poor thing teetered precariously past under such a back-breaking load that the girl felt it would have been a mercy to add the last straw and be done with it. After it bobbed what was apparently an animated load of hay, so completely were this other camel's legs hidden by his smothering burden.

Then the car shot impatiently forward, passing a dog cart full of fair-haired English children, the youngest clasped in the arms of a dark-skinned nurse, and behind the cart ran an indefatigable *sais*, bare-legged and sinewy, his red headdress and gold-embroidered jacket and blue bloomers flashing in the sun. On the sidewalk a party of American tourists were capitulating to a post-card vender, and ahead of them a victoria load of German sightseers careened around the corner in the charge of a determined dragoman.

Arlee smiled in happy superiority over these mere outsiders. *She* was not going about the beaten track, peeping at mosques and tombs and bazaars and windows; she was penetrating into the real life of this fascinating city, getting behind the grills and veils to glimpse the inner secrets.

She thought, with a deepening of the sparkle in her blue eyes and a defiant lifting of the pointed chin, of a certain sandy-haired young Englishman and how wrong and reasonless and narrow and jealous were his strictures upon her politeness to young Turks, and she thought with a sense of vindicated pride of how thoroughly that nice young man who had managed to introduce himself last night had endorsed her views. Americans understood. And then her thoughts lingered about Billy and she caught herself wondering just how much he did mean about coming up the Nile again. For upon happening to meet Billy that morning—Billy had devoted two hours and a half to the accident of that happening!—he had joyously mentioned that he was trying to buy out another man's berth upon that boat. It wasn't so much his wanting to come that was droll—teasing sprites of girls with peach-blossom prettiness are not unwonted to the thunder of pursuing feet—but the frank and cheery way he had of announcing it. Not many men had the courage of their desires. Not any men that little Miss Arlee had yet met had the frankness of such courage. And because all women love the adventurous spirit and are woefully disappointed in its masculine manifestations, she felt a gay little eagerness which she would have refused to own. It would be rather fun to see more of him—on the Nile—while Robert Falconer was sulking away in Cairo. And then when she returned she would surprise and confound that misguided young Englishman with her unexpected—to him—presence at the Khedive's ball. And after that—but her thoughts were lost in haziness then. Only the ball stood out distinct and glittering and fairylike.

Thinking all these brightly revengeful thoughts she had been oblivious to the many turnings of the motor, though it had occurred to her that they were taking more time than the car had needed to appear, and now she looked out the window and saw that they were in a narrow street lined with narrow houses, whose upper stories, slightly projecting in little bays, all presented the elaborately grilled façades of *mashrubiyeh* work which announced the barred quarters of the women, the *haremlik*.

Arlee loved to conjure up a romantic thrill for the mysterious East by reflecting that behind these obscuring screens were women of all ages and conditions, neglected wives and youthful favorites, eager girls and revolting brides, whose myriad eyes, bright or dull or gay or bitter, were peering into the tiny, cleverly arranged mirrors which gave them a tilted view of the streets. It was the sense of these watching eyes, these hidden women, which made those screened windows so stirring to her young imagination.

The motor whirled out of the narrow street and into one that was much wider and lined by houses that were detached and separated, apparently, by gardens, for there was a frequent waving of palms over the high walls which lined the road. The street was empty of all except an old orange vender, shuffling slowly along, with a cartwheel of a tray on her head, piled with yellow fruit shining vividly in the hot sun. The quiet and the solitude gave a sense of distance from the teeming bazaars and tourist-ridden haunts, which breathed of seclusion and aloofness.

The car stopped and Arlee stepped out before a great house of ancient stone which rose sharply from the street. A high, pointed doorway, elaborately carved, was before her, arching over a dark wooden door heavily studded with nails. Overhead jutted the little balconies of *mashrubiyeh*. She had no more than a swift impression of the old façade, for immediately a doorkeeper, very vivid in his Oriental blue robes and his English yellow leather Oxfords, flung open the heavy door.

Stepping across the threshold, with a sudden excited quickening of the senses, in which so many things were mingled that the misgiving there had scarcely time to make itself felt, Arlee found herself in a spacious vestibule, marble floored and inlaid with brilliant tile. She had just a glimpse of an inner court between the high arches opposite, and then her attention was claimed by Captain Kerissen, who sprang forward with a flash of welcome in his eyes that was like a leap of palpable light.

"You are come!" he said, in a voice which was that of a man almost incredulous of his good fortune. Then he bowed very formally in his best military fashion, straight-backed from the waist, heels stiffly together. "I welcome you," he said. "My sister is rejoiced.... This stair—if you please."

He waved to a stairway on the left, a small, steep affair, which Arlee ascended slowly, a sense of strangeness mounting with her, in spite of her confident bearing. She had not realized how odd it would feel to be in this foreign house with the Captain at her heels.

There was a door at the top of the stairs standing open into a long, spacious room which seemed shrouded in twilight after the sunflooded court. One entire side of the room was a brown, lace-like screen of *mashrubiyeh* windows; wide divans stretched beside them, and at the end of the room, facing Arlee, was a throne-like chair raised on a small dais and canopied with heavy silks.

By one of the windows a woman was squatting, a short, stout, turbaned figure, striking a few notes on a tambourine and crooning softly to herself in a low guttural. She raised her head without rising, to look at the entering couple, and for a startled second Arlee had the half hysterical fear that this squatting soloist was the *triste* and aristocratic representative of the *haut-monde* of Moslem which the Captain had brought her to see, but the next instant another figure appeared in a doorway and came slowly toward them.

Flying to the winds went Arlee's anticipations of somber elegance. She saw the most amazingly vivid creature that she had ever laid eyes on—a woman, young, though not in her first youth, penciled, powdered, painted, her hair a brilliant red, her gown a brilliant green. After the first shock of scattering amazement, Arlee became intensely aware of a pair of yellow-brown eyes confronting her with a faintly smiling and rather mocking interrogation. The dark of *kohl* about the eyes emphasized a certain slant *diablérie* of line and a faint penciling connected with the high and supercilious arch of the brows. Henna flamed on the pointed tips of the fingers blazoned with glittering rings, and Arlee fancied the brilliance of the hair was due to this same generous assistance of nature.

"My soul!" thought the girl swiftly, "they *do* get themselves up!"

The Captain had stepped forward, speaking quickly in Turkish, with a hard-sounding rattle of words. The sister glanced at him with a deepening of that curious air of mockery and let fall two words in the same tongue. Then she turned to Arlee.

"*Je suis enchantée—d'avoir cet honneur—cet honneur inattendu— —*"

She did not look remarkably enchanted, however. The eyes that played appraisingly over her pretty caller had a quality of curious hardness, of race hostility, perhaps, the antagonism of the East for the West, the Old for the New. Not all the modernity of clothes, of manners, of language, affected what Arlee felt intensely as the strange, vivid foreignness of her.

"My sister does not speak English—she has not the occasion," the Captain was quickly explaining.

"*Gracious*" thought Arlee, in dismay. She had no illusions about her French; it did very well in a shop or a restaurant, but it was apt to peeter out feebly in polite conversation. Certainly it was no vessel for voyaging in untried seas. There were simply loads of things, she thought discouragedly, the things she wanted most to ask, that she would not be able to find words for.

Aloud she was saying, "I am so glad to have the honor of being here. I am only sorry that my French is so bad. But perhaps you can understand— —"

"I understand," assented the Turkish woman, faintly smiling.

The Captain had brought forward little gilt chairs of a French design which seemed oddly out of place in this room of the East, and the three seated themselves. Out of place, too, seemed the grand piano which Arlee's eyes, roving now past her hostess, discovered for the first time.

"It was so kind of you," began Arlee again as the silence seemed to be politely waiting upon her, "to send your automobile for me."

"Ah—my automobile!" echoed the woman on a higher note, and laughed, with a flash of white teeth between carmined lips. "It pleased you?"

"Oh, yes, it is splendid!" the girl declared, in sincere praise. "It is one of the most beautiful I have ever seen."

"I enjoy it very much—that automobile!" said the other, again laughing, with a quick turn of her eyes toward the brother.

Negligently, rather caressingly, the young man murmured a few Turkish words. She shrugged and leaned back in her chair, the flash of animation gone. "And Cairo—that pleases you?" she asked of Arlee.

Stumbling a little in her French, but resolutely rushing over the difficulties, Arlee launched into the expression of how very much it pleased her. Everything was beautiful to her. The color, the sky, the mosques, the minarets, the Nile, the pyramids—they were all wonderful. And the view from the Great Pyramid—and then she stopped, wondering if that were not beyond her hostess's experience.

In confirmation of the thought the Turkish lady smiled, with an effect of disdain. "Ascend the pyramids—that is indeed too much for us," she said. "But nothing is too much for you Americans—no?"

Her curious glance traveled slowly from Arlee's flushed and lovely face, under the rose-crowned hat, down over the filmy white gown and white-gloved hands clasping an ivory card case, to the small, white-shod feet and silken ankles. Arlee did not resent the deliberate scrutiny; in coming to gaze she had been offering herself to be gazed upon, and she was conscious that the three of them presented a most piquant group in this dim and spacious old room of the East—the modern American girl, the cosmopolitan young officer in his vivid uniform, and this sequestered woman, of a period of transition where the kohl and henna of the *odalisque* contrasted with a coiffure and gown from Paris.

Slowly and disconnectedly the uninspiring conversation progressed. Once, when it appeared halted forever, Arlee cast a helpless look at the Captain and intercepted a sharp glance at his sister. Indeed, Arlee thought, that sister was not distinguishing herself by her grateful courtesy to this guest who was brightening the *tristesse* of her secluded day, but perhaps this was due to her Oriental languor or the limitations of their medium of speech.

It was a relief to have the Captain suggest music. At their polite insistence Arlee went to the piano and did her best with a piece of MacDowell. Then the sister took her turn, and to her surprise Arlee found herself listening to an exquisite interpretation of some of the most difficult of Brahms. The beringed and tinted fingers touched the notes with rare delicacy, and brought from the piano a quality so vivid and poignant in appeal that Arlee could dream that here the player's very life and heart were finding their real expression.

The last note fell softly into silence, and with her hands still on the keys the woman looked up over her shoulder at her brother, looked with an intentness oddly provocative and prolonged. And for the first time Arlee caught the quality of sudden and unforeseen attraction in her, and realized that this insolence of color, this flaunting hair and painted mouth might have their place in some scheme of allurement outside her own standards.... And then suddenly she felt queerly sorry for her, touched by the quick jarring bitterness of a chord the woman suddenly struck, drowning the laughing words the Captain had murmured to her.... Arlee felt vaguely indignant at him. No one wanted to have jokes tossed at her when she had just poured her heart out in music.

The Captain was on his feet, making his adieux. Now that the ladies were acquainted, he would leave them to discuss the modes and other feminine interests. He wished Miss Beecher a delightful trip upon the Nile and hoped to see her upon her return, and she could be sure that everything would be arranged for her. When she had had her tea and wished to leave, the motor would return her to the hotel. He made a rapid speech in Turkish to his sister, bowed formally to Arlee over a last *au revoir* and was gone.

Immediately the old woman entered with a tray of tea things, the same old woman who had been squatting by the window, but who had noiselessly left the room during the music. She was followed by a bewitching little girl of about ten with another tray, who remained to serve while the old woman shuffled slowly away. Arlee was struck by the informality of the service; the servants appeared to be underfoot like rugs; they came and went at will, unregarded.

The tea was most disappointingly ordinary, for the pat of butter bore the rose stamp of the English dairy and the bread was English bake, but the sweetmeats were deliciously novel, resembling nothing Arlee had seen in the shops, and new, too, was the sip of syrup which completed the refreshment.

Her hostess had said but little during the repast, remaining silent, with an air of polite attention, her eyes fixed upon her caller with a gaze the girl found bafflingly inscrutable. Now as the girl rose to go, the Turkish woman suddenly revived her manners of hostess and suggested a glimpse of some of the other rooms of the palace. "Our seclusion interests you—yes?" she said, with a half-sad, half-bitter smile on her scarlet lips, and Arlee was conscious of a sense of apologetic intrusion battling with her lively curiosity as she followed her down the long chamber and through a curtained doorway to the right of the throne-like chair, into a large and empty anteroom, where the sunlight streaming through the lightly screened window on the wall at the right reminded Arlee that it was yet glowing afternoon.

She lingered by the window an instant, looking down into the court which she had glimpsed from the vestibule. Across the court she saw a row of windows which, being unbarred, she guessed to be on the men's side of the house, and to the left the court was ended by a sort of roofed colonnade.

Her hostess passed under an elaborate archway, and Arlee followed slowly, passing through one stately, high-ceiled, dusty room into another, plunged again into the twilight of densely screening *mashrubiyeh*. There were views of fine carving, painted ceilings, inlaid door paneling, and rich and rusty embroideries where the name of Allah could frequently be traced, but Arlee was ignorant of the rare worth of all she saw; she stared about with no more than a girl's romantic sense of the old-time grandeur and the Oriental strangeness, mingled with a disappointment that it was all so empty and devoid of life.

This part of the palace was very old, her hostess said uninterestedly; these were the rooms of the dead and gone ladies of the dead and gone years. One of the Mamelukes had first built this wing for his favorite wife—she had been poisoned by her rival and died, here, on that divan, the narrator indicated, with a negligent gesture.

Wide-eyed, Arlee stared about the empty, darkened rooms and felt dimly oppressed by them. They were so old, so melancholy, these rooms of dead and gone ladies. How much of life had been lived here, how much of hope had been smothered with these walls! What aching love and fiery hate had vibrated here, only to smolder into helpless ennui under the endless weight of tedious days.... She shivered slightly, oppressed by the dreams of these ancient rooms, dreams that were heavy with realities.

Slowly she moved back after her hostess, who had pushed back a panel in one wall, and Arlee stepped beside her within the tiny, balcony-like enclosure the panel had revealed, one side of which was a wooden lacework of fine screening, permitting one to see but not be seen. Pressing her face against the grill, Arlee found she was looking down into a long and spacious hall, lined with delicate columns bearing beautiful, pointed arches, and brilliant with old gilding and inlay.

This was the colonnade which she had seen forming one side of the court; it was the hall of banquets, she was told, and connected this wing of the palace, the *haremlik*, with the *selamlik*, the men's wing, across the way. Here in old times the lord of the palace gave his feasts, and this nook had been built for some favorite to view the revels.

Arlee stared down into the great empty hall with an involuntary quickening of the breath. How desolate it was, but how beautiful in its desolation! What strange revels had taken place there to the notes of wild music, what girls had danced, what voices had shouted, what moods had been indulged! She thought of the men who had made merry there ... and then she thought of the women, generations of women, who had stood where she was standing, pressing their young faces against the grill, their bright eyes peering, peering down. She felt their soft little silken ghosts all about her, their bangles clinking, their perfumes enveloping her sense— lovely little painted dolls, their mimic passions helpless in their hearts....

Dreaming, she turned and in silence retraced her way after her hostess, loitering by the window in the anteroom to watch a veiled girl drawing water at the old well in the center, an old well rich in arabesques.

How much happier, thought Arlee, were these serving maids in the freedom of their poverty than the cloistered aristocrats behind their darkened windows. She wondered if that strange figure beside her, half Moslem, half modern, envied the little maid the saucy jest which she flung at a bare-footed boy idling beside a dozing white donkey. As she watched the old-world quiet of the picture was broken. Some one, the doorkeeper, she thought, from his vivid robes and yellow shoes, came running across the court, shouting something at the girl which sent her flying to the house, her jar forgotten, and another man, an enormous Nubian with blue Turkish bloomers, short red jacket and a red fez, hurried across the court toward the *haremlik*.

The lady stepped toward the screening and called down; the man stopped, raised his head, and shouted back a jargon of excited gutturals, waving his arms in vehement gesturing. His mistress interrupted with a brief question, then with another, then nodding her head indifferently to herself, she called down an order, apparently, and turned away.

"One of our servants is dead," she murmured to Arlee in explanation. "They say now it is the plague."

"The plague?" repeated the girl absently. She was thinking what a hideous creature that great Nubian was. Then, more vividly, "The *plague*?"

"You have fear?" said the negligent voice.

Arlee nodded frankly. "Oh, yes, I should be terribly afraid of it," she averred. "Aren't you?" And then she reflected, as she saw the inscrutable smile playing about the older woman's lips, that she must be witnessing that fatalistic apathy of the East that she had read about.

But there was nothing apathetic about the Captain. He followed on the very heels of the announcement, his sword clanking, his spurs jingling, as he bounded up the stairs and hurried through the long, dim drawing-room toward them.

"You have heard?" he cried in English as they came to meet him. "You have heard?"

"Of the plague!" Arlee answered, wondering at his agitation. "Yes, your sister just told me. Is it really the plague?"

"So say those damned doctors—pardon, but they are such imbeciles!" He made an angry gesture with his clenched hand. His face was tense and excited. "They say so. And there is another sick ... *Dieu*, what a misfortune! Truly, there was illness about us, a little, but who thought——"

"I shall run back to my hotel," said Arlee lightly, "before I catch one of your germs."

"To the hotel—a thousand pardons, but that is the thing forbidden." The young man made a gesture, with empty palms outspread, eloquent of rebellion and despair. "Those doctors—those pig English—they have set a quarantine upon us!"

CHAPTER IV
A SORRY GUEST

"A quarantine?" said Arlee Beecher, in a perfectly flat little voice.

Again the young man exercised his power of gesture, his dark eyes seeming to plead his own helpless desire to mitigate his words.

"Truly a quarantine. It is tyranny, but what can one do? They will hear nothing—they set their guard and it is finished—*bien simple*. We are their prisoners."

"Prisoners?" Her mind appeared but a hollow echo of his words. Her heart was dropping, dropping sickishly, into unending space. Then meaning stabbed her like a dentist's needle, and a pandemonium of incredulity and revolt clamored through every nerve in her body. "Why you can't mean— I'm going back to the hotel this instant! I haven't seen your servant!"

"That is nothing to them. They have no reason—heads of pigs! No one must leave or they shoot—the tyrants, the imbecile tyrants! But their day will not be forever—Islam will not endure——"

It was of no moment to Arlee Beecher what Islam would not endure. Her heart was galloping now like a runaway horse, but her voice rang with quick reaction from that first sickening shock.

"What nonsense," she said positively. "They wouldn't shoot *me*. Why didn't you call me when the English doctor was here. I could have explained then. But now—now I had better telephone, I suppose. Either to the doctor or the English ambassador—or the American consul. I'll make them understand in a jiffy. Where is your telephone, please?"

"Alas, not in the palace." The young captain's look of regret deepened.

"But—but you telephoned your sister! You telephoned her this afternoon."

"Ah, yes, but I spoke to a telephone which is in a palace near here— the palace of my uncle. I sent a servant with the message. But I can send a message to that palace," he offered eagerly, "and they can telephone for you. Or I can send notes out to all the people you wish. The soldiers will call boys to deliver them."

Across the girl's perfectly white face a tremor of panic darted; then she bit her lips very hard and stared very intently past the Captain's green and gold shoulder. She had totally forgotten the sister who had sunk on a divan beside them, her brown eyes rimmed in their dark pencilings turning from one to the other as if to read their faces.

"I'll just speak to those soldiers, myself," said Arlee decidedly. "I'll make them understand." She left them there, their eyes upon her and sped down the long room to the door which the Captain's hurried entrance had left half open. She disappeared down the steps.

In three minutes she was back, a flame in the frightened white of her cheeks, a flame in the frightened blue of her eyes.

"Captain Kerissen," she called, and he took a step nearer to her, his face alert with sympathy, "Captain Kerissen, that is a *native* soldier! He is at the bottom of the stairs—with a bayonet—and he will not let me pass. He doesn't know a word I say. Please come and tell him."

"Miss Beecher, it is useless for me to tell him anything," said the young Turk with a ring of quiet conviction. "I have been talking to that one—and to the others. They are at every entrance. It is as I told you—we are prisoners."

"Surely you can tell him that I am a guest—you can *bribe* him to turn his head, to let me slip by——"

"He would be shot if he let you out that street door. He has his orders to keep the ladies in their quarters and it is death to him to disobey. That is the discipline—and the discipline has no mercy—particularly upon the native soldiers." His tone held bitterness. "It is useless to resist the soldiers. You must resign yourself to remain a guest until I can obtain word to one who can render assistance.... Will it be so hard?" he added sympathetically, as she stood silent, her lips pressed quiveringly together. "My sister will do everything——"

"Of course I can't stay here," broke in Arlee in her clear, positive young tones. "I must get back to the Evershams—and we are going up the Nile to-morrow morning. Can you get a message to that doctor *at once*? And have someone go and telephone from the next house to the consul and ambassador—and I'll write them notes, too."

Her voice broke suddenly. On what wings of folly she had come alone to this place! Her bright adventure was a stupid scrape. Oh, what mischance—what mischance! She was chokingly ashamed of the predicament—to be penned up by a quarantine in a Moslem household. She was angry, defiant and humiliated at once. What would the Evershams say—and Robert Falconer——

She had never waited for anything as she waited for the answers to the passionately urgent notes she sent out. She had written the doctor, the ambassador, the consul, the Evershams. And then she walked up and down, up and down that long, dim room which grew darker and darker with the fading light and counted off the seconds and the minutes and the hours with her pulsing heart beats. She had never known there was such suspense in the world. It was comparable to nothing in her girl's life—the only faint analogy was in the old school-time when she thought she had failed in the history examination and her roommate had gone to the office to find out for her. She remembered walking the floor then, in a silly panic of fear. But she had not failed—she had just squeaked through and it would be like that now. Someone would come to tell her that everything was all right and laugh with her at her foolish fright. But underneath this strain of fervent reassurance ran a cold little current like an underground brook, a seeping chill of dread and vague fear and strange amazement that she should be here in this lonely palace, peering out of darkened windows, waiting and listening.

This time it *was* the Captain's steps, coming up the stairs. Perceptive of her impatience, he had left her to herself, till he could bring word. Now she stood, listening to the nearing jingle that accompanied his footsteps, her hands clasped involuntarily against her breast in rigid tension. And when she saw his face through the dusk, saw the courteous deprecation of it, the solicitous sympathy, she did not need his words to tell her that it was not yet all right.

There was nothing to be done. Legal and medical authorities united in insisting that no one, not even the guest, should leave the palace until the fear of spreading the infection was past. This might be modified in a day or two, but for the present they were too frightened to make exceptions.

And they were going up the Nile Friday morning, Arlee remembered numbly. And this was Thursday night.

"Did the Evershams—did they answer my letter?" she said with dry lips.

The Evershams, it seemed, had not been at the hotel. Perhaps when they had read the letter they would be able to do something about it.

"They'll just *talk*!" cried Arlee passionately, her breast heaving.

She wanted to scream, she wanted to rave, she wanted to fly down the stairs and hurl herself recklessly against that barring bayonet. But because there was pride and spirit behind her delicate loveliness she shut the door hard upon those imps of hysteria and with high-held head and palely smiling lips she thanked the Captain for the hospitality he was extending in his sister's name. Yes, thank you, she would rejoin them at dinner. Yes, thank you, she would like to go to her room now.

A serving maid, called by her hostess, conducted her—the blue-robed girl, she thought, that she had seen drawing water at the well. A black shawl hung from her head and dangling in its folds the *yashmak* ready to be slipped on at the approach of the men before whom she must appear veiled. Her bare feet were thrust into scarlet slippers, and as she moved silver anklets were visible, hanging loosely over slim, brown ankles. Shuffling slightly, yet with an erectly graceful carriage, the girl led the way into the ante-room again, pulled open one of the closed doors in the opposite wall and passed up an encased staircase wrapped in darkness. They emerged into the dusk of a long, dim hall, where hanging lamps from the ceiling shed a mild luster and a strong smell of oil, and passing one or two doors on the right, the maid pushed, open one that was rich in old gilding.

Crossing the threshold Arlee felt that she was crossing the centuries again into her own time.

The room was a glitter of white and rose; the windows, unscreened, admitted the warm glow of late afternoon, and windows and doorway and bed were smothered in rose and white hangings. A white triple-mirrored dressing-table gleamed with gold and ivory pieces; a white fur rug was stretched before a rose silk divan billowy with plump pillows, and an open door beyond gave a view of shining tile and a porcelain bath. Near her was a baby grand piano in white enamel—reminding her of one she had seen in the White House—and she noted absently a pile of gaudily covered music upon it betokening tunes different from the Brahms she had heard downstairs.

The maid indicated a pitcher of hot water in the bathroom—evidently pipes and faucets played no part with the shining tub—and then stepped outside, closing the door.

After an instant's hesitation, Arlee took off her hat and bathed her face and hands, then moved slowly to the dressing table to glance at her hair. Hesitantly she picked up the shining brush and stared at the flourish of an unintelligible monogram upon the back. Whose brush was this? Whose room was she in? The place, vivid, silken, scented, was fairly breathing with occupancy.

She laid down the brush without using it, touched her hair with absent fingers, and crossed to the windows. She looked down into a garden, a deep tangle of a garden, presided over by a huge lebbek tree that threw a pall of shadow upon the faintly moving flowers beneath.

The place seemed a riot in neglect, for across the white sanded paths thick creepers had flung their arms, and vines and climbers were scaling the gnarled limbs of the acacia trees and covering the high walls beyond. She was looking to the west where the rose and gold of sunset still hung breathless on the painted air, though the sun was hidden below the fringe of palms which rose above the wall, and for a moment that still brilliance of the sky above the sharply silhouetted palms made her heart quicken in forgetfulness.

And then her hands became aware of the bars she had been unconsciously clasping, white-painted bars extending across the window. They were of iron.

Not even here was there freedom, she thought with a throb of dread, not even here where one faced dark gardens and blank walls and the empty west.

Somehow that dinner had passed, that queer dinner in the candle light between the silent, painted woman and the politely talkative young man, and passed without a word from outside for the girl whose nerves were fraying with the suspense. The old woman and the little girl had served them with a meal which would have been judged delicious in any European hotel and though Arlee's nerves were tricky her young appetite was not and she ate and talked with a determined little air of trying to dissipate the strangeness of the situation.

And with the coffee came inspiration. She began to plan ... half listening to the Captain's amiable efforts to entertain her with an account of the palace, and of its history under Ismail, the Mad Khedive, who had occupied it for some months, tearing down and building in his feverish way, only to weary at the first hint of completion. She was wondering why in the world the inspiration had not arrived at once. Perhaps something in this fatalistic air, this stupid acceptance of authority had numbed her.

With alacrity she accepted the Captain's suggestion of a stroll in the garden, and was relieved when the silent sister did not rise to accompany them, but remained in the candle-light with her coffee and cigarette. She found the woman's lightly mocking, watchful eyes, the enigmatic smile upon the carmined lips, increasingly hard to bear. That woman didn't like her—she had failed, somehow, to propitiate her hostile curiosities.

Back through the old empty rooms of the past, the Captain led her, and passing by the screened alcove from which Arlee had looked down into the ancient banquet hall he came to a small dark painted door which he unlocked. The door opened upon a flight of worn and narrow stone steps descending into the garden.

It had been night in the palace of darkened windows but in the garden it was yet day, although the rose and gold of sunset had faded to paling pinks and translucent ambers and in the east the stars were shining in the deepening blue. It was the same garden on which her windows opened; Arlee recognized the huge lebbek tree in the center, the row of acacias, and the palms against the farthest wall. It was a very old garden. Those trees must have seen many, many years, she thought, and felt again that sense of vague oppression and melancholy which the lonely rooms of the palace had given her; that row of acacias which cast such crooked shadows over the path had been planted by very long-ago hands.

So she thought fleetingly, then stared about, her concern for other things. Captain Kerissen lighted a cigarette; over his cupped hands his eyes followed hers searchingly.

"That is the hall of banquets?" she said, pointing to the raised colonnade.

"Ah, yes—you are quick to learn!" he complimented.

"And could we walk through that into the courtyard?"

"Undoubtedly."

"And this side is the *haremlik*," she murmured, glancing up at the windows upon the third floor which she felt were those of that rose and white room. Much of the rest of the wing, she saw, extending down to the high wall at right angles to it, was in a ruinous and dilapidated condition. "What is there?" she asked.

"The rooms the Khedive Ismail left unfinished. They are of no use."

"And on the other side?" she persisted, pointing towards the wall that was the continuation of the men's wing, which stopped at the colonnade.

"On the other side is the palace of another man, and on the other side of that, ending the road is a *cimitère*—what you say, cemetery."

"And back of *that* wall?" She nodded at the one behind the palms, running parallel to the banquet hall.

"Back of that a canal, Mademoiselle, and across are other palaces.... You study the geography, it appears?"

"Indeed I do!" She turned towards him, her face bright with eagerness. Her light curls were blown about her forehead by a breeze, hot and dry, that seemed to mingle the odors of the desert with a piercing sweetness which it drew from the deep throats of the lilies swaying beside the path. "And I think *that* is going to be the way out for me." Her quick nod was for the wall behind the palms. "I want you to do me a great big favor, Captain Kerissen, that will make me your debtor for life! You must help me break out of this quarantine this very night?"

Not the ghost of a fear of failure to persuade him lurked in those bright, dancing eyes. Not the ghost of a fear of failure haunted those confident, smiling lips.

He sucked on his cigarette a moment, then slowly blew a thin ring of blue smoke. He appeared interested in watching it.

"What is it—this idea?" he murmured.

"Well, you may have a better one but mine is just to climb that wall, as soon as it gets dark. If you just get a ladder, or a pile of chairs I am sure I can manage it—and then I'll be back at the hotel in an hour!"

He took out his cigarette and shook his head at her. "You would drop, like the plum of Haydee, into the arms of the soldier who is guarding on the other side.... Shall I tell you the story of that plum?"

"A soldier guarding—a *native* soldier?"

"Yes."

"Then—then please won't you see if you can bribe him?" she shamelessly pleaded, anxiously clasping and unclasping her hands. "*Please*, Captain Kerissen, you must help me to run away to-night. I *can't* be shut up like this—I can't give up the Nile trip and besides—Oh, I really must be back at that hotel to-night!... If that soldier is sure no one else will see him I know you can persuade him to look away just a little minute while I slip down and run off!"

"Ah, no, no, my dear Miss Beecher, there is no hope of that." The young man started walking down the path and Arlee walked beside him, her eyes fixed on his face, incredulous of the denial that they were reading there. "He would think it a test, a trap—not for one minute is it to be thought of! Now could I let you go alone in that place by the canal. There is danger—you do not understand——"

"Oh, I understand, but I can take care of myself!" Across her pleading flashed the ironic thought of how excellently she had taken care of herself in coming there that very afternoon! "Just let me get over that wall and I can find my way—and if you cannot bribe the man we can wait till it is darker and then, when he is at the other end, why I can be down and off in a jiffy!"

"He would shoot," said the Captain. "He has his order. I have talked with them.... And what would the authorities say when they send here the doctor to-morrow and you are gone?"

"Say—say—Oh, what does it matter what they say? Tell them that I ran away without your knowledge. Surely——"

"But your name has been given as detained. They would not let you reappear in the world——"

"You leave that to me! I know it would be all right—once I was there. Please do this for me, Captain Kerissen—*please*! I know that in a great palace like this there must be many, many ways where one could slip into the streets——"

"In all this palace there are but three doors—the door in the vestibule by which you entered, the great door to its right, under the arch into the court, and the little door from the garden to the canal." He waved his cigarette at the wall ahead of them, towards which they were slowly walking. "And all those three doors are barred upon the outside and there is a soldier before each one—and the soldier that you saw within the vestibule, watching us there."

"But—but the windows." She remembered the *mashrubiyeh*, but went on resolutely, "I mean, the windows on the men's side. Aren't there any windows in that part which are open?"

"The *selamlik* is a short wing and looks into the court." A note of impatience sounded in his voice. He tossed away his cigarette which fell, a burning spark, in the shadows. Already, as they talked, it had grown darker, and the impatient tropic night was stealing on them. "It is no use," he repeated. "There is no way out for you—or any of us."

Into her heart stole the unthinkable perception that he did not want to help her—he was afraid of the authorities—or else—or else—Desperately she returned to the appeal.

"But do let me try to get over that wall. I will watch for the soldier—I will take the responsibility. Please, now—let us plan that attempt."

His answer held a quiet finality. "It is impossible.... And the wall is too high for such little feet."

The startled color flashed into her cheeks. Only Oriental language of course.... Perhaps she was unduly sensitive to any hint of familiarity in her predicament.

"I could manage it perfectly," she said with coldness.

He bent over her, as they walked. "Are you so unhappy here?"

"Of course I am unhappy," she gave back with a clear matter-of-factness that strove to ignore the sudden softening of his voice. "I am *very* unhappy. I realize that I should not be here, that I am intruding upon your hospitality— —"

"You are making me most happy."

"And I am making my friends most anxious and losing my trip on the Nile."

"The Nile," he said, "flows on forever. Who knows how soon you will see it and under what happier circumstances?"

"Our boat was to sail at ten. I simply must find a way out to-night— —"

"That is impossible." He spoke with sudden irritation, which he softened the next instant, with a light laugh. "You Americans—how you hurry!... Tell me—have you no heart for all this?"

She looked about her at the silent garden, the deepening shadows, the darkening sky. Above her head, now, high in the air were the faintly rustling palm leaves. Behind the palms stretched the wall, high and blankly impassable. She felt strange, unreal.... Her very fright was unreal.

"Tell me," he was saying, his voice low and caressing, "are there many girls like you—in your America?"

She tried to speak quite easily, quite simply. "You have been in England and France, Captain Kerissen, and you have seen many Americans traveling there."

"I have seen many—yes. But not like you." She looked swiftly at him, then more swiftly away. His eyes were glowing with a look of deep excitement; his teeth flashed white under his small, dark mustache. "Shall I tell you how you appear beside those others?"

"No, thank you," the girl answered with a hurried crispness which brought a stare and then a low laugh from him.

"You have been told so often?" he suggested.

"I never permit myself to be told at all!" Anger made her young voice imperious, but her heart was beating furiously. Involuntarily she quickened her steps and he reached his hand to her bare forearm and held her back.

"Pardon—but you are too quick."

She stood rigid, some deep instinct warning her not to resist. The situation had gone to the man's head, she felt dumbly; his courtesy was only a scant veneer over that Oriental cast of view which, like the Latin, reads every accident of propinquity as opportunity. His hand fell away and they walked on in slower time. When he spoke his voice betrayed the feeling quickening within him.

"Then I have a pleasure before me, for you will listen, please. To me your sister Americans are like big, bright flowers which grow by the wayside where every wind blows hard upon them. And each receives the dust of the footsteps of many men till comes the one who shall possess her. But he does not bear her away. He puts his name upon her, but leaves her out in the same field where every passerby may look and handle — —"

"You are dreadfully rude," said Arlee clearly. "You don't understand at all. I thought you knew better."

"Ah, I know! Was I not in England and did I not hear men talk — yes, of sisters and wives with bold words and laughter? Not so of our ladies — they are sacred names not to be spoken by another.... But I do not wish to speak of these others of your race. I speak of you."

"Really, I would rather you would not speak of me."

"But I wish to tell you." His voice was no louder; it was even lower, but it took on a note of authority. Arlee was silent, a chill creeping up about her heart — like a rising tide....

"You are a flower upon a height," he said, and his tones were soft again and gently caressing, "laughing at others because you know you are so high above them, and so proud. The blue of the skies is in your eyes, and the gold of the sun in your hair. You have a beauty that is too bright to be endured — it burns a man's heart like a flame.... It was never meant to shine in a common field. It must be guarded, revered, adored — a princess upon a height — —"

"You have an Oriental imagination," said Arlee Beecher, and prayed God her voice did not tremble. "I must ask you not to pay me such compliments while I am your guest."

"No?... Why not?"

"They — are embarrassing."

"Embarrassment is an emotion rare to find among your ladies — it is the dewy bloom upon your own perfect innocence.... Ah, I wish you spoke my language! I could tell you many things — —"

"Your English is excellent," said the white-faced girl. "Did you learn it at Oxford or before?"

He did not pause for such foolish questionings. "Why do you not wish me to tell you what you are?" he said reproachfully. "Is it because you doubt that I mean it?"

"Because I am not used to such compliments—and I would rather not hear them now. I am your guest and I am very tired. I must go in."

It was very dark in the garden. And it was still and unutterably lonely. Only the stars burned above them in the heavens; only the light wind of the desert stirred. From the far distance the muffled beat of the tom-tom sounded. Surely, thought Arlee, surely she was dreaming.... This could not be Arlee Beecher, here with this man—this Turk.

"I must go in," she repeated, with a heightening of assurance.

As he looked down at her for a moment that chill dread seemed to lay its icy hands on her very heart as she glimpsed something of the tumult within his eyes. She had a vision of him as a man capable of all, reckless, impassioned, poised upon the brink of some desperate plunge.... Then the hands of consequences seemed to lay compelling hold upon him; the fire was extinguished; the vision gone like a mirage. His eyes were friendly, his lips smiling, as he bowed to her, in deferential courtesy, to all appearances a gentleman of her world.

"I must not tire my guest," he said, and stood aside to let her pass up the narrow stone steps.

"We shall have other walks," he added, and the chill, delicate menace of those words went with Arlee Beecher to the rose and white room, and kept her sorry company through the long and restless hours.

CHAPTER V
WITHIN THE WALLS

Again the knocking, muffled but softly insistent, and Arlee's eyes, heavy with tardy sleep, came slowly open, resting blankly on the glittering strangeness of the room. The daylight was streaming in the wide windows, striking brightly on the white enameled furniture which had glimmered so ghost-like through the wakeful darkness of the night, and flung back in dancing points of color from the mirrors and the glass and gold of toilet pieces. The air was hot and close, as if the first freshness of the morning was already past.

Again through the heavy door came the knocking and the soft reassurance of a girl's voice. Arlee sprang from the couch where she had lain down that night, not undressed, but with her white frock exchanged for the negligée she had found laid out for her among other things, and hurried toward the door where she had piled two chairs to supplement the lock—a foolish-looking barricade in the shining light of day, she thought, her lips lifting whimsically.

The young Turkish maid entered with a huge jar of water which she emptied into the bath, returning to the door to take in another and yet another and another from some unseen porter, and pouring these into the bath, she added a spray of perfume and laid out powders and towels, smiling the while at Arlee, with the fascinated interest of a child.

"Do you speak English?" said Arlee eagerly.

But the girl laughed and shook her head at the question, and at the French and German with which Arlee next addressed her, and answered in soft Turkish, at which it was Arlee's turn to laugh and shake her head. But she felt a little rueful behind her pleasant smiling. She wished she could talk with the girl. She wondered about her. She had very handsome dark eyes, though perhaps overbold at times, but her lips were thick and her nose was flattened as if generations of *yashmak*-wearing women had crushed every hope of contour.

The cool freshness of the water was grateful to her senses. It was a plunge back into sanity and normal life again, drowning those ghosts of vague foreboding and anxieties which had kept such unpleasant vigil with her, and when the Turkish girl returned with a tray, Arlee was able to sit and eat breakfast with a trace of amusement at the oddity of the affair—sipping coffee in this Parisian boudoir overlooking an Egyptian garden.

As she was buttering a last crumb of toast the girl re-entered with a box from the florist. Her white teeth flashing at Arlee in a smile of admiring interest, she broke the cord with thick fingers and Arlee found the box full of roses, creamy pink and dewy fresh. The Captain's card was enclosed, and across the back of it he had written a message:

> I am sending out for some flowers for our guest and I hope that they will convey to her my greeting. If there is anything that you would have, it is yours if it is in my power to give. My sister is indisposed, but will visit you when her indisposition will permit. This afternoon I will see you and report the result of our protests to the authorities. Until then, be tranquil, and accommodate yourself here.

A tacit apology, thought Arlee, pondering the dull letter a moment, then dropping it to touch the roses with light fingers. The young man's wits had evidently returned with the sun. He had utterly lost them last night with the starshine and the shadows and his Oriental conception of the intimacy of the situation—but, after all, he had too much good sense not to be aware of the folly of annoying her. Her cheeks flushed a little warmer at the memory of the bold words and the lordly hand on her arm, and her heart quickened in its beating. She had certainly been playing with fire, and the sparks she had so ignorantly struck had lighted for her an unforgettable glimpse of the Oriental nature beneath all its English polish, but she imagined, very fearlessly, that the spark was out. She was not a nature that was easily alarmed or daunted; beneath her look of delicate fragility was a very sturdy confidence, and she had the implicit sense of security instinct in the kitten whose blithe days have known nothing but kindness. Yet she felt herself tremendously experienced and initiated....

She wrote back a word of thanks for the flowers and a request for writing paper and ink, and when they were brought she wrote three most urgent letters, and after an instant's hesitation a fourth—to the Viceroy himself. Feeling that his mail might be bulky, she marked it "Immediate" in large characters and gave them to the maid, who nodded intelligently and shuffled away.

It was very odd, she thought then, that she had no letters. By now the Evershams must surely have written—she had begged them to.... But she was *not* going to be silly and panicky, she determinedly informed that queer little catch in her side which came at the thought of her isolation, and humming defiantly she sat down at the white piano and opened the score of a light opera which she knew:

> Say not love is a dream,
> Say not that hope is vain ...

She had danced to that tune last night—no, the night before last—danced to it with that extraordinarily impulsive young man from home—for all America was now home to her spirit. And she had promised to see him last night. She wondered what he had thought of her absence.... She could imagine the Evershams dolefully deploring her rashness, yet not without a totally unconscious tinge of proper relish at its prompt punishment. They were such dismal old dears! They *would* complain—they must have made her the talk of the hotel by now. Robert Falconer would enjoy that! And his sister and Lady Claire would ask about her, and Lady Claire would say, "How odd—fancy!" in that rather clipped and high-bred voice of hers.... But she was *not* going to think about it!

She opened more music, stared wonderingly at the unfamiliar pages, read the English translation beneath the German lines, then pushed them away, her cheeks the pinker. They were as bad as French postcards, she thought, aghast. Whose room was this, anyway? Whose piano was this? Whose was the lacy negligée she had worn and the gossamer lingerie the maid had placed in the chiffonier for her? Was she usurping her hostess's boudoir?

She began to walk restlessly up and down the room, feeling time interminable, hating each lagging second of delay.

Then came a tray of luncheon, and lying upon it a yellow envelope. With an eagerness that hurt in its keenness she snatched it up and tore out the folded sheet. Her eyes leaped down the lines. Then slowly they followed them again:

> I think it very strange of you to leave us like that, but of course you are your own mistress. We are sorry and hope it will soon be over and you will join us again, unless you prefer your other friends, the Maynards. We have packed your clothes and sent them to Cook's for your orders, and we have paid your hotel bill. Let us know when you can join us.
>
> Mrs. Eversham.

That was all. No word of real sympathy—no declaration of help. Passive acceptance of her predicament—perhaps indeed a retributive feeling of its fitness for her folly. They were annoyed.... Packing her clothes must have been a bother—so was paying her hotel bill.

She crumpled the telegram with an angry little hand. Evidently they had done none of the telephoning she had begged of them. Surely there would have been time for that, if only they had hurried a little! She remembered with a sort of hopeless rage their maddening deliberateness.... Well, they were gone off to the Nile—the telegram, she saw, had been sent as they were on their way to the boat—and she had nothing more to hope from them! But surely the other people, the consul, the ambassador, the mysterious medical authorities, would understand when they had read her letters.

She sent another note to the Captain, asking to be called when the doctor came, and then she sat down at the little white table and began again to write.

But not to Falconer. Never would she beg of him, never, she resolved, with a tightening of her soft lips. She would never let him know how miserable she was over this stupid scrape; when she returned to the hotel she would carry affairs with a high hand and hold forth upon the interesting quaintness of her experience and the old-world charm of her hostess. She laughed, in angry mockery. Never to him, after their quarrel, would she confess herself.

The letter was to a young man whose gray eyes she remembered as very kind and whose chin as very vigorous. He would do things, she thought. And he would understand—he was an American. And dimly she felt that she didn't want him to think she had utterly forgotten her promise of the evening before last, and she didn't want him to be filled with whatever dismal impression the Evershams were giving out. So she dwelt very lightly upon her annoyance at being detained, and asked him please to see the consul or the English Ambassador or somebody in power and hurry matters up a little, as her rightful caretakers had taken themselves off to the Nile. And she said nothing stupid about the strangeness of her writing to him after only speaking to him twice and never being really presented. She merely added, "Please hurry things—I hate being a prisoner," and sealed and addressed it with a flourish to William B. Hill, and sent it off by the maid, and felt oddly comforted by the memory of Billy's vigorous chin.

The heat of the rose-and-white room was stifling now as the slant sun of afternoon burned through the closed blinds and drawn hangings. Languidly she curled up upon the sofa and pillowed her heavy head on the scented silk, and so, drowsing with fitful dreams, she lost the sense of the lagging hours.

She roused to find the maid at hand with more water jars, and, when she had bathed, the girl reappeared and beckoned her to follow. Perhaps the doctor was below, thought Arlee; perhaps the consulate had sent for her! With flying feet she followed down the dark old stairs and across the anteroom into the dim salon, only to find a candle-lighted table set for dinner in the middle of the room and Captain Kerissen bowing ceremoniously beside it.

In the blankness of her disappointment she scarcely grasped what he was saying about the dinner hour being early and his sister being indisposed. She interrupted with a breathless demand for news:

"And my letters—surely there has been time for answers!"

"Answers, yes," he replied, "but not such as I could wish for your sake."

"You mean——?"

"The English have written to me and request that I cease to trouble the department with my importunities. For I myself had written to them again, that I might find grace in your eyes by accomplishing your desires. They say to me that it is useless. The plague is more serious than the convenience of my visitors, and all must be done according to rule. When there is no danger you may depart."

The crash of hopes went echoing to the farthest reaches of her consciousness. But pride stiffened her to dissemble, and she tried to smile as she mechanically accepted the Captain's invitation to be seated at the little candle-lighted table.

"There was no word to me personally?" she asked.

"None, but the telegram which came this morning. I judged that it was not of a significance, for you did not send me a report."

"No—it was not of a significance," she repeated, with a ghost of a little smile. "It was from the Evershams."

"Ah! Their condolences, I think?... And is it that they still make the Nile trip?"

"Yes.... They went this morning." She spoke hesitantly, averse to having this eager-eyed young host perceive how truly deserted she was. "They expect me to take the express train later and join them."

"It is only a night's ride to Assouan." He spoke soothingly. "But you are not eating, Miss Beecher. I recommend this consommé."

It was worth the recommending. Miss Beecher spooned it slowly, then demanded, "Why was I not called when the doctor came?"

"But he does not come! Perhaps he is afraid"—the young man's brows and shoulders rose expressively—"but certainly he does not risk himself. If a servant is ill we are to tell a soldier and the sick one will be taken away to the house of plague—*bien simple*. It is so hard that I am helpless for you," he said, with sympathetic concern, then added, with an air of boyish confession, "although I do not deny that it is happiness for me to see you here."

The look in his eyes forced itself upon her. And the secret sense of discomfort intruded like a third presence at the little table.

In a clear voice of dry indifference: "That's very polite of you," she remarked, "but I imagine you are pretty furious, too, to be kept pent up in somebody else's house like this."

"But this is not somebody else's house," he smiled, his eyes observant of her quick glance and look of confusion. "I am *chez moi*."

"Oh! I thought—I was visiting your sister."

"My sister lives with me. She is a widow—and we are both alone."

"She does not seem to care for company."

"She is indisposed. She regrets it exceedingly." The young man looked grave and solicitous. "But I trust your comfort is not being neglected?"

"Oh, my comfort is being beautifully attended to, thank you, but my patience is wearing itself out!" Arlee spoke with a blithe assumption of humor.

"I wish that I could extend the resources of my palace for you."

"You must tell me about the palace. I shall want to picture it to my friends when I tell them about it. It's very old, isn't it? It must have seen a great deal of life."

"Ah, yes, it has seen life—and what life! *Quelle vie!*" A flash of real enthusiasm dispelled the suave indolence of his handsome features.

"Have you seen those old rooms? Those rooms that were built by the Mamelukes? There is nothing now in Cairo like them."

"I thought them very beautiful," said the girl. "Tell me about those Mamelukes who lived here."

"They were *men*," he said with pride, his eyes kindling, "men who lived as kings dare not live to-day!" The subject of those old days and those old ancestors of his was evidently dear to the young modern, and he launched into an animated sketch of those times, trying to picture for Arlee something of the glowing pageant of the past. And as she listened she found her own high spirit stirring in sympathy with the barbaric strength of those old nobles, riding to battle on their fiery Arab steeds, waging their private wars, brooking no affront, no command, working no other man's will.

"They knew both power and beauty," he declared, "like the Medici of Florence. There are no leaders like that in the modern world. To-day beauty is beggared, and power is lusterless.... And taste? Taste is a hundred-headed Hydra, roaring with a hundred tongues!"

"While in the old days in Cairo it only roared with the tongues of Mamelukes?" Arlee suggested, a glint of mischief in her smile.

He nodded. "It should be the concern of nobles—not of the rabble. That is why I should hate your America—where the rabble prevail."

"It's not nice of you to call me a rabble," said Arlee, busy with her plate of chicken. "But I want to hear more about your old Mamelukes. Is the story true about the Sultan's being so afraid of them that he had them taken by surprise and killed?"

"He did well to fear them," said Kerissen. "And he, too, was a strong man who had the power to clear his own path. Those nobles were in the path of Mohammed Ali. They were too strong for him, he knew it—and they knew it and were not afraid. On one day they were all assembled at the Citadel, at the ceremony which Mohammed Ali was giving in honor of his son, Toussoum. It was the first of March, in 1811, and my ancestor, the father of my father's father, rode out from this palace, through the gate by the court, which is the old gate, in his most splendid attire to greet his sovereign's son. The emerald upon his turban was as large as a man's eye, and his sword hilt was studded with turquoise and pearls and the hilt was a blazon of gold. His robes were of silk, gold threaded, and his horse was trapped with gold and silver and a diamond hung between her eyes.... The Mamelukes were fêted and courted, and then, as they were leaving the Citadel—you have been up there?" he broke off to question, and Arlee nodded, her eyes wide and intent like a listening child's, "and you recall that deep, crooked way between the high walls, between the fortified doors? Imagine to yourself that deep way filled with men on horseback, quitting the Citadel, having taken leave of their Sultan—they were a picture of such pride and pomp as Egypt has never seen again. And then the treachery—the great gates closed before them and behind them, the terrible fire upon them from all sides, the bullets of the hidden Albanians pouring down like the hosts of death—the uproar, the cries of horses, the shouts of the trapped men, and then all the tumult dying, dying, down to the last moan and hiccough of blood."

"But one escaped?" questioned the girl, breaking the silence which had followed the cessation of his voice. "Is it true that one really escaped?"

"Anym-bey—yes, he was the only one that escaped that massacre. He had a fierce horse which gave him pain to mount, and he was still in the courtyard of the palace when he heard the outburst of shots and then the cries. He comprehended. Stripping his turban from his head he bound it over the eyes of his stallion and, spurring to a gallop, he dashed out over the parapet of the Citadel and down—down—down! Magnificent! He did not die of it, but alas! he did not escape. Wounded as he was he managed to reach the house of a relative, but the soldiers of the Sultan tracked him there and seized him.... He was killed."

"Oh, the pity—after that splendid dash!" Arlee stopped and looked around her, at the strange shadowy room hung with its old embroideries and latticed with its ancient screening. "This room makes it all so real, somehow," she murmured. "I didn't believe it all when the dragoman told me—probably because he showed me the mark of the horse's hoof in the stone of the parapet! I thought it was all a legend—like the mark."

"Did he show you, too, the bulrush where Moses was found and the indentures in the stones in the crypt of the Coptic Church where Saint Joseph and Mary sat to rest after the flight into Egypt?" laughed the Captain. And, with a teasing smile, "Ah, what imbeciles they think you tourists!"

But Arlee merely laughed with him, while the old woman changed the plates for dessert. Her spirits had brightened mercurially. This was really interesting.... Uneasiness had vanished.

"Is that an old Mameluke throne?" she asked, pointing to the raised chair upon the dais, with its heavy, dusty draperies.

The Captain glanced at it and shook his head, smiling faintly. "No, that is the throne of marriage." He pushed away his sweet and lighted a cigarette. "That is where sits the bride when she has been brought to the home of her husband—there she holds her reception. Those are the fêtes to which the English ladies come in such curiosity." His smile was not quite pleasant.

"You cannot blame them for feeling a real—interest," said Arlee hesitantly.

"Their interest—pah!" he flung back excitably and made a violent gesture with his cigarette. "They peer at the bride with their haggard eyes, and they say, 'What! You have not seen your husband till to-day! How strange—how strange! Has he not written to you? Suppose you do not like him,' and they laugh and add, 'Fancy a girl among us being married like that!'... The imbeciles—whose own marriages are abominations!"

For a moment Arlee was silent, instinct and impulse warring within her. The man was a maniac upon those subjects, and it was madness to exchange a word with him—but her young anger darted through her discretion.

"They are *not* abominations!" she gave back proudly.

"But I know—I know—have I not been at marriages in England?" he declared, with startling fierceness. "Men and women crowd about the bride; they press in line and kiss her; bearded mouths and shaven lips, young and old, they brush off that exquisite bloom of innocence which a husband delights to discover. Her lips are soiled, *fanée*.... And then the man and woman go away together into a public hotel or a train, and the people laugh and shout after them, and hurl shoes and rice, with a great din of noise. I have heard!" He stopped, looked a moment at the flushed curve of Arlee's averted face, the droop of her shadowy lashes which veiled the confusion and anger of her spirit, and then, leaning forward, his eyes still upon her, he spoke in a lower, softer tone, caressing in its inflections.

"With us it is not so," he said. "We have dignity in our rejoicing, and delicacy in our love. The bride is brought in state to the home of her husband, no eyes in the street resting upon her, and there, in his home, her husband welcomes her and retires with his friends, while she holds a reception with hers. Later the husband will come home and greet her, and he wooes her to him as tenderly as he would gather a flower that he would wear. He is no rude master, no tyrant, as you have been taught to think! He wins her heart and mind to him; it is the conquest of the spirit!... I tell you that our men alone understand the secret of women! Is not the life he gives her better than what you call the world? The woman blooms like a flower for her husband alone; his eyes only may dwell upon the beauty of her face; for him alone, her lips—her lips——"

The young man's voice, grown husky, died away. A dreadful stillness followed, a stillness vibrating with unspoken thought. Her eyes lifted toward him, then fled away, so full of strange, dark, desirous things was the look she encountered. Abruptly he rose—he was coming toward her, and she struggled suddenly to her feet, battling against the cold terror which held her dumb and unready. She flung one arm out before her and found it grasped by hands that were hot and burning. The touch shot her with a fierce rage that cleared her brain and unlocked her lips.

"Is that—the conquest of the spirit?" she gasped, and for an instant the white-hot scorn in her eyes, flashing into his, hid any hint of the fear in her.

Involuntarily his grasp relaxed, and violently she wrenched her arm away and stood facing him, a little white-clad image of war, her eyes blazing, her breast heaving, a defiant child in her intrepidity who gave him back look for look.

In his eyes there glowed and battled a conflict of desires. For one moment they seemed flaming at her from the dark, like some wild creature ready to spring; the next moment they were human, recognizable. She read there grudging admiration, arrested ardor, irresolution, dubiety, and secret calculation.

Then he put both hands behind him and bowed with ceremony.

"The spirit," he remarked dryly, "is worth the conquest."

She said proudly, "You would not like your English friends to know how you treat a guest!"

At that she saw his lip curl in irony—at the mention of the English, perhaps, or in disdain at the appearance of fearing a threat, however powerful that threat might be. He answered with calmness, "It is not the English I am considering.... Nor have I treated my guest so ill, *chère petite mademoiselle*.... If for the moment I mistook my cue—that look within your face—I ask grace for my stupidity."

Suddenly she was frightened. He did not look like a man who wholly surrenders his desires. His eyes seemed to say to her, "Wait—the last word has not been spoken!" She felt her knees trembling.

With an effort she got out, "It is granted—but never again—must you misunderstand. An American girl——"

She stopped. There was a lump in her throat. Across a bright, familiar veranda she could hear a clear, sharp voice answer, "American goose!" She saw a lean tanned face burn red with anger. A wave of loneliness went through her. The irony of it was pitiless. How right Robert Falconer had been!

He was staring down at the table beside him, frowning, considering. She saw with peculiar distinctness how the cigarette he had dropped had burned a hole in the fine linen. One of the candles was dripping lopsidedly. She thought some one ought to right it. She wondered if that soft step, hesitating, behind the curtains, was the serving woman's, and she turned toward that doorway.

"I don't think I care for any coffee," she said, with an air of careless finality. "I think I will go back to my room. Good evening."

He followed her to the doorway, drawing aside the curtains as she passed into the anteroom, and opening the door at the foot of the steps, with an answering, "Good evening," and an added, "Till to-morrow,

Mademoiselle." And then, as the door closed below her, she paused on the dark stairs and huddled against the wall, listening to the faint footfalls from below, crossing and recrossing. Then, when the silence seemed continual, she tiptoed down the stairs again, softly pushed open the unlatched door, stole across the anteroom to the curtained doorway and peered in.

The salon was empty, and in its center the supper table stood stripped of its cloth and candles. Only the pale light from the windows dispelled the growing dark. Like a little white wraith Arlee fled through the room and turned the handle of the door at the head of the *haremlik* stairs. The door was locked.

She shook the handle, first cautiously, then with increasing violence, then she ran back into the room to the nearest window, staring down through the screen. It would have been a steep jump down into the street, but her tense nerves would have dared it instantly. Her hands tore at the *mashrubiyeh*, but the tiny spindles and delicate curves held sound and firm. She beat against it with fierce little fists; she leaped against it with all her trifling weight. It did not yield an inch. Was there iron in all that delicacy? Or was that old wood impregnable in its grim trust?

Wildly she glanced back into the room. Suppose she took a chair and beat at this carving—could she clear a way before the servants came? Could she take the jump successfully? She gazed down into the street, estimating the fall, trying to calculate the hurt.

As she gazed, her eyes grew fixed and filled with utter amazement. Down the street, on a black horse that arched his curving neck and danced on light, fleet feet, rode a man in a uniform of green and gold. He sat erect, his clear-cut profile toward her. The next instant his horse, side-stepping at a blowing paper, turned his face into view. It was Captain Kerissen.

Some one was stirring in the anteroom, and Arlee darted to the left of the throne-chair and through the door there which stood ajar. She was in a dim salon, like the one that she had left, but smaller, and across from her was another door. She flew toward it, wild with the hope of escape, and it opened before her eager hands.

From the shadows of the room it disclosed came a figure with a quick cry. So suddenly it came, so tumultuously it threw itself toward her that Arlee had a startled vision of bare arms, glittering with jeweled bands, arrested outstretched before her as the low gladness of the cry broke in an angry guttural. Slowly the arms dropped in a gesture of despair. She saw a face, distorted, passionate, grow haggard beneath its paint in the reversal of hope.

"Madame!" stammered Arlee to that strange figure of her hostess. "Madame—Oh, pardon me," she cried, snatching at her French, "but tell me how I can go away from here. Tell me— —"

"*C'est toi—va-t-en!*" the woman answered in a voice of smothered fury. She made a menacing gesture toward the door. "*Va-t-en.*" Suddenly her voice rose in a passion of angry phrases that were indistinguishable to the girl, and then she broke off as suddenly and flung herself down upon a couch. From behind her the old woman came shuffling forth and put a hand on Arlee's arm, and Arlee felt the muscles of that hand as strong and rigid as a man's. Utterly confused and bewildered, the girl suffered herself to be led back through the rooms to the foot of her stairs.

"Mariayah!" screamed the old woman, and after a moment the voice of waiting-maid answered from above, and then as Arlee dumbly ascended the stairs, the voice of the old woman rose with her in shrill admonition.

It was the voice of a jailer, thought the white-lipped girl, and that little, dark-skinned maid who waited upon her so eagerly, with such sidelong glances of strange interest, was the tool of a jailer. And though the turning of the key in her own hand gave her a momentary sense of refuge from them, it was but a false illusion of the moment. There was neither refuge nor safety here. She was being deceived ...

The quarantine was lifted.

How else could the Captain be cantering down the street? He did not look like a man escaping.... Perhaps he had bribed the doorkeeper—that which he had declared impossible for Arlee.... But certainly he was deceiving her.

Like a swollen river bursting its banks, her racing mind, wild with suspicion, surged out of its simple channels and swirled in every direction.... What did he mean? What was he trying to do? Keep her in ignorance of the outside world, detain her as long as he dared while the Evershams' absence left her friendless, and inflict his dreadful love-making upon her? Perhaps he thought that he could fascinate her!

She laughed aloud, but it was such a ghostly little laugh that it set her nerves jumping. She stopped in her feverish pacing of the floor; she tried to control her racing mind, she tried to be very calm and to plan.

Had he sent all those letters she had written? Steadily she stared at the possibility that he had not. But at least the Evershams knew where she was. Even the meager warmth of their telegram was like an outstretched hand through the dark. She clung tight to it.

It was absurd to be frightened. He would never dare to annoy her—never, in his sober senses. When they were alone together he had lost his head, but that was accident—impulse...

She rolled the divan against the locked door. She piled two chairs upon it.

No, of course, she had nothing really to fear from him. He was too wise not to understand the gulf between them. To-morrow she would confront him flatly with his deceit; she would array the power of the authorities behind her race. She would sweep instantly from that ill-omened palace. There would be no more philandering.

Her lips moved as she silently rehearsed the mighty speeches that she would make, and all the while as she leaned there against a window, staring strangely through the candle-light at the barricade before the door, she could think of nothing but how mad and unreal it all seemed—like some bad dream from which she would wake in an instant.

But she did not wake. The dream persisted, and the iron bars across her window were very tangible. Down below her in the garden the old lebbek tree rustled stealthily in the stillness. Gusty clouds hid the stars. In the distance the interminable tom-tom beat.

She cast herself into the bed and cried convulsively, like a desperately frightened child, while the awful sense of terror and utter loneliness seemed to be rolling over and over her, like an unending sea. Her sobbing racked her from head to foot. She cried until she was spent with weakness. Then, her wet face still pressed against the pillow and her tangled hair flung out in disordered curls, she fell at last into the deep sleep of exhausted youth.

She woke with a smothered cry. In the darkness a hand had touched her.

CHAPTER VI
A GIRL IN THE BAZAARS

Billy slapped on his hat with a clap of violence. She might have just *seen* him! Then he got up and marched down the steps. There was no more use in camping on that veranda. There was no more use in guarding that entrance. When a girl went whirling off in a limousine, "all dolled up" as his academic English put it, that girl wasn't going to be back in five minutes. And anyway he'd be blessed if he lay around in the way any longer like a doormat with "Welcome" inscribed upon the surface.

So this spurt of masculine shame at his swift surrender to her, and his masculine resentment at being ignored as she went by, sent him hurrying down the street resolved not to return till dinner.

From habit his steps took him to the bazaars. But the zest of that bright pageant was dulled for him. The color was gone even from the red canopies, and the excitement had vanished from the din of noises, the interest fled from the grave figures squatting in their cubby holes of shops draped with silky rags or sewing upon scarlet slippers. He listened apathetically to the warring shouts of the donkey boys and the anathemas of a jostled water carrier stooping under his distended goatskin, then dodged out of the way of a goaded donkey and turned into one of the passages where the four-footed could not penetrate.

For a few moments the bargaining over a silver bracelet between two beturbaned and berobed Arabs caught the surface of his attention, and as the wrangling became a bedlam of imprecations, and the explosive gestures made physical violence a development apparently of mere seconds, Billy's eyes brightened and he estimated chances. But as he picked his favorite there was one final frenzy of fury, and then—peace and joy, utter calm on the wild waters! One Arab counted out the coins from a little leather bag about his neck and the other passed over the bracelet, and with mutual salaams and smiling speeches, behold! the affair was accomplished.

Disgustedly Billy turned away. Then on the other side of him he heard a voice, a sweet and rather high voice, with a musical intensity of inflection that was as English as the Union Jack.

"Yes, it's *sweetly* pretty," the voice was saying irresolutely, "but I don't think I *quite* care to—not at *that* price."

"I—I will buy it for you—yes?" said another voice. "It is made for you—so 'sweetly pretty' as you say."

Billy turned. A slim, tall girl in a dark blue frock was standing before a counter of Oriental jewelry, her head turned, with an air of startled surprise, to the man on the other side of her who had just spoken. He was a short, stout, blond man, heavily flushed, showily dressed, with a fulsome beam in his light-blue eyes and an ingratiating grin beneath his upturned straw-colored mustaches.

The girl turned her head away toward the shop-keeper and put back the turquoise-studded buckle she held in her hand. "No, I do not care for it," she said in a steady voice whose coldness was for the intruder and turned away.

Billy had a glimpse of scarlet cheeks and dark lashed eyes before the blond young man again took his attention.

"You do not like it—no?" he said, blocking her path, his face thrust out to smile into hers. "But I buy you anything you wish—I make you one present——"

The girl gave a quick look about. But she was in a pocket; for there was no other exit to that line of shops but the path he was blocking. All about her the dark-skinned venders and shoppers, the bearded men, the veiled women, the impish urchins, were watching the encounter with beady eyes of malicious interest.

Billy took a quick step forward and touched the man on the arm. "Let this lady pass, please," he said.

The German confronted him with blood-shot blue eyes that ceased to smile and clearly welcomed the belligerency.

"Gott! Who are you?" he derided. "Get out—get out the way."

"Get out yourself," said Billy, and stepping in front of the fellow he extended a rigid arm, leaving a passage for the girl behind him.

"Oh, thank you," he heard her say, and as he half turned his head at the grateful murmur he felt a sudden staggering blow on the side of his face. He whirled about, on guard, and as the man struck again, lunging heavily in his intoxication, Billy knocked up the fist as it came.

"You silly fool!" he said impatiently, and as the man made a blind rush upon him he caught him and by main force flung him off, but his own foot struck something slippery and he lurched and went down, with a wave of intense disgust, into the dirt of the bazaars. He heard a chorus of cries and imprecations about him; he jumped up instantly, looking for his assailant, but the German was clinging to the front of the jewelry booth. "Meet you—satisfaction—honor," he was saying stupidly.

A native policeman elbowed his way through the throng, urging some Arabic question upon Billy, who caught its import and replied with the few sentences of reassurance at his command, pointing to the banana peel as the cause of all. A fat dragoman had suddenly appeared from nowhere and was hurriedly attempting to lead away the intoxicated one.

"You in charge of him? Take him to his hotel and throw him in the tub," said Billy curtly, and the dragoman replied with profound respect that he would do even as the heaven-born commanded.

Brushing off his clothes Billy shouldered his way out of the throng and was met by two bright and grateful eyes and a slim, bare, outstretched hand.

"Thank you *so* much—I am *so* sorry," said the musical voice.

"You shouldn't have waited," said Billy, with a prompt pressure of the friendly little hand. "It might have been a real row."

"I couldn't run away," she said in serious protest at such ingratitude. "I had to see what happened to you. And I am so sorry about your clothes."

"Not hurt a particle—I chose a fortunate place to drop," he returned lightly, but distinctly chagrined that he *had* dropped.

"It was so fine of you," she answered, "just to parry him like that—when he'd been drinking. I saw what you did." And then she added, very matter-of-factly, "And I'm afraid your nose is bleeding, too."

Billy put up a startled hand. In the general soreness he had not noticed that warm trickle. His whole face turned as scarlet as the shameless blood. Frantically he rummaged with the other hand.

The girl thrust a square of white linen upon him. "Please take mine—it will ruin your clothes if it gets on them."

Her immense practicality refused to be embarrassed in the least. Feeling immensely foolish Billy accepted hers, but then he discovered his own handkerchief and stuffed hers away into his pocket.

"You're a trump," he said heartily. "And it's all right now—all but the swelling, I suppose." He sounded rueful. He had remembered his engagement for the evening.

Her head a little aslant, the girl regarded him critically. "N-no, it doesn't seem to be swelling," she observed. "Of course it's a little red but that will pass."

They were walking side by side out of the narrow street and now, on a crowded corner, they paused and looked around. "I left Miss Falconer at the Maltese laces," she murmured, and to the laces they turned their steps.

Miss Falconer was still bargaining. She was a middle aged lady, Roman nosed and sandy-haired, and she brought to Billy in a rush the realization that she was "sister" and the girl was Lady Claire Montfort. The story of the encounter and Billy's hero part, related by Lady Claire, appeared most disturbing to the chaperon.

"How awkward—how very awkward," she murmured, several times, and Billy gathered from her covert glance upon him that part of the awkwardness consisted in being saddled with his acquaintance. Then, "Very nice of you, I'm sure," she added. "I hope the creature isn't lingering about somewhere.... We'd better take a cab, Claire—I'm sure we're late for tea."

"Let me find one," said Billy dutifully, and charging into the medley of vehicles he brought forth a victoria with what appeared to be the least villainous looking driver and handed in the ladies.

"Savoy Hotel, isn't it?" he added thoughtlessly, and both ladies' countenances interrogated him with a varying *nuance* of question.

"I remember noticing you," he hastily explained. "I'm not exactly a private detective, you know,"—the assurance seemed to leave Miss Falconer cold—"but I do remember people. And then I heard you spoken of by Miss Beecher."

The name acted curiously upon them. They looked at each other. Then they looked at Billy. Miss Falconer spoke.

"Perhaps we can drop you at your hotel," said she. "Won't you get in?"

He got in, facing them a little ruefully with his damaged countenance, and subtly aware that this accession of friendliness was not a gush of airy impulse.

"You know Miss Beecher then?" said Miss Falconer with brisk directness.

"Slightly," he said aloud. To himself he added, "So far."

"Ah—in America?"

"No, in Cairo."

Miss Falconer looked disappointed. "But perhaps you know her family?"

"No," said Billy. He added humorously, "But I'll wager I could guess them all right."

"Can you Americans do that for one another? That is more than we can venture to do for you," said the lady, and Billy was aware of irony.

"We know so little about your life, you see," the girl softened it for him, with a direct and friendly smile, and then gazed watchfully at her chaperon. She was a nice girl, Billy decided emphatically.

"How would you construct her family?" was the elder lady's next demand.

"Oh, big people in a small town," he hazarded carelessly. "The kind of place where the life isn't wide enough for the girl after all her 'advantages' and she goes abroad in search of adventure."

"Adventure," repeated Miss Falconer thoughtfully. She seemed to have an idea, but Billy was certain it was not his idea.

He hastened to clarify the light he had tried to cast upon his upsetting little countrywoman. "All life, you know, is an adventure to the American girl," he generalized. "She is a little bit more on her own than I imagine your girls are," and for the fraction of a second his eyes wandered to the listening countenance of Lady Claire, "and that rather exhilarates her. And she doesn't want things cut and dried—she wants them spontaneous and unexpected—and people, just as people, interest her tremendously. I think that's why she's so unintelligible on the Continent," he added thoughtfully. "They don't understand there that girlish love of experience as experience— enjoyment of romance apart from results."

"Romance apart from results," repeated Miss Falconer in a peculiar voice.

"I don't believe you quite get me," said Billy hastily. He felt foolish and he felt resentful. And if these English women couldn't understand the bright, volatile stuff that Arlee was made of, he certainly was not going to talk about it. But Miss Falconer had one more question for him.

"When you say big people in a small town do you mean her father would be a sort of country squire?"

"More probably a captain of industry," Billy smiled.

"A captain—Oh, that is one of your phrases!"

"One of our phrases," he laughed, and then parried, "I thought you were acquainted with Miss Beecher?"

"Quite slightly," said Miss Falconer in an aloof tone. "My brother came over on the same ship with her—he came to join us here."

Billy experienced a flood of mental light. The brother—at the hotel he had discovered that his name was Robert Falconer—was coming to join his elder sister and her young charge. He had come on the same steamer as Miss Beecher. Ergo, he was staying at the hotel where Miss Beecher was and not with his sister. Billy comprehended the anxiety of the lady with the Roman nose. He looked at Lady Claire with a certain sympathy.

He caught her own eyes reconnoitering, and they each looked hastily away.

Again Miss Falconer returned to her attack. "Then you really know nothing positive of Miss Beecher's family?"

"Nothing in the world," said Billy cheerfully. "But why not ask Miss Beecher?"

The lady made no reply. "Miss Beecher is a beautiful girl," said Lady Claire hastily. "She's *so* beautiful that I suppose we are all rather curious about her—of course people *will* ask about a girl like that!"

"Of course," said Billy, and Lady Claire, perceiving that he resented this catechism about his young countrywoman, and Miss Falconer perceiving that nothing was to be gotten out of him, the conversation was promptly turned into other channels, the vague, general channels of comment upon Cairo.

The Evershams dined alone. Alternately, from their table to the doorway went Billy's eager eyes, but no vision with shining curls and laughing eyes appeared. Evidently she had stayed to dine with whatever people she had gone to see. Robert Falconer was watching that table, too.... Perhaps she would not return till late; perhaps he would have only a tiny time with her that evening.... And he had not been able to buy out that man's berth upon the steamer....

Consommé and whitebait, *bœuf rôti* and *haricots vert* and *crème de cérises* succeeded one another in deepening gloom. The whole dinner over, and she had not appeared!

He went out to the lounge and smoked with violence. Presently he saw the Evershams in the doorway talking to Robert Falconer, and he jumped up and hurried to join them. As he approached he heard the word Alexandria spoken fretfully by Mrs. Eversham.

"Good evening, good evening," said Billy hurriedly to the ladies, and being a young man of simple directness, undeterred by the glacial tinge of the ladies' response—they had not forgotten his defection of the evening before when they were entertaining him so nicely—he put the question which had been tormenting him all evening, "Where is Miss Beecher to-night?"

"Alexandria," said Mrs. Eversham again, and this time there was a hint of malicious satisfaction in her voice.

"Alexandria?" Billy was incredulous. "Why I—I understood she was to go up the Nile to-morrow morning."

"She was, but she has changed her mind. She had word from some friends of hers while we were out this afternoon and she flew right off to join them."

"You mean she isn't going up the Nile at all now?"

"I haven't an idea what she is going to do. She is not in our care any longer. And I don't suppose the boat company will do anything about her stateroom at this late date—certainly she can't expect us to go to any trouble about it."

"She left us half her packing to do," Clara Eversham contributed, addressing Falconer with plaintive mien, "and her hotel bill to pay. She is the most unexpected creature!"

Two young men silently and heartily concurred.

"What was her hurry?" Billy demanded.

"Oh, she's going camping in the desert with them—that sort of thing would fascinate her, you know. Her telegram wasn't very clear. She just sent a wire from the station, I think, or from Cook's, with some money for her bill by the boy. So careless, trusting him like that!"

"I don't suppose he brought it all," Mrs. Eversham declared. "You see, she didn't say how much she was sending—just said it was enough for her bill."

Billy looked at Falconer. He admired the stolidity of that sandy-haired young man's countenance. He envied the unrevealing blankness of his eyes.

"May I ask where she is stopping in Alexandria?" he persisted.

Mrs. Eversham shook her head. "She didn't give any address—the best hotel, I suppose, whatever that is."

"The Khedivial," Falconer supplied.

"She just said to send her things to Cook's and to write to her there and she would write when she came back. She had been expecting to meet those friends, the Maynards, later, but we had no idea that she was going to run off with them like this. It's very upsetting."

"We shall miss her," said Clara Eversham suddenly, with a note of sincerity that made Billy warm to her a trifle. So he bestirred himself getting their after dinner coffee and remembered to send Mohammed for the cream for her, and listened with a show of attention to their interminable anecdotes and corrections. But his mind was off on the way to Alexandria....

Not a word of farewell. Of course, they had not exactly arrived, in those twenty-four hours, at a correspondence stage, but still she had made a positive engagement for that evening—and she had known he was trying to buy that berth. Only that morning she had listened to his account of his endeavors with a mischievous light in her blue eyes and a prankish smile edging her pink lips ... and she might, after that, have left just a line to tell him to cancel his arrangements.... But what could he expect from such a tricksy sprite of a girl? Only twenty-seven hours before he had seen her, flagrantly tardy, nonchalantly unrepentant, first mock and then annihilate the worthy and earnest young Englishman who had endeavored to correct her ways ... He had known then the volatile stuff that she was made of—and had succumbed to it!

But he *had* succumbed. On that point he was most disastrously certain. The memory of the young girl possessed him. Her beauty haunted him, that spring-like beauty with its enchanting youth and gaiety. And the spirit that animated that beauty, that young, blithe, innocently audacious spirit which looked out on the world with such sunnily trustful eyes, drew him with a golden cord.

He smoked many a pipe over it that night, his feet on the open window ledge, his eyes on the far-spreading flat roofs, the distant domes and minarets darkly silhouetted against the sky of softest, deepest blue. The stars were silver bright. They spangled the heaven with the radiance they never give to northern skies; they gleamed like bright, wild creatures on their unearthly revels.... It would be glorious camping in the desert on a night like this ... Heaven be praised, he had not bought that berth ... Alexandria ... the Maynards ... the desert ...

He knocked out the ashes from his last pipe and rose briskly. His decision was made, but its success was on the knees of the great god Luck.

CHAPTER VII
BILLY HAS HIS DOUBTS

The encounter in the bazaars that Thursday afternoon brought one more result to young Hill besides the bruise upon his chin and the privilege of bowing to Lady Claire and her vigilant chaperon, and the presence of Lady Claire's little handkerchief in his coat pocket.

It brought a young German, scrupulously sober, soberly apologetic, in formal state to Billy's hotel upon Friday morning, whose card announced him to be Frederick von Deigen and whose speech proclaimed him to be utterly aghast at his own untoward behavior.

"I was not myself," he owned, with a sigh and a melancholy twist of his upstanding mustaches. "I had been lunching alone—and it is bad to lunch alone when one has a sadness. One drinks—to forget.... But you are too young to understand." He waved his hand in compliment to Billy's youth, then continued, with increasing energy, "But when I find what *dummheit* I have done—how I have so rudely addressed the young Fräulein with you, and have used my fists upon you, even to the point of hurling you upon the street—I have no words for my shame."

"Oh, it wasn't exactly a hurl," Billy easily amended. "There was a banana peel where my heel happened to be—and I wasn't half scrapping. I could see you weren't yourself."

"Indeed no! Would I," he struck himself gloomily upon the breast, "would I intrude upon a young Fräulein, and attack her protector? It was that bottle—that last bottle.... I knew—at the time.... I offer you my apology. I can do no more—unless you would have satisfaction—no?"

"I guess I had all the satisfaction that was coming to me yesterday," said Billy. "You've got a fist like a professional. But there's no harm done.... Only you want to get over taking that last bottle and offering presents to young ladies," he concluded, with an accent of youthful severity.

The German nodded a depressed head. His melancholy, bloodshot eyes fixed themselves sadly upon Billy. "Ach, it is so," he assented meekly, "but when one has a sadness—" He sighed.

"Yes, of course, that's tough," agreed Billy sympathetically. "I hate a sadness."

"Perhaps you have known—?" The other's eyes lifted toward him, then dropped dispiritedly. "But, no, you are too young. But I—Ach!" He added in his own tongue a line of which Billy caught *geliebt* and *gelebt*, and so nodded understandingly.

"That geliebing business is bad stuff," he returned, and again the other tugged at his mustaches with a nervous hand and shook his big blond head.

"She was to have met me here," he said abruptly. "She wrote—I was to come quick—and then she comes not. That is woman, the *ewige weibliche*." He scowled. "But, Gott, how enchantment was in her!"

Billy heard himself sigh in unison. The phrase suggested Arlee. And the situation was not dissimilar. He felt a positive sympathy for the big blond fellow in his pronounced clothes and glossy boots and careful boutonnière.... He smiled in friendly fashion.

"She'll come along yet," he prophesied, "and if she doesn't, just you go out after her. I wouldn't take too many chances in the waiting game."

The German shook his head. His blue eyes swam with sentimental moisture. "You do not understand," he said. "She went with another—I must wait for her to come away. I have no address—so?"

"Well, that—that's different," stammered the young American. His sympathy became cynical. Fishy business—but even a fishy business has its human side. So presently he found himself gazing interestedly upon the photograph the German displayed in the back of his watch—the photograph of a decolleté young woman with provocative dark eyes and parted lips and pearl-like teeth, and he shook the caller's hand most heartily in parting, and prophesied, with fine assurance, the successful end of this fishy romance.

"You have a heart, my friend," said the German solemnly, and lifting hat and stick and lemon-colored gloves from the table, he bowed profoundly in farewell.

"And to the Fräulein—you will give my so deep apology?" he added earnestly, and Billy assured him that he would. And he found himself, for all his pre-occupation with the vision of Arlee's spring-like beauty, by no means displeased at the errand. A man must have something to do while he is waiting—if he is to avoid last bottles! He would seek her out that very afternoon.

But by afternoon he was tearing upstairs and downstairs through the hotel after a very different quarry, which at last he ran to earth at a tiny table behind a palm on the veranda. The quarry was further protected by an enveloping newspaper, but Billy did not stand on ceremony.

"I want to talk to you," said he.

Falconer looked up. He recognized Billy perfectly, though his gaze gave no admission of that. This tall young fellow with the deep-set gray eyes and the rugged chin and the straight black hair he first remembered seeing dancing that Wednesday evening with Arlee—after their own disastrous tea and its estrangement. Arlee had appeared on mystifyingly good terms with him, though he was positive from his own observations, and had corroboration from the Evershams, that she had never spoken to him until five minutes before. Then the fellow had fairly grilled the Evershams about the girl's whereabouts last night. And he had learned that the previous afternoon he had managed to take Claire's protection upon himself in the bazaars, actually convincing her that she ought to feel indebted to him, and had driven back with them.... An unabashed intruder, that fellow! He ought to have a lesson.

His air of unwelcome deepened, if possible, as Billy helped himself to a chair, drew it confidentially close to him and cast a careful glance about the veranda.

"I don't want anyone to hear this," he explained.

Falconer smiled cynically. He had met confidential young Americans before. There was nothing they could sell *him*.

"It's about Miss Beecher." Billy looked uncomfortable. He hesitated, blushed boyishly through his tan, and blurted, "There's something mighty queer about that departure of hers yesterday."

"Ah!"

"I don't feel right about it.... It's deuced queer. She isn't in Alexandria."

"Ah!"

"If you say 'Ah' again, I hope you choke," said Billy violently to himself. Aloud he continued, "I wired to the Khedivial and to all the other hotels—there are just a few—and she isn't registered there, and the Maynards are not, either."

"Possibly staying with friends," said Falconer indifferently. He regarded his paper.

"Very few Americans have friends in Alexandria. However, that might be so. But no ship has arrived from the Continent for three days, and it seems mighty odd, if they were there three days ago, for them to have wired at the last minute and had her tear off like that."

"I do not pretend to account for your compatriots," said the sandy-haired young man.

Billy looked at him a minute. "There's no use in your being disagreeable," he remarked. "I didn't thrust myself upon you because I was attracted to you, at all. But I thought you were a sensible, masculine human being who was interested in Miss Beecher's whereabouts."

"I beg your pardon," said the other young man. "I am—I mean I am interested—if you think there is anything really wrong. But I do not see your point."

"Well, now, see if you can see this. I wired the consul there and some other fellow at the port, and they wired back that no people of the name of Maynard have arrived on any of the boats for the past two weeks—that was as far back as they looked up. Now that's *queer*."

"He could be mistaken—or they could have bought some one else's accommodations—and that would account for the hastiness of their plans," Falconer argued.

"But what train did she go on?"

"What train? Why, the express for Alexandria."

"That left at eight-thirty. Now why in the world would she rush away in the middle of the afternoon, sending a telegram from the station and leaving her packing undone, for an eight-thirty train?"

"Why I—I really can't say. She may have had errands——"

"Where did she have her dinner? Did she dine with friends at some of the hotels? What friends has she here?"

"I really can't say as to that, either. I wasn't aware that she had any."

"And where did she send that telegram from? There isn't a copy of any such telegram at the offices I've been to—at Cook's or the station. It might have been written on a telegraph blank and sent up by messenger with the money—but why not come herself, with all that time on her hands? And nobody remembers selling her any ticket to Alexandria—and you know anybody would remember selling anything to a girl like that."

Falconer was silent.

"And nobody at Cook's paid out any money on her letter of credit—or cashed any express checks for her. Where did that money come from that was sent back to the hotel?"

"But what is the point of all this?"

"That's what I just particularly don't know.... But it needs looking into."

Falconer favored him with a level scrutiny. "How long have you known Miss Beecher?"

"I met her the night before last. That, however, doesn't enter into the case."

"It would seem to me that it might."

"Between three days and three weeks," said Billy, remembering something, "the difference is sometimes no greater than between Tweedledum and Tweedledee." He smiled humorously at the other young man, a frank, likeable smile that softened magically the bluntness of his young mouth. "That's why I came to you. You are the only soul I know to be interested in Miss Beecher's welfare. The Evershams are off up the Nile—and they'd probably be helpless, anyway. Besides, you know more about this blamed Egypt of yours than I do.... Have you any idea where she went yesterday afternoon?"

"Not at all."

"Neither have the Evershams. They were surprised when I asked them about it this morning. They didn't know she was going. Now she went somewhere in a limousine——"

"Probably to the station."

"American girls don't go to stations in floating white clothes and hats all pink roses. I particularly remember the pink rose," said Billy gloomily. "No, if she had been going to the station she would have had on a little blue or gray suit, very up and down, and a little minute of a hat with just one perky feather. And she'd have a bag of sorts with her—no girl would rush away to Alexandria without a bag."

"She could have sent it ahead of her or returned and dressed later for the station."

"Why the mischief did I tramp off to those bazaars?" said the young American. "But, see here—weren't you around the hotel after that yesterday—at tea time?"

"Er—yes—I——"

"And weren't you rather looking out for Miss Beecher? Wouldn't you have noticed if she had been coming or going?"

Falconer stroked his small mustache and shot a look at Billy out of the corners of his eyes which expressed his distinct annoyance at these intrusive demands.

"I don't remember to have met you," said he slowly.

"You haven't. I know your name, but you don't know mine. I am William B. Hill."

"Ah—Behill."

"No—B. Hill. The B is an initial."

"Of what?" said the other casually, and Billy's cheeks grew suddenly warm.

"Of my middle name," said he, with steady composure. "If we are to do any team-work you will have to let it go at the William and the Hill."

"What team-work do you suggest?"

"Find out where she went yesterday. Find out where she is now. What worries me," he burst out, with ungovernable uneasiness, yet with a hint of humor at his own extravagant imaginings, "is her talking to that Turk fellow yesterday—that Captain Kerissen, I think she called him. She had told me the night before that he was going to get her some ball tickets or other, and I didn't think anything of it, but yesterday I thought he had his nerve to come and call upon her. You see, I passed through the hall and saw them talking. I went out to the veranda and after he had gone I came in again, but she was nowhere in sight. Then I went back to the veranda, and in a few moments she came out, in white with a rose on her hat, and went off in a car that was ready. Of course Kerissen wasn't in the car, and I haven't any proof of his connection with the thing, but he might easily have induced her to look at some mosque or other off the 'beaten track'— —"

"But she returned, for later she sent that telegram from the station," Falconer argued.

Billy was silent. Then he burst out, "But all the same there is a mystery to this thing.... She—she's too confoundedly young and pretty to run around alone in this painted jade of a city."

"This city has law and order—much more of them than there are in your national hotbeds of robbery and murder."

"H'm—well, I don't hold any brief for Chicago—I suppose Chicago is the target—so I won't defend that. But I've heard stories."

"Queer ones, I should say."

"*Devilish* queer ones!... How about that young Monkton or Monkhouse who dropped out of things last winter?"

Falconer looked annoyed. "Oh, there are rumors——"

"Yes, rumors that he flirted with a Turkish lady—that he was on horseback just outside her carriage during the jam at the Kasr-el-Nil bridge, and they looked and smiled and afterwards met in a shop. And rumors that she gave him a *rendezvous* at her home and that he told another man about it at the club, who warned him sharply, and he only laughed.... But it's no rumor that he disappeared. He's gone, all right, and nobody knows where he went, and nobody seems to want to know. Officially they said he was drowned out swimming—or lost in a sandstorm riding in the desert—or spiked on top of an obelisk or something equally reasonable—but, privately, people say other things.... No international law intrudes into the Turkish woman question."

"What of it?" Falconer looked stubborn. "I daresay the fellow received his deserts.... But the case hardly applies—what?"

"Well—it makes one feel that anything can happen here—that the city is quicksand where a chance step would engulf one." Billy stared frowningly out on the vivid street ahead of him. A pretty English bride and her soldier husband were out exercising their dogs. Two ladies in a victoria were advertising their toilettes. A blond baby toddled past with his black nurse. It was all very peaceful and charming. It did not look like quicksand.... Into the picture came a one-eyed man with a stuffed crocodile on his head, stalking slowly along, scanning the veranda with his single, penetrating eye, calling his wares in harsh gutturals, and with him came suddenly the sense of that strange background before which all this bright tourist life was played, that dark watching, secret East, curious and incalculable.

Falconer folded his paper with a sharp crackle that recalled young Hill's wandering thought. "That's all very well, but it doesn't apply," he observed, with conviction.

"Then where is she?" Billy was bluntly belligerent.

The other put his paper in his pocket. "In Alexandria, to be sure, and not at all pleased, either, to have you bring her name into such questioning." He looked squarely at Billy as he said that, and the eyes of the two young man met and exchanged a secret challenge of hostility.

Billy rose. "Oh, all right," he returned. "I daresay I am as much a fool as you take me for.... She may be all right. But if not—I thought I'd give you a chance to take a hand in it."

"The sporting chance," said Falconer, with an appreciable smile. "I'm much obliged—but I don't at all share your misgivings.... And what in the world do you propose to do about it?"

For a minute Billy's gaze blankly interrogated the sunlit distances. His eyes were fixed, but empty; his forehead knitted in an uncertain frown. Then quite suddenly he turned and flashed at Falconer a look of odd and unforeseen decision.

"I'm going to buy a crocodile," he imparted, with a wide, boyish grin. "I'm going to buy a crocodile of a one-eyed man."

Stolidly Falconer eyed his departing back. Stolidly, definitely, comprehensively, he pronounced judgment. "Mad," said he. "Mad as the March Hare."

CHAPTER VIII
THE MIDNIGHT VISITOR

That stealthy touch brought Arlee half upright, shot with ghastly alarms. Her heart stopped beating; it stood still in the cold clutch of terror. The breath seemed to have left her body.

Once more she felt the hands gropingly upon her. It came from the back side of her bed, reaching apparently from the very wall. And then she heard a voice whispering, "Be still—I do not hurt you. Be still."

It was a woman's voice, soft, sibilant, hushed, and the frozen grip of fear was broken. She was trembling now uncontrollably.

"Who is there?"

"S-sh!" came the warning response, and then, her eyes staring into the shadowy recess, she saw the curtains at the back side of the bed were parting as a figure appeared between them.

"Give me a box, a book—somethings to put here in this lock," commanded the voice peremptorily, and in a daze Arlee found herself extending a magazine across the bed toward the half-seen figure, who turned and busied herself about the curtains a moment, then came straight across the bed into the room beside Arlee.

"Now you see who I am," said the astonishing intruder calmly.

Mutely Arlee shook her head, seeing only a figure about her own height clad in a dark negligée. Dumfounded she stood watching while her visitor deliberately lighted a candle.

"So—that is better," she observed, and in the light of the tiny taper between them the two stood facing each other.

Arlee saw a girl some years older than herself, a small, plump, rounded creature, with a flaunting and insouciant prettiness. Her eyes were dark and bright, her babyish lips were full and scarlet, her nose was whimsically uptilted. Dark hair curled closely to the vivid face and fell in ringlets over the white neck.

"You don't know me?" she said in astonishment at Arlee's eyes of wonder. "He has not told you?" Incredulity, impertinent and mocking, darted out of the dark eyes. "What you think then—you what got my room?"

"Your room?" Arlee echoed faintly. She flung a quivering hand toward the bed. "How did you get in here? I locked the door——"

"You see how I came—I came by the panel," She waited a moment, watching the wide blue eyes before her, the parted lips, the white cheeks in which the blood was slowly stealing back, and incredulity gave way to astonished acceptance. "You don't know that, either? That is very funny."

"Did you lock it?" was Arlee's next breathless question. "What was that you said about putting in a magazine? Did you leave it open?"

The other girl reached quickly and caught her arm, as Arlee turned toward the bed. "No, no, if it goes shut we cannot open it inside," she warned. "It does not open this side unless you have the key. It opens from without. But he will not come in now—he is at the Khedive's palace. We are all right."

"But I want to get away," cried Arlee. She turned upon this other girl great eyes of pitiful entreaty, eyes where the dark shadows about them lay like cruel bruises on the white flesh. "I must get away at once. Won't you help me?"

"Help you? I would help myself, if I could. But there is no way out. It is no use." The unknown girl spoke with a bitterness that brought conviction. Piteously the flare of hope and spirit wilted.

"You are sure?" she questioned faintly. "There is no way out?"

"No way, no way!" The other shook her head impatiently. "Do I not know? Let us talk of that again. Now I came to see you, to see what pretty face had sent me packing!" She laughed, but there was ugliness in the laughter, and catching up the candle she held it before Arlee, her face impudently close, her eyes black darts of curiosity.

"Well you are pretty enough," she said coolly. "Hamdi has always the good taste. But do you think you will keep my room from me—h'm?"

"I do not want your room," said Arlee with passionate intensity. "I do not want to stay here. I want only to go away. Oh, there must be a way. Please help me—please." She choked and broke down, the tears hot in her eyes.

"'I do not want to stay here'"

The other girl abruptly drew her down on the couch and settled herself beside her among the cushions. "Here—be comfortable—let us be comfortable and talk," she said. "Do not cry so—What, you are so soon sorry? You want to be off?"

Desperately Arlee steadied her shaking voice. "I must go at once."

"You got enough so soon?"

"Enough!" was the quivering echo.

"What you come for then?"

"Come for? I did not know what I was coming into. I thought—but tell me," she broke off to demand, "tell me about the plague. Was there any quarantine at all? How soon was it over? What is really happening?"

"Quar—quar—what you mean?"

"The plague? Has there been a plague here? Have people had to stay in the palace on account of it?"

"Oh—h!" The indrawn breath was eloquent of enlightenment. "Is that somethings he said to you?"

"Yes, yes. Isn't it true? Wasn't there any plague?"

With eyes of dreadful apprehension she saw the other shake her head in vigorous denial. "No plague," she said decisively. "My maid—she know everything. No sickness here."

"Then it was all a lie." Arlee's eyes fixed themselves on the dancing candle flame, swaying in the soft night air. She tried to think very coolly and collectedly, but her brain felt numb and fogged and heavy. The sight of that tortured candle flame hypnotized her. Faintly she whispered, "Then it was all—an excuse," and, at that, sharp terror, like a knife, cleaved her numbness. She turned furiously to her visitor.

"But he would not dare make it all up!"

She saw the callousness of the shrug. "Why not—he is the master here!" Her own heart echoed fearfully the words. She stammered, "But—but I wrote—I had a letter—there must——"

"What in all the world are you saying?" demanded the other. "What is this story?" and as Arlee began the quick, whispered narration she listened intently, her little dark head on one side, nodding wisely at intervals.

"So—you came to have tea," she repeated at the close, in her quaintly inflected, foreign-sounding English. "And you stay because of the plague? So?"

"But I wrote—I wrote to my friends and——"

"And gave him the letters!"

"But I had a letter from my friends—or a telegram rather." Arlee knitted her brows in furious thought. "And it sounded like her."

"Does he know her, that friend?" questioned the other and at Arlee's nod, "Then he could write it himself—that is easy on telegraph paper. He is so clever, that devil, Hamdi."

"But my friends knew where I was going"—slowly the mind turned back to trace the blind, careless steps of that afternoon. "At least he said he'd leave a note—Oh, what a fool I was!" she broke off to gasp, seeing how that forethought of his, that far-sighted remark, had prevented her from leaving a note of her own. And she remembered now, with flashing clearness, that upon her arrival he had carelessly inquired if she, too, had left a note of explanation. How lightly she had told him no! And what unguessed springs of action came perhaps from that single word! For so cleverly had the trap been swiftly prepared that if anything had gone wrong, if anyone had become aware of her intentions, it could have passed off as a visit and she would have returned to her hotel prattling joyously of her wonderful glimpse into the seclusion of Turkish aristocracy!

"But the soldier with the bayonet," she said aloud. "There was one on the stairs."

"A servant."

"Oh, if I had passed him!"

"You could not—he would run you through on a nod from Hamdi. They watch that stairs always—day and night."

Day and night—and she was alone here, in this grim palace, alone and helpless and forsaken.... What were her friends thinking about her? Where did they think she was? Her thoughts beat desperately upon that problem, trying to find there some ray of hope, some promise that there were clues which would lead them to her, but she found nothing there but deeper mystery and fearful surmise. He was clever enough to cover his traces. No one had known of his connection with her departure.... Perhaps he had sent them some false and misleading message like the one he had sent her.... What were they thinking? What did they believe? This was Friday night, and she had been gone since Thursday afternoon.

In that moment she saw with merciless clarity the bitter straits that she was in.

"Oh, he is a devil!" her companion was reaffirming with an angry little half-whisper sibilant with fury. "Look how he treat me—me, Fritzi Baroff! You do not know me? You do not know that name? In Vienna it is not so unknown—Oh, God, I was so happy in Vienna!" She stopped, her breast heaving, with the flare of emotion, then went on quickly, with suppressed vehemence, "I was a singer—in the light opera. I dance, too, and I was arriving. Only this year I was to have a fine rôle—and it all went, zut, it all went for that man! I was one fool about him, and his dark eyes and his strange ways.... I thought I had a prince. And he worship me then, too—he follow me, he give me big diamonds.... So he take me here—it was to be the vacation!"

She gave a strangling little laugh. Arlee was listening with a painful intensity. She was living, she thought, in an Arabian nights.

"I stay at the hotel first till he make this like a private apartment for me," went on the little dancer, "and when I come here he do everything for me. I have luxury, yes, jewels and dresses and a fine new car. Then, by and by, I grow tired. It was always the same and he was at the palace, much. And he would not let me make acquaintance. We quarrel, but still I have a fancy for him, and then, you understand, money is not always so easy to find. Life can be hard. But I get more restless, I want to go back on the stage and I, well, I write some letters that he finds out. *Bang*, goes the door upon me! He laugh like a fiend. He say that I am to be a little Turkish lady to the end of my life. Oh, God, he shut me up like a prisoner in this place, and I can do nothing—nothing—nothing!"

She beat out angry emphasis on the palm of one hand with a clenched little fist. "I go nearly mad. I lose my head. He laugh—he is like that. He is a devil when he turns against you, and, you understand, he had somethings new to play with now.... Sometimes he seem to love me as before, and then I would grow soft and coax that he take me to Europe some day, and then when I think he mean it—Oh, how he laugh!" She drew in her breath sharply. "Sometimes I think he will take me again—sometime—but I cannot tell. And the days never end. They are terrible. My youth is going, going. And my youth is all I have."

She looked at Arlee with eyes where her terror was visible, and all the lines of her pretty, common little face were changed and sharpened, and her babyish lips dragged down strangely at the corners.

A surge of pity went through Arlee Beecher. "Oh, you will escape," she heard herself saying eagerly. "And I will escape—or—or——"

"Or?"

"Or I will kill myself," she whispered quiveringly.

The little Viennese stared hard at her, and a sudden crinkle of amusement darted across the bright shallows of her eyes. "Come, love is not so bad," she said, "and Hamdi can be charming." Then as she saw a shudder run through the young girl before her, "Oh, if you do not fancy him!" she cried airily, yet with a keen look.

But Arlee's two hands sought and covered up the scarlet shame in her face. She did not cry; she felt that every tear in her was dried in that bitter flame. Her whole body seemed on fire, burning with fury and revulsion and that awful sense of humiliation.

The other stirred restively, "Come, do not cry—I hate people to cry. It makes everything so worse. And do not talk of killing. It is not so easy anyway, that killing. Do I not think I will die and end all when my rage is hot—but how? How? I cannot beat my head out against the wall like a Russian. I cannot stick a penknife in my throat or eat glass. To do that one must be a monster of courage. And I have no poison to eat, no gas to turn on.... Then the mood goes and the day is bright and I look in the glass and say, 'Die? Die for you? Kill all this beautiful young thing that has such joy to dance and sing? Never! Some day I will be out of this and laugh at the memory of such blackness.' And so I practice my voice and my steps—and I wait my chance. When you came, yesterday, first I was furious to be pushed out, then I think it is the chance, maybe. I think you would be glad to help me to get out and not to stay to make you jealous. But if you are also in the trap——" Her voice fell dispiritedly. She drew a long, weary breath.

"But I shall not stay in the trap." Arlee spoke with desperate resolve, her eyes on the sputtering candle, her palms against her burning cheeks, her finger tips pressed into her throbbing temples. "I shall not let him make me afraid like this. He must know he will be found out—he cannot play like this with an American girl! I shall face him to-morrow. I shall demand my freedom. I shall tell him that I did tell people at the hotel—that he will be discovered. I will make *him* afraid!"

"You cannot. He watches what happens on the outside—he knows."

After a pause, "Oh, why did I come!" said Arlee in choking bitterness.

The little dancer turned, and, sitting there cross-legged on the couch like a squat little idol, her chin sunk in her palm, her dark eyes staring unwinkingly at Arlee, gave the girl a long, strange scrutiny.

"You do not like him?" she said.

"I hate him!"

"But you came to tea?"

"To meet his sister. To see the palace."

"His sister? Did he show you one?"

"Yes—a woman with red hair. A Turkish woman. She spoke French to me."

"Ah—that would be Seniha!"

"Seniha? I don't know. She played the piano. Has he more than one sister?"

But as she put the question a sudden flash of intuition forestalled the dancer's mocking cry of "Sister!" And as Fritzi hurried on, "He has no sister—not here, anyway," Arlee's thoughts ran back to the beginning of that very evening which seemed so long ago when she had plunged wildly into those unknown rooms, and saw again that painted, jeweled woman with her outstretched arms.

"She is his wife," the Viennese was saying.

"I—I did not know that he was married."

"Oh, Turkish marriages." The other shrugged, with a contempt a trifle droll in one who had dispensed with every ceremony. "She was his second. The first was a little girl, he said. The match was made for him. She is dead. This Seniha was her cousin, a cousin who was divorced and she lived with the wife. And our pretty Hamdi made love to her, and she was mad about him and so, presently, it happens that he must marry her, for it would be terrible to have disgrace upon the wife's family. Besides the first wife had no children. So he married her. But *she* had no children. It was all one fairy story." Fritzi laughed under her breath in great enjoyment. "So Hamdi was cheated and he has been a devil to her. The first little wife dies and he shut the second up here, teasing her sometimes, sometimes making love when he is dull, but forcing her to his will for fear he will divorce her.... How she must have hated you, when she had to play that sister. Except that she was glad that *I* was being put aside," the dancer added with quick spite. "I think she would put poison in my meat if she did not fear Hamdi so.... And always she hopes that he will come back to her. I have seen her waiting, night after night— —"

And Arlee thought of the jewels and the silks ... and the long, long, silent hours.... Slowly she put out her hand and snuffed out the smoking wick, then raised her eyes to where the painted bars stretched black across the starry square of sky. "Won't *she* help?" she asked.

"Not she! Hamdi would find her out.... Not through her can you get word to your friends. For you have friends here? And they will help you? And then you will help me?"

"Oh, yes, if I can get help," promised Arlee. "But I am afraid my friends have gone up the Nile—and there are just—just one or two left in Cairo that would help. And I must get word to them *at once*. What is the best way? Couldn't I push a note through the windows on the street? Someone might see that!"

"Yes, the doorkeeper. No, that is not safe.... If only that girl were sure— —"

"Mariayah?" cried Arlee.

"No, the other—the little one with the wart over her eye. Have you seen her? Well, watch for her, then. She has an itching palm—she may help. But only in little things, of course, for she is afraid. And I have no money left and she is afraid to take a jewel."

"I have almost no money," said Arlee blankly. "Only a letter of credit——"

"A letter of nothing here! But promise her your friends will give much."

"Would she mail a letter?"

"Have you stamps? No? She is so ignorant that is an obstacle. And the post is distant and she dare not go far. But sometimes the baker sends a little boy, and if you had money to give she might get a note to him to carry—though, maybe, she burns the note and keeps the money," the Viennese ended pessimistically.

"But I must get help *at once*," Arlee iterated passionately. Before——"

"Before?" the other repeated curiously, "He makes love to you—h'm?"

"He—is beginning."

"Only beginning?"

"Only—beginning." Arlee felt the girl's strange, hard scrutiny through the dark. Then she heard her draw a quick breath as if her eyes on Arlee's flower-like face had convinced her of something against all her sorry little reason.

"Well, that is good then," she said. "Try to keep him off. What does he promise you?"

"Promise me? He does not promise anything."

"But he must say something—what is between you—what?" demanded the other impatiently.

Briefly, her shamed cheeks grateful for the shadows, Arlee told of that walk in the garden, of the flowers and the letter, the scene after dinner. And the other girl's eyes grew wider and wider, and then finally she burst into a smothered little laugh.

"Oh, he is mad, that Hamdi!" she whispered. "He is a monster of vanity—'conquest of the spirit'—h'm, I comprehend. That young man has a pride beyond all sense. You dazzle him—he is in love again like a boy. And he must dazzle you. His pride demands a victory not of force alone.... Some men are like that.... Well, that is your chance!"

"My chance?"

"Play with his vanity—fight his force with that!" said this strange initiator into terrible secrets. "He will believe anything of his fascinations—I know him. And if he is so mad for you that he dares all this trouble to have you here, then he is so mad that you can fool him and make him hold back in hopes to gain more from you. Make him think you are coming, as he wishes, heart and body, but still you would wait a little. So you gain time.... Oh, you must be careful! If he loses hope, if you anger him, why the game is over. But if you are careful you can gain a few days— —"

"A few days," said Arlee in a tense little voice.

"Well, that is something—since you hate him so!"

"Yes, that is something." Arlee drew a shivering breath, her head drooping, her lashes on her cheeks. Then suddenly, amazingly, her chin came pluckily up, her soft lips set with desperate decision, her eyes turned on her counselor a look of flashing spirit. She was like some young wild thing at bay, harried, defiant, tensely defensive. Something of the pathos of her innocent presence there, in that evil palace, utterly alone, hopelessly defiant, penetrated for an instant the callous acceptances of the little dancer and her eyes softened with facile sympathy, but the impression dulled, and she only nodded her head encouragingly.

"Good! That is the way! Women can always act!" she murmured, slipping off the divan and drawing her fluttering robes about her. "But it is very late and I must go—it is not safe to stay so."

"Where is your room? Could I get to you?"

"No—for you cannot open that panel on the inside—unless you can steal the key from him as I could not! My room—for this present, little one," and her eyes laughed suddenly in challenge, "is up on the top—a little old room all alone. My doors are locked, but there is a panel in my room, too, a panel at the top of tiny stairs, and the lock on that panel is so old and rusty that a knife make it open. So I pushed it open and came down the tiny stairs that end out there in the passage way, and I opened your panel. Now I must steal back, but I shall come again, and we must plan."

"But where does this secret passage go?" Arlee had followed over the bed, and held aside the heavy draperies while the little Baroff was pushing the panel softly and carefully open. Eagerly Arlee peered out into the darkness beyond. "Where does it go?" she repeated.

"It runs above the hall of banquets and into the *selamlik*," whispered the Viennese. "It opens into Hamdi's rooms, he says, and I know that a servant sleeps always at his door and another is at the foot of the stairs. So it would be madness to try that way."

But Arlee stared thoughtfully into the secret place. "I am glad I know," she said.

"Well, good-by, little one." The Viennese was standing outside now, softly closing the door. For a moment her face remained in the opening. "You will not tell Hamdi that I came—no?" she demanded sharply, and then on Arlee's quick reassurance she nodded, whispered good-by again, and drew back her little face.

The wall rolled into place and a gentle click told of the caught lock. The curtains fell back over the wall. And Arlee was left huddling there alone, feeling that it had all been a dream, but for the heavy scent that lingered in the air and the wild fear beating in her heart.

CHAPTER IX
A DESPERATE GAME

Very slowly the black night grayed down into a wan, spectral morning, and slowly the gray morning paled into a dim mother-of-pearl dawn. And then suddenly the mother-of-pearliness brightened into a shimmering opal, and the ray of pale gold light slanted through the barred window and the bright face of new day peeped over the sill, staring out of countenance the lurking shadows of the night.

And then Arlee's eyes closed, and the heart which had been beating like a frightened rabbit's at every sound and shadow steadied into a rhythm as regular as a clock. She slept like a tired baby; while the light grew brighter and higher, and reached in over the shining dressing table, over the white piano, to rest upon the oblivious face upon the couch and to play with the bright, tangled hair.

The first knocking upon the door did not disturb that sleep, and it was a long time before the knock was again sounded. Then Arlee heard and sprang to her feet in a lightning rush of consciousness. It was Mariayah again, and the water jars which already looked familiar to her, and after the water jars appeared more roses and with the roses a letter.

Those roses came, the letter explained, to droop their heads before her loveliness, which put theirs to shame. They would greet her as humbler sisters greet a fairer. For they were roses of a day, but she was the Rose of Life. The capitals were Kerissen's own. And then abruptly the letter demanded:

> Did I frighten you last night? Is it so strange to you that you have magic to make a man forget all the barriers of your convention? Do you not know you have an enchantment which distills in the blood and changes it to wine? You are the Rose of Life, the Rose of Desire, and no man can look upon you without longing. But you must not be angry at me for that, for I am your slave, and would strew roses always to soften the world for your little feet.... Fortune has made you my guest. Will you not smile upon me while Fortune

smiles? Luncheon will be in the garden, for it is cool and fresh today.

The mask was slipping. Only a flimsy veil of sentiment now over his rash will. Only a light pretense of her freedom, of his courtesy. He was beginning to declare himself....

But she must not let him suspect that she knew. She must *not*.

Her spirit responded fiercely to this tense demand upon it. The dread, the panic of the night was gone. The fear that had shaken her was beaten down like a cowardly dog. Excitement burned in her blood. Everything depended upon her coolness and her wit, upon a look, perhaps, the turn of a phrase, the droop of an eye, and she was passionately resolved that neither coolness nor wit should fail her, nor words nor looks nor eyes betray the heart of her. She would play her rôle with every breath she drew.

She crossed the room at the luncheon summons in the nervous tensity of mood that an actress might go to play a part in which her career would live or die. Every half hour with Kerissen was now a duel, every minute was a stroke to be parried, and she flung herself into that duel with the desperate exhilaration of such daring. Her hands were icy, and her cheeks were flaming with the excitement which consumed her, but she revealed no other trace of it, and she wondered to herself at the inscrutable fairness of the face which, looked back at her from the glass.

None of the record of those frightened, sleepless hours was written there, none of her furious pride, her fixed intensity. Only the soft shadows under the blue eyes gave her face a look of added delicacy for all the unnatural flare of brilliant color, and a faint wistfulness in those eyes seemed to overlay the smiles she practiced, like a cloud shadow on a brook. And never, never, in all her glad, care-free days, had she been as distractingly pretty as she was that moment. With an angry little pang she recognized it, pinning on the lace hat with its enchanting rose, and then desperately she resolved to employ it and added two of Kerissen's pink roses to the costume.

She thought the scene was very like a stage, when she came out through the narrow door which the old woman unlocked from a key she carried on a girdle, and slowly descended the stone steps. Beneath the wide-spreading lebbek a low table was laid for luncheon with two wicker chairs beside it. The green of the fresh turf was as vivid as stage grass; the lilies loomed unreally large and white; the poinsettias flaunted like red paper flowers behind the vivid picture that the Captain made in a dazzling buff and green uniform picked out with gold. His bow was theatric, so was the deep look of exaggerated admiration he bent upon her—it was strange to remember that her danger was not theatric also. But that was deadly real, and real, too, was the sudden surge of color into the young man's sallow face.

"You are kind to my roses—if not to me," he said quickly, and held out his hand for the brief little clasp she accorded.

"Your roses are dumb and have said nothing to make me cross," she laughed lightly, and looked swiftly about her. "How lovely this is," she ran on, "and how charming to feel a breeze. That room is rather warm and close.... Is you sister still too ill to come?"

And scarcely waiting for the assent which he began to frame with his searching eyes upon her, she added, "I am afraid I made her angry last night by intruding upon her. But I heard her voice and ran back to her room to ask after her. She wouldn't let me stay at all."

It was droll how natural her voice sounded, she thought. His eyes held their fixed scrutiny in an instant, then dropped carelessly away, as he drew forward the wicker chairs. "She is a *nerveuse*, you understand," he said with an air of indolent resignation, "and one can do nothing for that sort of thing. A crisis comes—one must wait for it to pass.... She regrets that condition.... And she wished me to present her regrets to you," he added suavely, "for that reception of you last night. She was ill and did not expect you—and she did not wish you to see her in that condition."

"I should not have gone," acknowledged Arlee, "but, as I said, I heard voices from the ante-room and thought I would like to see her.... That pretty little maid she gave me does not speak any English, so I cannot send any messages."

"But you can write them."

"My French spelling is worse than my pronunciation!" She laughed amusedly. "I wish you would find me an interpreter to put my polite remarks into polite sounding phrases. I know I put things like a First Reader!"

He smiled. "You do not put them like a First Reader to me. *We* do not need an interpreter.... Unless I need one to speak to you?"

"Oh, no, your English is wonderful!" She waited an instant, then took a breathless plunge. "Have you any more news for me?" she demanded, forcing the note of expectancy. It would be suspicious, indeed, if she did not ask that. But what if he had decided to throw the pretense aside— —

"Not one word of news more," he said slowly.

She felt him watching her as she looked down on her plate. The pretty little girl was passing a platter of pigeon: Arlee did not speak until she had helped herself, then she said in a voice touched faintly with chagrin, "Well, the English are not very gallant toward ladies in misfortune, are they? I feel furiously snubbed.... Of course Mrs. Eversham never was much of a writer, but they might send over my letters from the hotel. The last mail ought to have brought a lot from that big brother of mine."

"Ah, yes, that big, grown-up, married brother who is so satisfied with all you do!"

She felt she had been unfortunate in her rash confidences.

"He won't be so pleased when he learns how I wasted a perfectly good Nile ticket," she remarked. "And Big Brother is rather fierce when he isn't pleased."

His eyes smiled, as if he understood and despised her suggestion. "Cairo and your America are not so near," he observed negligently, "that an incident here is a matter of immediate knowledge there."

She felt the danger of seeming to threaten him. "Oh, I'd 'fess up," she said lightly, playing with her food. "There—shoo—go away!" she cried suddenly, with a militant gesture about her plate. "That's one thing I hate about Egypt—the flies!"

"I hope that is the only thing you hate," said the young man blandly.

"Isn't that enough? There are so many of them!"

He laughed with real amusement at her petulance. "Is there netting enough in your room?" he inquired. "Would you like more for your bed?"

"Oh, no, I'm all right, thank you. The flies are chiefly bothersome at meals. This is certainly their paradise."

"But is there anything you would like—to make you happy here? I will get it for you. Would you not like some books, some music, some new clothes——"

"I don't wonder you ask! But really this white gown will last a little longer—Cairo is so clean. No, thank you, there is nothing I need bother you about—Oh, yes, there really is one book that I would like—a Turkish or an Arabic dictionary. I have always meant to learn a little of the language and this would seem the opportunity."

In the pause in which he appeared to be consuming pigeon she could feel him weighing her request, foreseeing its results.

"I shall be most happy to teach you," was what he said, but she knew she would never have that dictionary. And so one plan of the morning went flying to the winds. But she snatched at the next opening she saw and plunged into interested questions about the Turkish language, asking the words for such things as seemed spontaneously to occur to her—wall, palace, table—numbers—days of the week—repeating the pronunciation with the earnestness of a diligent young pupil, until she felt that her memory had all it could hold. And distrust, always ready now like a prompter in the box, suggested most upsettingly that perhaps he was not giving the right words. She resolved to experiment upon Mariayah.

He reverted, with increasing emphasis, upon his desire to make her happy in the palace, to surround her with whatever she desired, and swiftly she availed herself of this second opening.

"Yes, indeed, there is something that would make me happier, if you don't mind, please," she added with a droll assumption of meekness. "You don't know how horrid it is for me to be caged in one room and not be out of doors, and I would love to come down into the garden when I want to. Won't you give me a key to that door? That is, if it is always locked."

"Generally it is not," he said readily, "but now with the soldiers about it is safer. You see, the soldiers can approach the garden through the open banquet hall"—and he nodded to the colonnade behind them—"and though it is forbidden, one cannot foretell their obedience."

To one who knew those soldiers were chimerical acquiescence was maddening.

"But, dear me, can't you have some one in the banquet hall to shoo the soldiers away?" Arlee argued persuasively. "Since the rest of the household has the court, it seems awfully selfish not to let the ladies have the garden for their airing."

"It may be managed," he assented. "It has always been done, for the garden is for the ladies. Whenever you wish to be in the garden you have but to send word, and the household will remain in the court, as is, indeed, the custom."

"It would not be so terrible, you know, if a gardener or a donkey-boy did see my face!" laughed Arlee. "Plenty of them have had that pleasure before this."

She saw that the young man's face changed. Every clear-cut line of it was sharp with repugnance. "You need not remind me of that," he said with muffled fierceness, staring down at his plate.

"The danger line!" she thought while shaking her head at him, with the tense semblance of an amused little smile…. "You aren't the least bit English," she rebuked, "and I thought you were."

"Not in that…. And some day England will see her folly."

"America is seeing her folly now," thought Arlee with secret bitterness. But when she raised her eyes they were gently contemplative. She spoke musingly.

"In things like that you aren't at all what I thought you were—about our social customs, I mean. Yet fundamentally, I think you are."

"That I am what?"

"What I thought you were."

He waited, palpably waited, but Arlee continued to peel a tangerine with absorption, and the question had to come from him. He put it with an air of indolent amusement, yet she felt the intent interest in leash.

"And what did you think I was like, *chère petite mademoiselle?*"

"Very handsome for one thing, Monsieur! You see, I owe you a compliment for calling me such a pretty name as this!" With a mischievous smile she touched the roses nodding in her girdle. "And very autocratic for another, with a very bad temper. If you can't get your way you would be shockingly disagreeable!"

"But I always get my way," he assured her lazily, his teeth showing under his small, black mustache.

"I believe you do!" Ingenuous admiration, simple and sustained, was in the look she gave him. Her hands were not half so icy now, nor her nerves so tense. She felt strangely surer of herself; the actual presence of the danger calmed her. She must make good with this, she thought simply, in strenuous American.

"And yet," she went on thoughtfully, the pretty picture of fascinated absorption in this most feminine topic—the dissection of a young man—"yet, you are chivalrous. And I think that is the quality we American girls admire most of all."

"The quality—of indulgence?" he questioned, with a half-railing air.

"The quality—of gentleness."

"But is there not another quality which you American girls would admire more than that gentleness—if you ever had the chance in your lives to see it? The quality of dominance? The courage of the man who dares what he desires, and who takes what he wills? Is not that——"

"Ah, yes, we love strong men," Arlee flung into the speech that was bearing him on like a tide, "but we don't think them strong unless they are strong enough to fight themselves. They may take what they will—but they mustn't crush it.... There is a gentleness in great strength—I can't explain what I mean——"

"Ah, I see, I see." He smiled subtly. "I am not to crush you, little Rose of Desire," he said softly.

She met the sly significance of his gaze with a look of frank, unfaltering candor. "Of course not," she said stoutly. "When you—you make me afraid of you, you make me like you less. You seem less like the friend I knew on the boat."

"Ah, that boat!... You were my friend, then!" he added suddenly, with a note of question sounding through the affirmation, and she answered quickly, looking away with an air of petulant reproach. "Why, you know I was, Captain Kerissen. And here in Cairo——"

"Yes, here in Cairo," he interrupted triumphantly, "in the face of those eyes and tongues—I saw that red-headed dog of an Englishman looking his anger at you! But you smiled on me before them all—those fools, those tyrannic fools——"

"But you mustn't abuse my other friends! They were only—stupid!"

"Stupid as their blood brother, the ox!... But they are not in the picture now—those other friends!" Disagreeably he laughed. "And you do not grieve for them—no? The world has not touched you? There is no one out there,"—he made a gesture over the guarding walls—"no one who holds a fragment of your thought, of your heart in his hands?"

She looked at him as if puzzled, then burst into a bubbling laugh. "Why, of course not! I've just had a nice time with people. There has never been a bit of sentiment about it!"

"Not on your side," he said meaningly, and because this was hitting the truth smartly on the head she looked past him in some confusion.

"Oh—boys!" she said with a deprecating little laugh. "I've never listened to them."

He leaned back in his chair, feeling for his cigarette case, and the contentment of his look deepened. "You have been a child, asleep to life," he murmured complacently. "I told you you were a princess—let us say a sleeping princess waiting for the prince, like that old fairy tale of the English." He was looking at his cigarette as he tapped it on the arm of his chair, and slowly struck a light, then, after the first breath, "But do you not hear his footsteps in your sleep?" he added, and gave her a glance from the corner of his eyes.

She looked up and then down; she stared out into the sun-flooded garden and laughed softly. "Even princesses dream," she demurely acknowledged, and thought the line and her fleet, meaning glance went very well with this mad opera-bouffe which fate was forcing her to play.

Kerissen seemed to think that went very well, too, for his flashing teeth acknowledged his pleasure in her aptness; then his smile faded and she felt him studying her over his cigarette, studying her averted gaze, the bright color in her cheeks, the curves of her lips, and he was puzzled and perturbed by the sweet, baffling beauty of her. A wild elation began to swell his heart. His eyes glowed, his blood burned with the triumph, not so much of his daring capture of her, but of the flattering tribute that her pretty ways were paying toward his personality alone. Wary as he was, cynical of subterfuge, he did not penetrate her guard. His monstrous vanity whispered eager flattery in his ears.

And still he continued to stare at her, finding her unbelievably lovely. "My grandfather would call you an *houri* from paradise," he told her, the warmth of admiration deepening in his eyes.

"And your grandfather's grandson knows that I am only an *houri* from America!... But that *is* paradise for *houris*!"

"And not for men, no!... Sometimes I have wished that those English would restore in me that young belief in the heaven of the Prophet," he continued, smiling, "and now that wish is granted. It is here, that paradise," and his smile, flashing about the lonely garden, came to dwell again upon the girl before him.

She laughed. "But does one *houri* make a paradise?" she bantered, while the beating, hurrying heart of her went faster and faster till she thought his ears would hear it. "We have a proverb—one swallow does not make a summer."

"*Cela dépend*—that depends upon the *houri*.... When *you* are that one it is paradise indeed." He leaned toward her, speaking softly, but with a voice that thrilled more and more in its own eloquence.

She was the Rose of Desire, he reminded her, and beside her all other flowers drooped in envy. She was as lovely as young Dawn to the eyes of men. She was the ravishing embodiment of gaiety and youth and delight. He quoted from the poets, not from his own Oriental poets, but snatches from Campion and Wilde, vowing that

> "There was a garden in her face,
> Where roses and white lilies grow,"

and adding, with points of fire dancing in his heavy lidded eyes,

"Her neck is like white melilote,
Flushing for pleasure of the sun,"

and went on to add praise to praise and extravagance to extravagance, till a sudden little imp of mirth caught Arlee by the throat, hysterically choking her. "I shall never like praise or poetry or—or men again," she thought, struggling between wild laughter and hot disgust, while aloud she mocked, "Ah, you know too much poetry, Captain Kerissen! I do not recognize myself at all! You are laughing at me!"

"Laughing at you?... I am worshipping you," he said tensely, his eyes on hers, and the fierce words shattered her light defenses to confusion.

Silence gripped her. She tried to meet his look and smile in mock reproof, but her eyes fled away affrighted, so full of desperate, passionate things was the dark gaze they touched. She gripped her cold little hands in her lap and looked out beyond the lebbek's shade into the vivid garden. The hot sunshine lay orange on the white-sanded paths; the shadows were purple and indigo. A little lizard had come out from a crack in a stone and was sunning himself, while one bright eye upon them, fixed, motionless, irridescent, warned him of their least stir. She envied him the safety of his crack.... She herself must meet this crisis—must turn this tide....

"It is—so soon," she faltered.

"Soon?" He had risen and was standing over her. "Soon? I was with you on the boat—I walked by your side—I danced with you and held you against my heart. And here in Cairo I walked and talked with you.... And now for three days you have been under my roof, eating at the table with me, alone within these walls, and you call it soon! Truly, you are beyond belief! *Soon!*"

"But soon—for *me*!" she interrupted swiftly, and sprang to her feet to face him with eyes and lips that smiled without a trace of fear. Only her cheeks were no longer crimson but white as chalk. "Too soon—for me to be sure—how *I* feel! I hadn't realized—I hadn't known—Oh, you mustn't hurry me! You mustn't hurry me!" She broke off in a confusion he might well misconstrue, and moved nervously away, her back to him.

He stood staring after her, a man not in two minds but in three and four. Her broken words—her smiles—her emotion—these might well arouse the most flattering surmise, and his vanity and his curiosity were stirred to swift delight. He broke into a storm of words, of protestations, of eager persuasion and honied flattery, drawing nearer and nearer to her, while she slipped continually away from him.

"You mustn't hurry me," she echoed defensively. "I am not like you—you Southerners. I——"

"You are asleep—I have told you that you are that sleeping princess," he broke in, and following after as she turned away from him, he put a quick arm about her, and bending over her, tried to turn her about toward him. "Do you know how that little sleeping princess was awakened by her prince?" he murmured fatuously, bending closer.

The hat saved her, that coquettish little hat with its jealously guarding brim which bent obstinately lower and lower between them. And in the instant of his indecision, while he waited for the surrender his vanity expected before exerting the force that would conquer brutally, she broke unexpectedly from his clasp and darted a few steps away from him, whirling about to face him with her head flung back, her eyes on fire, her lips parted in a breathless excitement.

"Captain Kerissen," she cried, and there was a ring of gaiety in her voice, "do I understand that you are proposing to me?"

Very formally he bowed, a bow that hid the astonishment and the cynical humor which zigzagged across his handsome face. "I am doing myself that honor," he most suavely returned, and eyed her with an astonished curiosity that checked his passion.

"Really?... So soon?" she cried very childishly, and again he bowed. But this time she caught his smile.

"Really so soon, little Arlee."

To his amazement she burst into prankish laughter.

"Oh, you *are* romantic!" she gave back. "And if I can believe you truly in earnest—last night I was furious at you," she went on rapidly, interrupting the speech forming on his lips, "for I thought you a dreadful flirt, just taking advantage of my being here, and yet—and yet you *didn't* seem that kind. You seemed a *gentleman*! And now if you really mean—all you are saying—but you can't, you can't! I know your words are running ahead of you!"

"My words—let my heart speak—I——"

"But I don't know whether I ought to listen or not!" she burst out, and with great naïveté, "I'm afraid it would be very silly to let myself care for you."

"Silly? An adorable silliness! Could you not be happy with me here in this palace? You would be a princess, indeed, a queen of my heart. I would put every luxury at your command." In mingled eagerness and wariness he watched her, incredulous of her assenting mood, but with a hope that lured him on to believe. And in his eyes, dubious, desirous, calculating, watchful, she read the fluctuations of his thought. If afterwards there should happen to be any trouble about this affair, how wonderfully it would smooth things to have the girl infatuated with him, to show that she had been a party to the intrigue! And how spicily it sweetened the taste of success to his lips!

He had caught her two hands in his, and clasping them tightly he bent forward, trying to scan the changes in her hesitating look, while his words poured forth in a stream of praise and promise. She would live like a little princess. His love and his wealth were at her feet. Other women were eager for him, but he was hers alone. She would adore Egypt, the Egypt that he would reveal to her, and when she wearied they would go to the Continent and live always as she desired. Only she must be kind to him, be kind and sweet and lift her eyes and tell him that she would make him happy. She must not keep him waiting. He was not a man with whom one amused oneself.

"And I am not a girl whom one commands!" she gave back with a flash of spirit and a childish toss of her head. "I like you, Monsieur, at least I did like you before you hurt my fingers so horribly"—the tight grasp on her hands relaxed and she drew them swiftly away, rubbing them in mock ruefulness—"and I could like you better and better—perhaps"—her blue eyes flashed a look into his—"if you were *very* nice and polite and give me time to catch my breath! You are such a *hurrying* sort of person!" Her whimsical little smile enchanted him, even while he chafed at such delay.

"I am mad about you," he said in a low tone.

"And only me?" she laughed, her dimples showing.

So, teasing and luring, she held him off, and her heart beat exultantly as she saw that she had given him the thought of marriage for that of conquest, the dream of a perfect idyll for that of an enforced submission.... It was a desperate play, but she played it valiantly, and her fearfulness and the spell of her beauty sweetened the rôle of beseeching suitor for him, and gave a glamour to this pretty garden dalliance.... The memory of time came to him at last with a start, and frowningly he stared at the watch he drew out to consult.

"I must hurry away—to another part of the palace," he amended swiftly, "where I have an engagement.... I shall not be at liberty till to-night—rather late. I will send word to you, then——"

She shook her head at him. "To-morrow," she substituted gaily. "Let us have luncheon to-morrow under the trees again like this.

"To-morrow is too far away — —"

"No, it is just right for me. And if you really want to please me — —"

"But does it please you to make me miserable — —?"

"You can't be very miserable when you have a luncheon engagement," she insisted. "*I'm* not!"

He shrugged. "Till luncheon then—unless I should be back earlier than I think." He gave her a quick look, but her face did not betray awareness of the slip.

"Oh, of course, if you are at liberty sooner—And while you are busy won't you manage things so I can stay out here awhile? I shall love this garden, I know, when I am better friends with it," and after an imperceptible pause he promised to send a maid back to keep watch over her, and with a lingering pressure of hands and a look that plainly said he was but briefly denying himself a more ardent farewell, he hurried away through the banquet hall into the court.

She dared not run after to spy upon his departure. She could only wait, hoping in every throbbing nerve that the maid would prove to be the little one with the wart over her eye. And as she hoped she feared, lest all her frail barrier of cards should be swept away by a single breath.

If he should learn that the little dancer had visited her! If he should discover that she was playing a game with him!

CHAPTER X
A MAID AND A MESSAGE

The March hare would have been a feeble comparison for Billy Hill's madness if Robert Falconer could have seen him that Saturday morning, that same Saturday on which Arlee was essaying her daring rôle, for Billy Hill was sitting in the sun upon a camp stool, a white helmet upon his head, an easel before him, and upon the easel a square of blank canvas, and in Billy's left hand was a box of oils and in his right a brush. And the camp stool upon which Billy was stationed was planted directly before the small, high-arched door of the Kerissen palace and in plain view of the larger door a few feet to the right.

It had all followed upon acquaintance with the one-eyed man.

Taciturn in the beginning and suspicious of Billy's questionings, that dark-skinned individual had at first betrayed abysmal ignorance of all save the virtues of stuffed crocodiles, but convinced at last that this was no trap, but a genuine situation from which he could profit, his greed overcame his native caution, and through the aid of his jerky English and Billy's jagged Arabic a certain measure of confidence was exchanged.

The one-eyed man then recollected that he had noticed a Turkish officer and an American girl returning together to the hotel upon that Wednesday afternoon. He had stared, because truly it was amazing, even for American madness—and also the young girl was beautiful. "A wild gazelle," was his word for her. The man was Captain Kerissen. He was known to all the city—well known, he was—in a certain way. It was not a good way for the ladies. Yes, he had a motor car—a grand, gray car. (Billy remembered that the fatal limousine had been gray.) It was well known that he had bought it for a foreign woman whom he had brought from over-seas and installed in the palace of his fathers. Yes, he knew well where that palace was. His brother's wife's uncle was a eunuch there, but he was a hard man who held his own counsel and that of his master.

Could a girl be shut up in that palace and the world be no wiser? The one-eyed man stared scathingly at such ignorance. Why not? The underworld might know, but native gossip never reached white ears.

What was the best way of finding out, then? The one-eyed man had no hesitation about his answer.

A native must use his eyes and ears for the American. Through his subtle skill and the American's money the discovery could be made. The women servants would talk.

That was the way, Billy agreed, and quoted to the Arab his own proverb, "A saint will weary of well-doing and a braggart of his boasts, but a woman's tongue will never stop of itself," and the one-eyed man had nodded, with an air of resigned understanding, and quoted in answer, "There is nothing so great and nothing so small, nothing so precious and nothing so foul, but that a woman will put her tongue to it," and an understanding appeared to have been reached.

The one-eyed man was to loiter about the palace, calling upon the brother's wife's uncle if possible, and discover all that he could without arousing suspicion. And Billy determined to do a little loitering himself and quicken the one-eyed man's investigations and keep watch of Kerissen's comings and goings, and a donkey boy was hired by the one-eyed man to follow the Captain when he appeared in the street and report the places to which he went.

It was all very ridiculous, of course, Billy cheerfully agreed with himself, but by proving its own folly it would serve to allay that extraordinarily nagging uneasiness of his. If he could just be *sure* that little Miss Beecher wasn't tucked out of sight somewhere in the power of that barbaric scamp with his Continental veneer!

Meanwhile the Oriental methods to be employed in the finding out appealed to the young American's humor and his rash love of adventure. He was grinning as he sat there on that stool and stared at the blank canvas before him. He had felt the rôle of artist would be an excellent screen for his loitering, but he had done no painting for a little matter of twenty years, not since he was a tiny lad, flat upon his stomach in his home library, industriously tinting the robes and beards of Bible characters and the backgrounds of the Holy Land—this work of art being one of the few permitted diversions of the family Sabbath. Now he reflected that the scenes for his brush were decidedly similar.

With humorous interest he fell to work, scaling off the palace on his left, blocking off the cemetery ahead, and trying to draw a palm without emphasizing the thought of a feather duster. His engineering training made him critical of his lines and outlines, but when it came to the introduction of color he had the sensation of a shipwrecked mariner afloat upon uncharted seas.

The color that his eyes perceived was not the color which his stubborn memory persisted in reminding him was the actual hue of the events, and the color that he produced upon canvas was no kin to any of them. But it sufficed for an excuse, and he worked away, whistling cheerily, warily observant of the dark and silent façade of the old palace and alertly interested in the little groups his occupation transiently attracted. But these little groups were all of passers-by, shawl-venders, package-deliverers, beggars, veiled desert women with children astride their shoulders, and the live hens they were selling beneath their mantles, and these groups dissolved and drew away from him without his being able to attract any observation from the palace.

But at least, he thought doggedly, any girl behind those latticed windows up there could see him in the street, and if Arlee were there she would understand his presence and plan to get word down to him. But he began to feel extraordinarily foolish.

At length his patience was rewarded. The small door opened and the stalwart doorkeeper, in blue robes and yellow English shoes, marched pompously out to him and ordered him to be off.

Haughtily Billy responded that this was permitted, and displayed a self-prepared document, gorgeous with red seals, which made the man scowl, mutter, and shake his head and retire surlily to his door, and finding a black-veiled girl peering out of it at Billy, he thrust her violently within. But Billy had caught her eyes and tried to look all the significance into them of which he was capable.

Nothing, however, appeared to develop. The door remained closed, save for brief admissions of bread and market stuff from little boys on donkey-back or on a bicycle, all of whom were led willingly into conservation, but none of whom had been into the palace, and though Billy pressed as close to the door as possible when the boys knocked, he was only rewarded with a glimpse of the tiled vestibule and inner court.

To the irate doorkeeper he protested that he was yearning to paint a palace court, but though he held up gold pieces, the man ordered him away in fury and spoke menacingly of a stick for such fellows.

Now, however cool and fresh it was in the garden that Saturday, it was distinctly hot in the dusty street, and by noon, as Billy sat in the shade beside the palace door, eating the lunch he had brought and drinking out of a thermos bottle, he reflected that for a man to cook himself upon a camp stool, feigning to paint and observing an uneventful door, was the height of Matteawan. He despised himself—but he returned to the camp stool.

Nothing continued to happen.

Travelers were few. Occasionally a carriage passed; once a couple of young Englishmen on polo ponies galloped by; once a poor native came down the road, moving his harem—a donkey-cart load of black shrouded women, with three half-naked children bouncing on a long tailboard.

Several groups of veiled women on foot proceeded to the cemetery and back again.

The one-eyed man sauntered by in vain.

In the heat of the afternoon the wide door suddenly opened and Captain Kerissen himself appeared on his black horse. He spurred off at a gallop, intending apparently to ride down the artist on the way, but changed his mind at the last and dashed past, showering him with dust from his horse's hoofs. The little donkey-boy, lolling down the road, started to follow him, crying out for alms in the name of Allah.

Billy stared up at the windows. Not a handkerchief there, not a signal, not a note flung into the street! In great derision he squirted half a tube of cerulean blue upon his canvas.

This, he reflected, was zero in detective work. It was also minus in adventure.

But one never knows when events are upon the wing. Almost immediately there came into the flatness of his bored existence a victoria containing those two English ladies he had met—in the unconventional way which characterized his meetings with ladies in Cairo—two days before.

The recognition was mutual. The curiosity appeared upon their side. To his horror he saw that they had stopped their carriage and were descending.

"How interesting!" said Miss Falconer, with more cordiality than she had shown on the previous occasion. "How very interesting! So you are an artist—I do a little sketching myself, you know."

"You do happen in the most unexpected places," smiled Lady Claire.

The English girl looked very cool and sweet and fresh to the heated painter. His impression of her as a nice girl and a pretty girl was speedily reinforced, and he remembered that dark-haired girls with gray-blue eyes under dusky lashes had been his favorite type not so long ago ... before he had seen Arlee's fairy gold.

"We've just been driving through the old cemetery—such interesting tombs," said the elder lady, and Lady Claire added, "I should think you could get better views there than here."

By this time they had reached the easel and stood back of it in observation.

Blue, intensely blue, and thickly blue was the sky that Billy had lavished. Green and rigid were the palms. Purple was the palace. Very black lay the shadows like planks across the orange road.

Miss Falconer looked as if she doubted her own eyes. Hurriedly she unfolded her lorgnette.

"It—it's just blocked in," said Billy, speaking with a peculiar diffidence.

"Quite so—quite so," murmured the lady, bending closer, as if fascinated.

Lady Claire said nothing. Stealing a look at her, Billy saw that she was looking it instead.

Miss Falconer tried another angle. The sight of that lorgnette had a stiffening effect upon Billy B. Hill.

"You get it?" he said pleasantly. "You get the—ah—symphonic chord I'm striking?"

"Chord?" said Miss Falconer. "Striking," she murmured in a peculiar voice.

"It's all in thirds, you see," he continued.

"Thirds!" came the echo.

"Perhaps you're of the old school?" he observed.

"Really—I must be!" agreed the lady.

"Ah!" said Billy softly, commiseratingly. He cocked his head at an angle opposite from the slant of the lorgnette and stared his own amazing canvas out of countenance.

"Then, of course," he said, "this hardly conveys——"

"What are you?" she demanded. "Is this a—a school?"

"I?" He seemed surprised that there could be any doubt about it. "I am a Post-Cubist."

Miss Falconer turned the lorgnette upon him. "Oh, really," she said vaguely. "I fancy I've heard something of that—you're quite new and radical, aren't you?"

"Oh, we're old," he said gently, "very, very old. We have returned to Nature—but not the nature of mere academicians. We paint, not the world of the camera, but the world of the brain. We paint, not the thing you think you see, but the way you think you see it—its vibrations of your inner mentality. To paint the apple ripening on the bough one should reproduce the gentle swelling of the maturing fruit in your perception.... Now, you see, I am not trying to reproduce the precise carving of that door; I do not fix the wavings of that palm. I give you the cerebellic——"

"Quite so," said Miss Falconer, dropping her lorgnette and giving the canvas the fixity of her unobstructed gaze. "It's most interesting," she said, a little faintly. "Are there many of you?"

"I don't know," said Billy. "We do not communicate with one another. That always influences, you know, and it is better to work out thought alone."

"I should think it would be." Something in her tone suggested that the inviolated solitude of the asylum suggested itself to her as a fitting spot. "Well, we won't interrupt you any longer. You've been most interesting.... The sun is quite hot, isn't it?" and with one long, lingering look at the picture, a look convinced against its will, she went her way toward the victoria.

But Lady Claire stood still. Billy had fairly forgotten all about her, and now as he turned suddenly from the clowning with her chaperon, he found her gaze being transferred from his picture to himself. It was a very steady gaze, calm-eyed and deliberate.

"I'm afraid you're making game of us!" she said, in her musical, high-bred tones, her clear eyes disconcertingly upon him. "Aren't you?" she gently demanded.

"That's not fair." Billy was uncomfortable and looked away in haste. He felt a grin coming.

Perhaps he was a shade too late, for Lady Claire laughed suddenly and with a note of curious delight.

"You're *too* amusing!" she said. "What made you?... How did you think of it all?... Are you just beginning?"

"Oh, I began twenty years ago," he smiled back, "but I haven't done anything in the meantime."

Again she laughed with that ring of mischievous delight. "However you could think of it all! I shan't tell on you—but she'll *never* be done wondering." She turned away, her pretty face still bright with humor, and then she turned back hesitantly toward him.

"It *is* hot here in this sun," she said. "It *can't* be good for you. Shall we drive you back?"

She had lovely eyes, dark, smoky-blue under black lashes, and when they held a gentle, half-shy, half-proud invitation, as they did then, they were very unsettling eyes.... And it was hot on that infernal camp stool. And there was a crick in the back of his neck and his errand was glaringly a fool's errand....

He half rose, and as he did so the door in the palace opened a crack and a veiled face peered furtively out. Billy sat down again.

"No, thank you," he said, "I think I'd better do a little more of this."

In such light ways is the gate of opportunity closed and opened. Everything that happened afterwards with such appalling startlingness hung on that instant's decision.

For the moment he felt himself a donkey as Lady Claire turned quietly away and the victoria rattled off with brisk finality. Then the door opened again, and again the girl peered out, and furtively, stealthily slipped just outside.

Billy caught up a pad and a pencil and called out a request to sketch her, holding up some silver. Instantly she assumed a fixed pose, with a nervous giggle behind her veil, and he came quickly near her, pretending to be drawing. Her dark, curious eyes met his with questioning significance, and he threw all caution aside and plunged into his demands.

Did she want to earn money, he said quickly, in the Arabic he had been preparing for such an encounter, and on her eager assent, he asked if there was a foreign lady in the palace, an American.

The flash of her eyes told him that he had struck the mark before her half-frightened words came.

His heart quickened with excitement. He might have suspected this thing—but he had not really believed it! He asked, stammering in his haste, "Does she want to get away?"

Again that knowing nod and the quick assent. Then the girl burst into low-toned speech, glancing back constantly through the door she held nearly shut behind her. Billy was forced to shake his head. It was one thing to have picked up a little casual Arabic, and another, and horribly different, thing to comprehend the rapid outpourings behind that muffling veil.

Baffled, he went hurriedly on with his own questionings. Was this lady safe? Again the nod and murmur of assent. Did she want help? Vehement the confirmation. He repeated, with careful emphasis, "I will reward you well for your help," and this time the direct simplicity of her reply was entirely intelligible:

"How much?"

"One pound.... Two," he added, as she shook her head.

"Four," she demanded.

It was maddening to haggle, but it would be worse to yield.

"Two—and this," said Billy, drawing out the gold and some silver with it.

She gave a frightened upward glance at the windows over them and stepped closer. "I take it," she said. "Listen—" and that was all that Billy could understand of the swift words she whispered to him.

"Slower—slower," he begged. "Once more—slower."

She frowned, and then, very slowly and distinctly, she articulated, "*T'âla lil genaina ... 'end eltura.*"

He wrote down what he thought it sounded like. "Go on."

"*Allailade,*" she continued.

"That's to-night," he repeated. "What else?"

"*Assâa 'ashara,*" she added hurriedly, and then, intelligible again, "Now, quick, the money."

"Hold on, hold on." He was in despair. "Go over that again, please," and hastily the girl whispered the words again and he wrote down his corrections. Then with a flourish he appeared to finish the sketch and held out the gold and silver to her, saying, "Thank you," carelessly.

Quick as a flash she seized the money, leaving a little crumpled ball of white linen in his hand, and then, apparently by lightning, she secreted the gold, and with the silver shining in her dark palm she came closer to him, urging him for another shilling, another shilling for having a picture made. In an undertone she demanded, "Is it yes? Shall I say yes to the lady?"

"Yes, yes, yes," said Billy, desperately, to whatever the unknown message might be. "Take a note to her for me?" he demanded, starting to scribble one, but she drew back with a quick negation, and as a sound came from the palace she slipped back through the door and was gone like a shadow when a blind is thrown open.

Only the crumpled little ball of linen remained in Billy's hand. He straightened it out. It was a lady's handkerchief, a dainty thing, delicately scented. In the corners were marvels of sheer embroidery and among the leaves he found the initial he was seeking. It was the letter B.

As he stared down on it, that tiny, telltale initial, his face went white under its tan and his mouth compressed till all the humor and kindliness of it were lost in a line of stark grimness. And then he swung on his heel and packed up his painting kit in a fury of haste, and with one last, upturned look at those mocking windows, he was off down the road like a shot.

There were just two things to do. The first was to discover the message hidden in those unknown words.

The second was to do exactly as that message bade.

CHAPTER XI
OVER THE GARDEN WALL

Two oil lamps flared in the little coffee-house. In one circle of yellow light two bearded Sheiks were playing dominoes with imperturbable gravity; the other lamp flickered over an empty table beneath which the thin, flea-bitten legs of a ragged urchin were showing in the oblivion of his tired sleep. In the shadow beyond sat a young American with a keen, impatient face, and a one-eyed Arab shrouded in a huge burnous.

"I make fine dragoman?" the Arab was saying proudly. "This is ver' old coffee-house. Many things happen here, ver' strange——"

"Yes, but I'm sick of the doggone place," said Billy fiercely. "I can't sit still and swallow coffee any longer. Can't we start now?"

"Too soon—too soon before the time. You say ten? Come, we go next door. Nice place next door, perhaps—dancing, maybe."

There was noise enough next door, certainly, to promise dancing. The strident notes of Oriental music came shrieking out the open doorway, but as Billy stepped within and stared over the heads of the squatting throng, he saw no sinewy dancers, but only two tiny girls in bright colors huddled wearily against the wall. The music which was absorbing every look came from the brazen throat of a huge instrument in the corner.

"Lord—a phonograph!" thought the young man in disgust, resenting this intrusion of the genius of his race into foreign fields.

The squatting men, their dark lips parted in pleased smiles, were too intent upon the innovation to turn at his entrance, but the little girls caught sight of him and ran forward, begging clamorously, their bracelets clanking on their outstretched arms.

With a little silver he tried to soften the vigor of the one-eyed man's dismissal. "This cheap place—no good dancers any more," the Arab uttered in disgust. "New man here—no good. Maybe next door better—eh?"

But next door was only a flight of steps and a lone little doll of a sentinel, painted and hung like a bedizened idol. Only the dark eyes in the tinted sockets were alive, and these turned curiously after the strange young white man who had dropped a coin into her outstretched hand and passed on so hurriedly.

"I don't want any more of these joints," Billy was saying vehemently to his harassed guide. "It's dark as the Styx now—let's be on our way."

The street they were on was narrow enough for any antiquarian, but the one into which the Arab guide now turned was so narrow that the jutting bays of the houses seemed pushing their faces impudently against their neighbors. A voice in one room could have been heard as clearly in the one over the way. It was a mean little street, squalid and poor and pitiful, but it maintained its stripped dignities of screened windows and isolation. It was better not to wonder what nights were like in those women's rooms in summer heat.

The lane-like path stopped at a rickety sort of wharf, and at their approach a black head bobbed quickly up from a waiting boat. It was the little boy who had shadowed the Captain that day—reporting his arrival at the Khedivial palace—and he climbed out now and sat on the wharf, watching curiously while Billy and his guide bestowed themselves in the long canoe, and pushed silently away.

It was an eerie backwater in which they were paddling, a sluggish stream which moved between dark houses. Sometimes it scraped against their sides and lapped their balconies; sometimes it was held in check by walls and narrow terraces. For Billy the water between the dark houses, the mirrored stars, the unexpected flare of some oil lamp and its still reflection, the long windings and the stagnant smells held their suggestions of Venice for his senses, and he thought the business he was going about was very similar to the business which had brought so many of the gentry of Venice to sudden and undesired ends.

The flies were horribly thick here. They settled upon the faces and arms of the paddlers, totally unapprehensive of rebuff. Billy's flesh crawled. He finished the swarm with a ringing slap that brought a low caution from his guide.

Now the canal was wider and shallower. The houses receded, and a field or so appeared, and frequent walls hedged the way. Then suddenly the houses came down again to the water, and the ruins of old mosques and palaces lined the banks for a time; to be replaced by walls again. The windings were interminable, and just when he was thinking that his silent guide was as confused as he was, the man made a sudden gesture to the right bank where a tiny strip of land showed above the water clinging to a high brick wall, and with careful, soundless strokes they brought the canoe up to that land.

Billy looked at his watch. It was nearly ten. Hurriedly he climbed out, taking out the stout, notched pole and the knotted rope with the iron hook at the end which he had prepared. The message which had been so unintelligible to him was very simple. "Escape by canal to-night—come to garden at ten," had been the words, and Billy, on hearing the description of the canal from the one-eyed man, had felt he understood.

"You're sure this is the place?" he demanded, and on the man's much injured protestation, "Because if it isn't I'll wring your neck instead of Kerissen's," he cheerfully promised and set his pole against the wall, showing the man how to steady it. It was not the best climbing arrangement in the world, but time had been extremely limited, and the one-eyed man not inclined to pursue any investigations which would advertise their expedition.

Wrapping the rope about his shoulders, he started to pull himself up that notched pole the Arab was holding against the wall, feeling desperately for any hold for toes and fingers in the rough chunks between the old bricks, and breathing hard he reached the top and threw one leg over. He felt something grind through the serge of his trousers and sting into the flesh.

"Ground glass—the Old Boy!" said Billy through his teeth. He hoisted himself cautiously, and with his handkerchief swept the top of the wall as clean as he could. He heard the little pieces fall with a perilously loud tinkling sound, and flattened himself upon the wall, and strained his eyes through the darkness of the garden, but no alarm was raised. The shadows seemed empty.

He hoped to the Lord that no disturbance would break out in the garden, for the man below would be off in the canoe like a flash. He had no illusions about the one-eyed man's loyalty, but the fellow was already in the secret; he was needy and resourceful and as trustworthy as any dragoman that he could have gone to. And a dragoman would have had a reputation and a patronage he'd fear to lose. This melancholy Arab, hawking crocodiles for a Greek Jew, had more to gain than lose.

By now he had caught the end of the rough hook over the top of the wall, and let down the knotted rope into the garden below. It was long enough, thank goodness, he thought, wondering under what circumstances and in what company he would ascend it again. Then with one more keen look into the garden, and a reassuring touch of the pocket where his revolver bulged, he gripped the rope and swiftly lowered himself.

Keeping close to the wall he pressed toward the buildings on the right, which he had been told was the wing of the harem, and as he stepped forward a flat black shadow near the wall came suddenly to life. It sprang to its feet, revealing a shrouded little form, wrapped and hooded in black, and ran to him with steps that stumbled in excitement.

"Quick, quick!" breathed an almost inaudible voice of terror, and Billy flung one strong arm about the girl and dashed toward the dangling rope. Gripping it with one hand he flung the light figure over his left shoulder, and with a cheerily whispered "Hang tight," he threw himself into the ascent. It was arm-wrenching, muscle-racking work, with that dead weight upon him, but the touch of those soft arms clinging childishly about his neck seemed to double and treble his strength, and with incredible quickness he lifted her to the top of the wall, and then, catching her by the wrists, he lowered her into the upreaching clasp of the Arab.

An instant more and he had reversed his rope ladder and climbed down beside her as she stood waiting, and in the throbbing triumph of that moment he flung his arm grippingly about her to sweep her into the boat. But as she raised her face to his, the shrouding mantle fell away, and he found himself staring down into the exultant face and bright, dark eyes of a girl he had never seen before.

Back of them beyond the wall, pandemonium was breaking out.

"He found himself staring down into the bright dark eyes of a girl he had never seen"

CHAPTER XII
THE GIRL FROM THE HAREM

He was dumb with the shock. Then, "Who are you?" he demanded. "And where is she—where is Arlee Beecher?"

On her own face the astonishment grew. "What you mean? Frederick—he not send you?" she gasped, and then as the outcries grew louder and louder behind them she gripped convulsively at his arms. "Oh, quick! come away—quick, quick!" she besought.

"I came for Arlee Beecher—an American girl. Isn't she held here? Isn't she back there?"

"What you going to do? What——"

"I'm going to get her!" he said fiercely. "Tell me——"

He had caught her and unconsciously shook her as if to shake the words out of her. Furiously she struggled with him.

"Let me go. No, no, she is not there! No one is there! You are gone crazy to stay! They will kill me if they catch me—they will fire over the wall. Oh, for God's sake, help me quick!"

"She's not there?" he repeated stupidly, and then at her vehement "No, no! I tell you no!" he drew a breath of deep astonishment and chagrin, and turned to stow her safely low in the boat. Hurriedly he and the one-eyed man bent over their paddles, and very swiftly the long, dark canoe went gliding down the stream, but not any too swiftly, for in an instant they heard a triumphant yell behind them, and then light, thudding feet along the path.

Steadily Billy urged the canoe forward with powerful strokes that seemed to be lifting it out of the water at each impulse, and they swept past a wall that reaching to the river bank must block their pursuers for a time, and though there was a path after that, there was soon another wall, and no more pursuit along the water edge. But every opening ahead now might mean an ambush, and as soon as a narrow lane showed between the houses to the left, the one-eyed man steered swiftly there and Billy sprang out with the girl and they raced through the lane into the adjoining street.

He looked up and down it; either they had got out at the wrong lane or the cab they had ordered to be in waiting had failed them, but there was no time for speculation and they walked on as fast as they could without the appearance of flight. The stray loiterers on the dark street stared curiously as they passed, to see a young American in gray tweeds, his cap pulled over his eyes, with a woman in the Mohammedan wrap and mantle, but no one stopped them, and in another minute they saw a lonely cab rattling through the streets and climbed quickly in.

"And now, for Heaven's sake, tell me all about it!" besought Billy B. Hill, staring curiously at his most unforeseen companion.

With a deep-drawn sigh of relief she had snuggled back against the cushioned seat, and now she flung off the shrouding mantle and looked up to meet his gaze with a smile of excited triumph.

She had the prettiest teeth he had ever seen, lovely little rows of pearls, and the biggest and brightest of dark eyes with wide lashes curling dramatically back. Even in the thrill and elation of the moment there was a spark of provocation in those eyes for the good-looking young man who stared down at her, and Billy would have been a very wooden young man, indeed, if he had not felt a tingling excitement in this unexpected capture, for all the destruction of his romantic plans. So this, he thought rapidly, was the foreign girl in Kerissen's house, and Arlee, bless her little golden head, was safe where she planned, in Alexandria. A warm glow of happiness enveloped him at that.

"Now tell me all about it," he demanded again. "You are running away from Kerissen?"

"Oh, yes," she cried eagerly. "You must not let him catch us. We are safe—yes?"

"I should rather think so," Billy laughed. "And there's a gun in my pocket that says so.... And so you sent me that message to-day by that little native girl? How in the world did that happen?"

"That girl is one who will do a little for money, you understand," said the Viennese, "and I have told her to look sharp out for a foreign gentleman who come to save me. You see I have sent for a friend, and I think that he—but never mind. That girl she come running this afternoon to where I am shut in way back in the palace, and she say that a foreign gentleman is painting a picture out in the street, and he stare very cunning at her. So I tell her to find out if he is the one for me, and to tell him to come quick this night. She was afraid to take note—afraid the eunuch catch her. So she went to you. She told afterwards that you ask her if there is any strange lady there anxious to get away, and she give you the message and my handkerchief and you say you will come—and my, how you give me one great surprise!"

"And a great disappointment," said Billy grinning.

"Oh, no, no," she denied, eyes and lips all mischievous smiles. "I say to myself, 'My God! That is a fine-looking young man! He and I will have something to say to each other'—h'm?"

"Now who in the world are you?" demanded Billy bluntly. "And how did you happen to get into all this?"

Volubly she told. She dwelt at picturesque length upon her shining place upon the Viennese stage; she recounted her triumphs, she prophesied the joy of the playgoers at her return to them. Darkly she expatiated upon the villainy of the Turkish Captain, who had lured her to such incarceration. Gleefully she displayed the diamonds upon her small person which she was extracting from that affair.

"Not so bad, after all—h'm?" she demanded, in a brazen little content. "Maybe that prison time make good for me," and Billy shook his head and chuckled outright at the little baggage.

But through his amusement a prick of uneasiness was felt. The picture she had painted of the Captain corroborated his wildest imaginings.

"You're dead sure you know all that was going on in that palace?" he demanded. "There wasn't any American girl coaxed into it on some pretext?"

He wanted merely the reassurance of her answer, but to his surprise and growing alarm she hesitated, looking at him half fearfully and half ashamedly. "Oh, I—I don't know about that," she murmured, with evasive eyes. "An American girl—very light hair—yes?"

"Very light hair—Oh, good God!" He leaned forward, gripping her wrist as if afraid she would spring out of the carriage. "You said she wasn't there," he thrust at her in a voice that rasped.

"I said I don't know—don't know any such name you say. I never hear it. You hurt me—take your hand away."

"Not till you tell me." But he loosened his harsh grip. "Now tell me all you know—*please* tell me all you know," he besought with a sudden melting into desperate entreaty. Worriedly he stared at this curious little kitten-thing beside him on whose truth now that other girl's life was resting.

"Well, I tell you true I do not know that name," began Fritzi Baroff, with a little sullen dignity over her shame. "And I saved your life, for it was death for you to go back to that palace. You heard them coming for us. You would have got yourself killed and that little girl would be no better. Now I can tell you how to help her."

"All right—tell me," said the young American in a tense voice. "Tell me everything you know about it," and Fritzi told him, throwing aside all pretense of her uncertainty about Arlee, revealing every detail of the situation that she knew.

And from the heights of his gay relief Billy Hill was flung back into the deeps of desperate indignation. The anger that had surged up in him that afternoon when he had felt his fears confirmed flamed up in him now in a fire of fury. His blood was boiling.... Arlee Beecher in the power of that Turkish devil! Arlee Beecher prisoned within that ghastly palace! It was unreal. It was monstrous.... That radiant girl he had danced with, that teasing little sprite, half flouting, half flirting. Why, the thing was unthinkable!

He put a hand on the dancer's arm. "We must go to the consul at once," he said. "We must get her out to-night."

"Consul!" The girl gave a short, derisive laugh. "This is no matter for consuls, my young friend. The law is slow, and by the time that law will stand knocking upon the palace doorstep, your little girl with the fair hair will be buried very deep and fast—I think she would not be the first woman bricked into those black walls.... You must go about this yourself.... You are in love with her—yes?" she added impertinently, with keen, uptilted eyes.

"That's another story," Billy curtly informed her. He made no attempt to analyze his feeling for Arlee Beecher. She had enchanted him in those two days that he had known her. She had obsessed his thoughts in those two days of her disappearance. Now that he was aware of her peril every selfish thought was overwhelmed in burning indignation. He told himself that he would do as much for any girl in her situation, and, indeed, so hot ran his rage and so dearly did his young blood love rash adventure and high-handed justice, that there was some honest excuse for the statement!

"Zut! A man does not risk his neck for a matter of indifference!" said the little Baroff sagely, her knowing eyes on Billy's grim young face. "So I am to be the sister to you—the Platonic friend—h'm?" she observed with droll resignation. "Never mind—I will help you get her out as you got me—*Gott sei dank!* There is a way, I think—if you are not too particular about that neck. I will tell you all and draw you a plan when we get to a hotel."

But before they got to a hotel there was an obstacle or two to be overcome. A lady in Mohammedan wraps might not be exactly *persona grata* at fashionable hotels at midnight. Casting off the wrap Fritzi revealed herself in a little pongee frock that appeared to be suitable for traveling, and with two veils and Billy's cap for a foundation she produced an effect of headgear not unlike that of some bedraped tourists.

"I arrived on the night train," she stated as they drew up before the shining hotel. "It is late now for that night train—but we waited for my luggage, which you will observe is lost. So I pay for my room in the advance—I think you had better give me some money for that—I have nothing but these," and she indicated her flashing diamonds.

"My name," said Billy, handing over some sovereigns with the first ray of humor since her revelation to him, "my name, if you should care to address me, is Hill—William B. Hill."

"William B. Hill," she echoed with an air of elaborate precision, and then flashed a saucy smile at him as he helped her out of the carriage. "What you call Billy, eh?"

"You've got it," he replied in resignation.

"Hill—that means a mountain," she commented. "A mountain of good luck for me—h'm? And that B—what is that for?"

"My middle name," said Billy patiently, as they reached the door the Arab doorman was holding open for them.

Absently she laughed. Her dark eyes were sparkling at the vision of the safe and shining hotel, the dear familiar luxury, the sounds and sights of her lost Continental life. A few late arrivals from some dance gave a touch of animation to the wide rooms, and Fritzi's eyes clung delightedly to the group.

"God, how happy I am!" she sighed.

Billy was busy avoiding the clerk's knowing scrutiny. It was the same clerk he had coerced with real cigars to enlighten him concerning Arlee Beecher, and he felt that that clerk was thinking things about him now, mistaken and misguided things, about his predilections for the ladies. Philosophically he wondered where they had better try after this.

But he underestimated the battery of Fritzi's charms, or else the serene assurance of her manner.

"My letters—letters for Baroff," she demanded of the clerk. "None yet. Then my room, please.... But I sent a wire from Alexandria. That stupid maid," she turned to explain to Billy, her air the last stand of outraged patience. "She is at the train looking for that luggage she lost," she added to the clerk, and thereupon she proceeded to arrange for the arrival of the fictitious maid whom Billy heard himself agreeing to go back and fetch if she did not turn up soon, and to engage a room for herself—a much nicer room than Billy himself was occupying—then handed over Billy's sovereigns and turned happily away jingling the huge key of her room.

"It is a miracle!" she cried again, exultant triumph in every pretty line of her. "My heart dances, my blood is singing—Oh, if I were on the stage now, the music crashing, the lights upon me, the house packed! I would enchant them! I would dance myself mad.... Ah, what you say now—shall we have a little bottle of champagne to drink to our better acquaintance, Mr. Billy?"

"Not this evening," said the unemotional young man. "You are going to sit down at this desk and draw me those plans of the palace."

Petulantly she shrugged at her rescuer. "How stupid—to-morrow you may not have that chance for the champagne," she observed. "You think of nothing but to go back and get killed, then? And I must help you? Very well. Here, I will draw it for you and I will tell you all I know."

She sat down at a desk and began working out the diagrams, and at last she handed the paper to Billy, who sat beside her, and pointed out the rooms and scribbled the words on them for his aid.

"It is very simple," she said. "That first square is for the court, and the next square is for the garden. The hall of banquets comes so, between them, and the hall is two stories tall, and across the top of that, from the *selamlik* to the harem, runs that little secret passage. And at the end of it, here, is the little panel into the rose room where she is, and beside the panel outside in the passage are the little steps that go up to that tower room, where they put me on the top. And from that top room I broke out a locked door on the roof—that is how I got away. I climbed down at the end of the harem from one roof to another where it is unfinished.... The rose room is here on the garden, but the windows have bars, and those bars are too strong for breaking. I have tried it! There is no way out but the secret way by that passage into the men's wing, or the other way through the door into the long hall and down the little stairs into the anteroom below. How Seniha hated me when I made laughter and noise and talk going up and down those stairs to my motor car!"

She laughed impishly, pointing out Seniha's rooms, facing on the street, and contributing several bizarre anecdotes of the palace life. But Billy was not to be diverted, and went over the plans again and again, before the diminished number of lights and the hoverings of the attendant Arabs recalled the lateness of the hour to his absorption.

But late as they were they were not the only occupants of the lift. Returning from a masquerade, a domino over his arm, stood Falconer.

Civilly enough he returned Billy's greeting, with no apparent awareness of the little lady in pongee, but Billy was conscious that her flaunting caliber had been promptly registered. And to his annoyance the actress raised big eyes of reproach to him.

"No champagne for me, after all, Mr. Billy!" she sighed. "You are not very good for a celebration—h'm?... Well, then—good night."

Her parting smile as she left the car adroitly included the tall aristocratic young Englishman with the little moustache.

Sharply Billy turned to him. "Come up to my room, please. I have something to say to you."

In silence Falconer followed. Billy flung shut the door, drew a long breath, and turned to him.

"Do you know where I got that girl?" he demanded.

It took several seconds of Falconer's level-lidded look of distaste to bring home the realization.

"Oh, see here," he protested, "wait till you understand this thing.... I pulled that girl over Kerissen's back wall at ten o'clock to-night. I thought she was Miss Beecher, but a mistake had been made and the wrong girl arrived. But the point is this—*Arlee Beecher is in that palace.* This girl saw her and talked with her last night. Now we've got to get her out. It's a two-man job," said Billy, "or you'd better believe I'd never have come to you again."

He had given it like a punch, and it knocked the breath out of Falconer for one floored instant. But he was no open-mouthed believer. The thing was more unthinkable to him than to Billy's romantic and adventurous mind, and the very notion was so revolting that he fought it stoutly.

From beginning to end Billy hammered over the story as he knew it, explaining, arguing, debating, and then he drew out the plans of the palace and flung them on the table by Falconer while he continued his excited tramping up and down the room.

Falconer studied the plans, worried his moustache, stared at Billy's tense and resolute face, and took up the plans again, his own chin stubborn.

"Granted there's a girl—you can't be sure it's Miss Beecher," he maintained doggedly. "This Baroff girl had no idea of her name. Now Miss Beecher would have told her name, the very first thing, it appears to me, and the names of her friends in Cairo, asking for the Baroff's offices in getting a letter to me—us."

"She may have been too hurried to get to it. She had so many questions to ask. And she probably expected to see the girl again the next day or night."

"Possibly," said Falconer without conviction.

"But where, then, is Miss Beecher?"

"We may hear from her to-morrow morning."

"We won't," said Billy.

Falconer was silent.

"Good Lord!" the American burst out, "there can't be two girls in Cairo with blue eyes and fair hair whom Kerissen could have lured there last Wednesday! There can't be two girls with chaperons departing up the Nile! Why—why—the whole thing's as clear to me—as—as a house afire!"

"I don't share your conviction."

"Very well, then, if you don't think it is Miss Beecher, you don't have to go into this thing. If you can feel satisfied to lay the matter before the ambassador and let that unknown girl wait for the arm of the law to reach her, you are at perfect liberty, of course, to do so." Billy was growing colder and colder in tone as he grew hotter and hotter in his anger.

Falconer said nothing. He was a very plucky young man, but he had no liking at all for strange and unlawful escapades. He didn't particularly mind risking his neck, but he liked to do it in accredited ways, in polo, for instance, or climbing Swiss peaks, or swimming dangerous currents.... But he was young—and he had red hair. And he remembered Arlee Beecher. These three days had not been happy ones for him, even sustained as he was by righteous indignation. And if there was any chance that this prisoned girl was Arlee, as this infatuated American was so furiously sure—He reflected that Billy was doing the sporting thing in giving him the chance of it.

"I'll join you," he said shortly. "I can't let it go, you know, if there's a chance of its being Miss Beecher."

"Good!" said Billy, holding out his hand and the two young men clasped silently, eyeing each other with a certain mutual respect though with no great increase of liking.

"Now, this is my idea," Billy went on, and proceeded to develop it, while Falconer carefully studied the plans and made a shrewd suggestion here and there.

It was late in the morning when they parted.

"You must muzzle that Baroff girl," was Falconer's parting caution. "We must keep this thing deuced quiet, you know."

"Of course. He shan't get wind of it ahead."

"Not only that. We mustn't have talk afterwards. It would kill the girl, you know."

Billy nodded. "She would hate it, I expect."

"Hate it? My word, it would finish her—a tale of that kind going the rounds.... She could never live it down."

"Live it down? It would set her up in conversation for the rest of her life!" Billy chuckled softly. "That is, if it comes out all right—and that's the only way I can imagine its coming out."

With one hand on the door Falconer paused to stare back at him. "You don't mean she'd want to *tell* about it!" he ejaculated with unplumbed horror.

Billy was suddenly sobered. "Well, nobody but you and I and the Baroff know it now," he said, "and I think we can keep the Baroff's mouth shut.... I'll see her in the morning. You'd better get in a nap to-morrow, and I will, too, for we'll want steady nerves. Good night; I'm glad you're going with me."

"I'm damned if I'm glad," said the honest Englishman, with a wry grin. "If we get our throats cut, I hope Miss Beecher will return from the desert in time for our obsequies."

"Something in that red-headed chap I like after all," soliloquized Billy B. Hill, as he turned toward his long-deferred repose. "Hanged if he hasn't grit to go into a thing on an off chance!... Now, as for me, I'm *sure*."

CHAPTER XIII
TAKING CHANCES

Late as he went to sleep, Billy B. Hill was up in good season that Sunday morning. The need for cautioning Fritzi Baroff haunted him, and he was not satisfied until he had had breakfast with that lively young lady and laid down the law to her upon the situation.

She was very loath not to talk about herself at first. She wanted to tell her tale to the papers and see if one of them would be hardy enough to publish the story of the outrageous incarceration; she wanted to cable the Viennese theater where she had played of her sensational detention—in short, she wanted to get all the possible publicity out of her durance vile and to advertise her small person from Cairo to the Continent.

But Billy was urgent. "You just bide a wee on this publicity stunt," he demanded. "Cable your manager and press agent all you want to—but don't talk around the hotel here—and whatever you do and whatever you say, keep Miss Beecher's name and mine out of it."

He was very decided about that, and because she was very grateful to him and because she liked him and because she lacked other friends and other pocketbooks, the little Viennese held her tongue as directed. And she borrowed as much money as Billy would lend her, and drove off to the small shops which were open that day, and found a frock or two and a hat which she declared passable, and returned transfigured to the hotel and rendered the table where she lunched with Billy, with the air of possessing him, quite the most conspicuous in the room. The ladies gazed past them with chill eyes; the men stared covertly, with the surreptitious envy with which even the most virtuous of men surveys a lucky devil. And Billy sadly perceived that he was acquiring a reputation.

He did not blame Miss Falconer for turning haughtily aside as he and his vivid companion went past them in the veranda. But he did think her disdainful lack of memory a little overdone.

His cheeks were still red as he looked away from her and encountered the direct eyes of the girl who followed her.

"Oh, how do you do, Mr. Hill?" said Lady Claire, as clear as a bell. "It's *such* a nice day, isn't it?" she added, a little breathlessly, as she went by.

"It's much better than it was," said Billy, and he turned back to open the door for her.

"Claire!" said Miss Falconer from within.

"Coming, dear," said Lady Claire, and with a little smile of defiant friendliness at the young American she was gone.

But the memory of that plucky little smile stayed right with Billy. The girl liked him, she liked him in spite of his unknown antecedents, his preposterous picture, his conspicuous companion. She had a mind of her own, that tall English girl with the lovely eyes and the proud mouth. In a warm surge of friendliness his thoughts went out to her, and he wished vaguely that he could let her know how fine he thought she was.

Within an hour that vague wish came true. He had packed Fritzi off, with a newly acquired maid, for a drive up and down the safe public streets and he had re-interviewed the one-eyed man and the native chauffeur that the one-eyed man introduced for the evening's work, and he was at one of the public desks in the writing room, inditing a letter to his aunt, which, he whimsically appreciated, might be his last mortal composition, and reflecting thankfully that it was highly unnecessary to make a will, when Lady Claire strolled into the room and over to a desk.

She tried a pen frowningly, and Billy jumped to offer another. "Oh, thank you," she said. She seemed not to have seen him before.

"That was rather nice of you, you know," he said gravely.

She looked up at him.

"I'm not really a wolf," he continued, the gravity surrendering to his likable, warm smile, "and I'm glad you recognized it."

Her reply took him unawares. "I think you're *splendid*," said Lady Claire. "I thought so in the bazaars when you came to my help and stood up to that *beastly* German."

"Oh, he wasn't such a beastly German, after all," Billy deprecated. "And here I've had a message to you from him and never remembered to give it. The fellow called on me the next morning in gala attire and offered every apology and satisfaction in his power—even the satisfaction of the duel, if I desired it. I didn't. But I promised to express his deep apologies to you. He was horribly shocked at himself. He'd been drinking, he said, to forget a 'sadness' which possessed him. His lady love had failed to keep her tryst and life was very dark."

"I don't wonder at her," said Lady Claire unforgivingly. "I'm sure he must have been horrid to her!"

"I rather think she was horrid to him," Billy reflected, "although she was a very sprightly looking lady love. He showed me her picture in the back of his watch.... By *George*!" he uttered violently.

"What is it?"

"Oh—an idea, that's all. Something I must really attend to before I—this afternoon, I mean. But there's no hurry about it," he added cheerily.

Oh, Billy, Billy! Not even with his blood hot with thoughts of the evening's work, not even with his memory ridden with Arlee's gay witchery, could he keep his restless young eyes from laughing down at her. But there wasn't a notion in the back of his honest head as to the picture he was making in Lady Claire's eyes as he leaned, long-limbed, broad-shouldered, lazily at ease against the desk, his gray eyes very bright between their dark lashes, his dark hair sweeping back from his wide forehead.

"Are you sure?" she asked of him, with the smile that he drew from her. "Is it the inspiration for another picture?"

"No, no—that was my first and my last. That was the one purple bloom of my art. I have laid my brushes by.... But I'm keeping you from that letter you were going to write."

"It's just a few lines for Miss Falconer," Lady Claire unnecessarily explained. "We are going to drive out to the Gezireh Palace Hotel for tea, and she thought her brother might like to go out with us if he came in in time."

She did not add why Miss Falconer was unable to write her own notes, but slanted her blue-hatted head over the desk and then hastily blotted her brief lines and tucked the sheet into an envelope. Hesitantly she looked up at Billy.

"Have you been out to the Gezireh Palace?" she very innocently inquired.

"Alone," said Billy.

"It's very jolly there," said she. "It's so gay—and the music is *quite* good."

"H'm," meditated Billy. "The condemned man ate a hearty tea of Orange Pekoe and cress sandwiches," he reflected silently. He also reflected that Miss Falconer would be furious—and that invited him—and that time was interminable and that this expedition was as good a way of getting through the afternoon as any other. Thereupon he turned to the English girl, with a humorous challenge in his gaze. "I wonder if you and Miss Falconer would let this be my tea party?" he suggested.

"Miss Falconer will be delighted," said Lady Claire mendaciously.

The traces of that delight, however, lay beneath so well schooled an exterior that they were decidedly non-apparent. Nor did Robert Falconer's mien reveal any hint of joy when he returned to the hotel and found the two ladies starting with Billy. He joined them with rather the air of a watch dog, but that air soon wore away during the long drive under the spell of young Hill's frank friendliness and gay good humor. For Billy was extravagantly in spirits. Excitement stirred in him like wine; his blood was on fire with thoughts of the evening.

"It's the fool *lark* of the thing," he said, half apologetically, to Falconer's wonder when the two young men were alone for a minute on the Gezireh verandas. "Didn't you ever want to be a pirate?"

The red-headed young man nodded. "Yes, but this business doesn't make me feel like a pirate—more like a second-story man!"

"I've left letters with Fritzi Baroff," said Hill, "and if we're not back by morning, she's to go to the authorities with them."

"That won't do us any good," said the Englishman grimly.

But after the ladies returned it was a very merry-seeming tea party. Even Miss Falconer unbent to the artist, as she persisted in calling Billy, though he had dutifully enlightened her that engineering was his true and proper life work, and art but a random diversion, and she promised to show him the sketches which she had been making, and piled him with questions about his mysterious America.

And Lady Claire was very prettily animated, and rallied Falconer upon his absent-mindedness and told Billy tales of her English home and how her father had threatened to change the name of the Hall to *Mädchenheim* because there were five daughters of them. "*Five* girls near an age, Mr. Hill, and all poor as church mice!" she had blithely asserted.

But from what Billy heard of balls and hunters and "seasons," he gleaned that being poor as church mice, for these five titled girls, meant merely an effort in keeping up with the things they felt should be theirs by right divine. And as Billy listened, feeling the force of the girl's attraction, the charm of her serene confidence and the pleasant air of security and well-being that hedged her in, he stole a covert glance at Falconer's unrevealing countenance and reflected that it was rather a stormy day for that young man when he became entangled with the fortunes of little Miss Beecher. It was also a stormy day for himself, but he felt that storms belonged more naturally to his adventurous lot.

But it was characteristic of Falconer when once committed to a plan not to open his mind to the objections which besieged it. So that night, at the fall of dark, as the two young men motored forth together, he maintained a stolid resolution which refused to look back. The approach of the danger was tuning up his nerves, and whatever his common sense might think about it, his youth and pluck greeted the adventure with a quickening heart and a rash warmth of blood.

Both young men were resolute and confident. Either would have been more than human if he had not looked a trifle askance upon the other and wished to thunder that he had been able to go into it alone and to have tasted the intoxication of delivering the girl single-handed out of the den of thieves. But the success of the plan was paramount, as Billy reminded himself.

He found himself hoping wildly that she would see him as well as Falconer.

"She has probably forgotten all about me," he thought ruefully. "She won't remember that dance with me, nor that chat next morning. I'm just an Also Met. She won't even perceive me. She'll see that sandy-haired deliverer—and she'll tell him how right he was and how good to come after her——"

Thus jealousy darkly painted his undoing. "But, darn it, I had to ask him!" Thus he downed his ungenerous thoughts. "It needed two men at least—and besides, I don't want any handicap of gratitude in this."

They left the automobile in the Mohammedan graveyard with exact and impressive instructions. And then they stole back among the gloomy trees and ghostly tombs to where the canal washed the foot of the little terraces, and there the one-eyed man sat waiting in the canoe, a figure of profound misanthropy.

Silently he lifted a stricken but set countenance, and they climbed in and the three paddled off, approaching the back of the palace with wary eyes, for they were afraid that a guard might now be set upon the walls. But Billy had argued that Kerissen was unaware of Fritzi's knowledge of Arlee's identity; in fact she had at first supposed her a willing supplanter like herself, and so he would not be apprehensive of any of her revelations. And he did not dream that Fritzi's rescuers were interested in Arlee.

At the strip of path the canoe made softly to shore and the two young men climbed out, while the Arab remained in the canoe, his single eye peering into the darkness. This time Billy had provided three stout, but narrow, ladders, constructed of two poles nailed together with occasional cross pieces that gave narrow room for a foot. He set one of these in place against the wall now, grounding its ends deep in the soft earth, so that it would remain in readiness for any sudden descent. Then from the top of the wall they reconnoitered the scene before them.

It was very dark. The garden was full of blotting shadows, and the long wing of the harem lay almost in darkness, with only a faint beam from two adjacent windows to reveal a sign of life. Those windows were on the third story, next the angle made by the union of the banquet hall and the harem, and Billy's heart quickened as he recognized the location of the rose room.

"That's it—that's her room," he whispered excitedly to Falconer.

Falconer stared and nodded. "I wish that beastly hall wasn't in the way ahead of us. I'd like to see what lights are in the windows in that court beyond."

"We might both go and take a look," said Billy doubtfully, "but I guess you had better make, straight for your roofs. It wouldn't do to have us both nabbed. Do you hear anything?"

They listened, crouching flat upon the wall, straining their eyes toward the palace. There was a high wind blowing and above them the leaves of the palm trees were slapping against each other, and below the shrubs and flowers were stirring restlessly. But the noise of the wind, they felt, was helpful to cover the sounds of their approach.

"Why can't I make my way around on top of this wall and climb on the roofs from the start?" Falconer questioned, and Billy answered, "I asked her that. She said it couldn't be done. You'd have to climb through some unsafe rubbish. The best way is down and up again in that angle that she showed me. Shall we start?"

The same impulse made both men examine their revolvers, then drop them in readiness into their right-hand coat pockets. They moved along the top of the wall till they reached the angle with the wall on their right, and then they lowered the same knotted rope which Billy had used the night before, but now another rope added to it made it into a rope ladder. Suspending that over the top of the wall by iron hooks, they slipped down it, each with a pole ladder in his arms, and with another hook of iron they drove the ends down into the earth, so that the rope would not wave out in the wind and either betray them or become displaced.

It was insecure enough, anyway, but they felt it ought to be left in readiness for a flight that might have no second to waste. Now, with eyes sharply challenging the shadows, they stole along the edge of the palace.

Staring up at the building, Billy stopped. "Here's a place a story and a half high—you could almost climb up by those carvings without any ladder. And there's the next higher roof back of it—and then you must go there to the left."

"I can make it," said Falconer, surely. "Now how much time shall I allow you for your sawing—fifteen minutes?"

"Guess you'd better," Billy reflected, and they compared watches.

It was tremendously difficult to arrive at any sort of concerted action on this bewildering expedition, but they were hoping to achieve it. Their plan had the simplicity of all desperate measures. One from below and one from above they were to make their way to that rose room and fight the way out with the girl. They considered it wiser to come from two directions, for if one were discovered and the alarm raised, the other had still a chance of getting off with Arlee, and if one were trying to escape, the other could cover his flight. They had drawn straws for their positions, and Billy had been slightly relieved that the entrance from below, which he considered a trifle more difficult, had fallen to him. He felt responsible, as well as he might, for Falconer's neck.

Now he steadied one narrow ladder of poles while Falconer crept up it and then drew it up after him; and after a few moments of waiting, crouched in the shadow, Billy saw the Englishman's figure reappear against the sky on top of a higher roof. The route over the old buildings had been found, so Billy turned and crept forward along the wall, carrying the last long ladder of poles in his hand. It was an unwieldy thing to carry and it distracted his attention harassingly.

"My job," said he to himself, "is evidently to make a racket and draw their fire from below while that red-headed chap carries Arlee off from above. Well, I hope to the Lord he does. When I think of her here——"

But it was unnerving to think of her here, so he didn't. He kept his mind steadily on the plan. He had reached the stone steps that led from the garden to the harem now, and laying down his pole-like ladder he slipped up them and turned the handle.

But the door was locked. Fearful lest the grating of the knob should have roused some watcher, he ran down the steps and hurried into the shadow of the banquet hall, where he stood close beside a pillar until he satisfied himself of the objects in the court beyond. He saw an edge of light along the crack of a closed door to the left on the ground floor of the *selamlik*, and in the higher stories above that a couple of windows showed a pale illumination. On the right, in the harem, only one window betrayed a ray of light. Altogether the old pile was as gloomy and gruesome as a tomb.

Billy stared across the court to where the columned vestibule, uniting the two Ls, indicated the door. He had been told a watchman slept there, but he could see nothing now but vague outlines of the arches of the vestibule. To the left was the open passage left for the entry of the automobile and horses, but this, too, was roofed so that a black shadow lay over it. But for that watchman Billy would have made his way to those doors to draw back the bars in readiness, but fearful of raising an alarm, he judged it was better to leave escape to chance and turn his attention to his entry.

He went back now for his ladder, and on the right side of the banquet hall, up under the arched roof, he discovered the wooden grating where Fritzi had described it. Against this wall he placed his ladder and climbed to the top, from which he could reach up and clasp the spindles of the grating above him.

He drew himself swiftly up to this, and the end of his pole was dislodged by his departure and fell to the inlaid pavement with a bang that seemed to him to carry to the farthest echoes of the sounding court. Instantly there was an answering clatter of steps.

Like a monkey Billy clung to the grating, thrusting his toes desperately into the first openings they could find, hanging on with his hands for dear life, holding himself as close up in the darkness as he could, and nearly twisting his neck off in the effort to watch what was going on below him.

The steps sounded nearer and nearer, and a huge Nubian in baggy bloomers and a short jacket was outlined in the court. His bare feet were thrust into clattering English shoes. He peered about him for a time, with one hand pointing the muzzle of a revolver. Billy caught the unpleasant gleam of it; then the man stepped in underneath the arches of the hall and made a slow way across it.

Directly in his path lay that fatal pole. It lay along the shadow of a column, but its end protruded beyond that shadow and would surely catch his eye. Billy tried to free his right hand to get at a gun of his own. To be caught ridiculously like this, clutching like a monkey on a stick— —!

Another man, shorter and bent, in a long robe and carrying a lantern, now emerged from that door along whose closed edge Billy had noticed the crack of light, and the Nubian diverged toward him. The pole was unnoticed and the two joined forces and made a slow circle in the garden. Billy remembered that dangling rope, and with a thumping heart he hoped that it would hang unregarded in that shadowed angle, overrun with vines.

Apparently it did, for he heard the footsteps passing on without a stop as he clung there to his grating, his muscles cramped, his sockets strained. Slowly the two recrossed the hall, talking together in low gutturals and not apparently of unpleasant things, for a note of laughter sounded. They lingered in parley in the court, but by the time that he thought that he could not hang on a minute longer and would drop like a peach from the wall, they separated and each moved slowly away. The man with the lantern shut the door after him and all was darkness there and the great Nubian was blotted out beneath the arches of the vestibule.

The fear that Falconer was in the palace alone made Billy desperate. Clinging with his feet and his left hand, he drew out a clasp knife with a razor edge and hacked furiously at the delicate spindles and frail carved work of the screen till he could thrust one arm through the opening. The work was easier then, but he had to resist the temptation to seize the brittle stuff and break it in pieces, for fear the splintering sound would be too sharp.

Torn between caution and impatience he worked on, and as soon as the hole was large enough he pulled himself cautiously up and dropped over the edge into the cage-like balcony on the other side. The panel which separated it from the rest of the old room was half open, and he stepped through it into what appeared utter darkness.

He stood listening keenly, for he knew that he was standing below the rose room; the very spot where he was must be almost exactly beneath that secret passage outside the panel in the rose room's wall. Not a sound came down to him and he dared not wait longer, but turned to the left and passed through the arched doorway into the next great salon.

As his eyes grew accustomed to the dark he saw that it was not utter blackness, but that some wan light from the paler night without faintly penetrated through those jealously guarded windows—windows not so heavily screened, he had been told, as those upon the front of the palace, for these were upon the court. He found time for a flash of horror at this stifling barricade as he made his hurried way through the room and stepped out into the little anteroom beyond.

Here he paused, for he knew that to the left, ahead of him, was the curtained opening into the long salon upon the street, and within that, Fritzi had warned him, a eunuch sometimes slept or Seniha occasionally came from her small salon to play on the piano there and lingered apparently in wait. But no one seemed stirring, and Billy stole to the door on his right, opening on the encased stairs, and found it locked. Hurriedly he pried at it with a burglarious tool, and then a sudden outburst sounded overhead.

There was a racket of hurrying feet and then a muffled explosion of a shot. A hoarse voice yelled. Another shot, and then a thud of something falling.

Desperately Billy fired his gun into the lock. The noise did not matter now and might serve to divert the fight from Falconer. Throwing his weight against the shattered lock, he bounded up the narrow stairs and raced down the long hall to the door that was brightly gilded. From beyond, but fainter now, came the sounds of conflict. With a heart beating to suffocation he flung open the door and rushed into that room.

CHAPTER XIV
IN THE ROSE ROOM

Candles flared on the table but not a figure greeted his eye. The room was deathly still; nothing stirred but the long draperies fluttering in the wind.

"Arlee!" he whispered in a voice strained with excitement. "Arlee Beecher, are you here?... Arlee!"

No voice answered. No motion revealed her. Only the candle flames danced drunkenly in a puff of air, flaunting their secret knowledge of the tenant they had lighted.

He darted to the tumbled bed and flung aside the covers; he looked beneath it and beneath the couch; he sent a candle's light traveling about the empty whiteness of the bath. No little figure, pitifully silenced, was, hidden there. The room was empty. And all the while that din sounded somewhere beyond them—running feet and strident yells.

"He's got her!" thought Billy, and first his heart leaped and then it sank. For very dear to that boy's heart had been the dream of rescuing her himself. And then he hated himself for that base envy. For what did it matter as long as little Arlee was safe, and that she was gone with Falconer, the empty room and the signs of hasty departure all spoke in witness. He wondered sharply how they had gone and whether he had better try to follow them and then thought it was shrewder to go back the way he had come and from below to try to guard whatever descent they must make.

He turned swiftly and crossed to the door. With a hand outstretched toward it he caught suddenly, beneath all the distant din, the click of a sliding lock, and he whirled about, dropping his right hand into his pocket, to see a pale face staring at him from the other side of the bed.

"Not a move—or you drop!" said Captain Kerissen. The candle lights glinted on the muzzle of a gun leveled steadily at him.

"Stay where you are," the Captain added, and Billy stayed, and through the dusk the two men stood eyeing each with a glare of hatred. But Kerissen's eyes held hatred triumphant.

"So, Monsieur," said the Turk. "This is the midnight call you gentlemen pay—in the chamber of my wife."

"Your wife!" Billy gave a snort of unbelief. "She says you did not marry her!"

"When you are found dead—if you are found," the other continued, looking lovingly along the sight, "there will not even be a question into the cause. You will be carted off like carrion—carrion that prowled too near."

"Just the same you've made a mistake," said Billy in a dogged and argumentative tone. "I'm not interested in visiting any wife of yours. The lady I'm representing says you didn't marry her. But she says you did keep back most of her jewelry and she's giving the story to the papers to-morrow unless I return with the stuff to-night."

He could not guess what impression this speech was making.

"I am not interested in your stories, Monsieur," the Turk returned blandly. "I am interested only in your dispatching—which I feel should be prolonged beyond the mercy of a shot."

"Look here, I'm not a common robber and you know it," said Billy, and his voice sounded rough and angry. "I'm here to collect the property of the lady you detained here, while she was under contract in Vienna. I don't want anything more than *belongs* to her. She left——"

"With a great deal more upon her than she brought! But am I to suppose, Monsieur, that you have made your way here, at some personal inconvenience, I should say, to discuss the generosity of my remuneration to the lady?" There was a tense silence and the Captain continued in a low, almost purring voice, "You do not appear, even now, to comprehend the thing you have done. I shall do my best to make you comprehend—and before I have finished it may be that I shall have a clearer explanation of this impulsive call. You have no notion, Monsieur, how certain things unloose the tongue—but you shall discover."

Billy saw his white teeth show in a deadly smile. Back of him a dark, heavy figure appeared and the Captain, without turning his head or moving his eyes or his gun from Billy, gave some rapid directions in Turkish and the figure disappeared. It occurred to Billy like a flash that from that secret passage where the figure had appeared there was a panel into the room on the right and that room had a door opening into the hall outside. The next moment he felt the door behind him open.

Then he pulled the trigger of that gun in his pocket in which his hand had been so lightly resting. The Captain seemed to fire the same instant, but Billy had jumped aside as he shot his own gun and he heard the bullet singing past his ear, and now, with his revolver out of his pocket, he shot again with an aim so true that the other man's right hand gave a spasmodic jerk and the revolver went spinning to the ground.

Across the room he hurled himself, springing from the onslaught of the assailant entering behind him, and thrusting the cursing Captain from his path he leaped through the sliding panel. The lock clicked home and he paused even in that moment of hammering pulses and pounding heart to fumble in the darkness to shut that other panel into the next room, remembering Fritzi's warning that those locks needed a key to open them from within. The minute's delay for the key would mean many minutes for him.

He stumbled against the tiny stairs that led to the tower room through which Falconer had descended, but he did not dash up those stairs for he heard the noise of feet overhead, as if returning from pursuit, and he darted straight on through the long, narrow, unlighted corridor, running like a hare.

At the other end he crashed against a half-open door and fell headlong down a flight of stairs. From his astonished fingers the revolver went clattering and though he picked himself up, battered but unbroken, at the foot, he dared not waste a minute to go back and hunt for the gun in the dark. He was totally at a loss for directions; he had expected to find himself in the Captain's rooms, and the stairs were unknown. Now he could just make out a door ahead of him and sent it flying open, smash in the face of an astonished black boy who went stumbling backwards.

Out went Billy's fist and caught the unguarded chin a staggering blow, and as the boy reeled back he flung one hurried glance about the big, lamp-lit chamber in which he found himself, the room evidently of Captain Kerissen, and darted to an arsenal of weapons that glinted against the inlaid panels. Wrenching down the shortest scabbard he jerked out a most villainous looking two-edged knife and gripping this piratical weapon he bounded out the door, fled through the dim hall to his right, rounded a corner, to the right again, hearing the sounds of pursuit louder and louder now behind him, shot through a vast reception hall and plunged down a flight of stairs.

From the darkness below a figure rose up to receive him with a grip like iron. Billy's right arm was doubled at his side; the blade of that villainous old dagger was pressed against the yielding softness of the fellow's sash, but for the life of him Billy could not drive home that knife against the human flesh. With a convulsive movement he tore himself from those gorilla arms and sent up a desperate kick, then leaped past the staggering man, and with the unused knife in his teeth, he tore at the bars of the great gate in the wall at his left. The bars were stiff and primitive and resisted his furious fingers, and the big gate-keeper, gasping for a moment against the stairs, suddenly straightened and sprang toward him.

"Here's one hero that didn't open the door 'in the nick of time'!" raced through Billy's grimly humorous mind, as he dodged the savage thrust of a knife the man had drawn and turned and scuttled across the court with the other on his heels. Through the arches he darted and then down into the garden, sprinting as he had never sprinted before, on, on to the southwest angles of the wall, thanking Heaven fervently, as every step outdistanced his pursuer, that the man had evidently no gun.

The rope ladder was still there, blown free at the bottom now and waving merrily in the wind. He snatched at it, dropping his knife in his pocket, praying that the top hooks had not become dislodged, and after him came the other man, hand over hand. Billy drew up his legs in a horrid fear of having them gripped or hacked at, and gained the top just as the other's head appeared below, his knife gleaming in his teeth.

Like a flash Billy drew out his knife and cut the rope. There was a wild yell from below and a screech of curses and imprecations following a rather sickening sounding thud, which persuaded Billy, peering down from above, that the victim's lungs at least were unimpaired, and then to his great amazement a shot went winging up past his ear.

"Had a gun all the time—too fighting mad to think of it—knife more natural!" he thought amazedly, sliding down the other side in a jiffy and then jerking his ladder down flat on the ground.

Out in the shadows the one-eyed man was paddling earnestly to safety. The shot so close at hand had been his sign for departure; he did not look back at Billy's shrill whistling nor his wilder shouts, and as the yells on the other side of the wall were bringing the inmates of the palace upon him, Billy had no more time for persuasion.

Off went his shoes and out into the canal he flung them, then headlong he plunged into the dark and uninviting water and struck out to the right, in the same direction in which the canoe was going, keeping carefully in the shadow of the bank, on the other side.

In a few moments the canoe was lost from sight and Billy was left alone, swimming between two steep walls of old palaces, weighed down by his tweeds, and maddened through and through with his inability to wring the neck of the one-eyed canoeist. The distance seemed unending to his slow progress but at last the palms of the cemetery appeared upon the right hand bank, and he struck across the widening waters and climbed out on the first foot of the graveyard that presented itself.

A dozen rods farther on the Arab was awaiting him in the canoe. Billy's mood did not invite conversation and he did not linger now for the other's explanations, but calling to him to wait he made in through the cemetery, dodging warily from tomb to tomb, till he reached the entrance of the main road.

The motor was gone. He satisfied himself of that, and a wave of rejoicing surged through him. That motor was to wait till one or the other arrived with the girl and then leave with all speed, while the other was to be left to the slower canoe. He was sure, now, that Falconer had succeeded in carrying the thing through and Billy's heart warmed to him. Then, for the first time, he felt something numb and queer about his left arm and putting his hand on it he found the sopping sleeve was torn and a warm ooze of blood welling through the cold water from the canal.

"Gosh, the chap winged me!" was his startled exclamation. "Feels as if it's going to sleep—glad it didn't go back on me in the ditch, there." Then he pressed back into the shadows for he saw a figure edging forward beyond the corner of a tomb. After a moment's hesitation it came directly toward him. He saw it was Robert Falconer.

Foreboding gripped him and he could scarcely keep himself from shouting his eager question, but he hurried forward till the two stood face to face and then, "Where is she? Did you get her?" burst from him, and "Have you got her? Is she all right?" came at the same instant from Falconer.

Blankly they stared at each other and a cold sense of failure went over and over Billy like a sea. His voice shook with this new, sickening fear. "Didn't you see her at all?"

"Did you?" counter-demanded Falconer, and Billy stammered, "Why no I—I found the room empty. And I thought you were safely off with her."

"Safely off!" said Falconer grimly. "I got in all right, though there must be a new lock on the door of that room up top, but I made some noise about it and ran plump into a fellow half way down the stairs. I threw him the rest of the way down, and he fired and brought a couple of others swarming up at me but I got out on the roofs again and gave them the slip. They went tearing back along the wing toward the garden the way I'd come and I went toward the street and got down."

"Got down! *How* did you get down?"

"Over those bay-window places," said the Englishman briefly. "I tied that cord I had to one of the doddering old cornices to start with. It wasn't any trick at all."

"Three stories," Billy shot in.

"And you'd no better luck, it seems?" Falconer inquired.

"No, I came up from below and found the room empty—but disheveled, so I thought you were off with her sure. And just then the Captain came in the panel places—just back from chasing you along the roof, I guess, for I'd been hearing the racket—and another fellow with him and we had a scrimmage and I got away through the men's wing."

"You're wet."

"That was a bit of canal bathing—our Arab put off with the canoe when I was needing it badly. I left him waiting here all right, however, and came here to find the motor gone."

"Naturally—being paid in advance."

"Only half paid."

"Half pay was enough for him. I knew it would be.... The thing was all rot in the first place."

Billy was too bitter of soul to reply. He was remembering what he ought to have done. He ought to have put that pistol to the Captain's head and forced him through the palace inch by inch.... He wondered if it would do any good to go back. His arm was rousing from its numbness, however, and raising a little racket all its own.

"We might as well get out of this," the Englishman advised, and Billy's reason acquiesced in spite of his rage. In silence they went down to the water's edge and embarked. The homeward course, from caution, was not past the palace but upstream through a remote and unknown region where they finally landed upon a bank and struck through unfamiliar and unfriendly looking byways toward the city.

Their walk was silent. Fierce gloom enveloped Billy; furious chagrin bestrode him. Chump that he was to have jumped at such positive conclusions! He ought to have stayed there. If only that second Turk had not been coming up behind him! He could think now of a number of brilliant ways out of his difficulties.... Morosely he trudged on through the interminable streets, his chilly wetness like an outward aspect of his gloom-soused mind.

He could not bear to think of Arlee. He felt now that, warned by Falconer's approach from above, they had snatched her from her room and hidden her away. He wondered if he deceived the Captain about the motives for his presence. He wondered what in the world could be done now—if all effort was to resolve itself into the futility of an official search-party. He wondered where in all that baffling prison Arlee was hidden.

Upon that tormenting question he unlocked his lips. "Where is she?" he muttered worriedly. "That's the question—where is she?"

"In Alexandria."

Plainly the Englishman's wrath had been smoldering. Billy turned upon him fiercely.

"In that palace, I tell you."

"So you say."

"And I say, too," and Billy's exasperation strained its bonds, "that if you don't believe she was there—if you think I got up this little party to while away an idle evening, why it was most uncommonly good of you to come! But I can't think why you did it if you weren't convinced of the necessity. Certainly it was not from love of me."

"Rather not."

"That goes double.... But you couldn't deny the facts and you *did* come. Because we failed doesn't change the facts at all. She's there—only *where*? Had we better go straight to the consul now?"

"I think," said Falconer coldly, "that we had better telegraph the Evershams to see if they have had any word from her before we stir up any hue and cry."

"All right," said Billy, and then he gave a short laugh. "Lord, we shall be quarreling like a couple of backyard dames next ... Of course, we're chagrined. It's poor satisfaction to reflect that we did our best—and if you are still uncertain about Miss Beecher's danger there I can't blame you for seeing the folly of the business."

After this effort of pleasantness Billy subsided into the cab that was most welcomely discovered, rousing after some minutes of violent progress to change their direction to the English doctor's.

"Winged," he said briefly, to Falconer's question. "Watchman chap as I was getting over the wall. Nothing wrong, I know, but it feels like—fire," he substituted.

Falconer was instantly concerned, but his sympathy went against the grain. Billy was too stirred for consolation. At the doctor's he refused to have Falconer enter with him.

"No use in having both of us traced if there is to be any trouble about this," he said with decision. "Go ahead and telegraph the Evershams and get an answer as soon as possible."

He had no earthly belief in that answer, and great, therefore, was his astonishment when, as he was walking the floor with his tingling arm in the early morning hours, a telegram was sent to him which Falconer had just received. His wire had caught the boat at Rhoda where it tied up for the night and Mrs. Eversham had promptly answered.

"We have heard from Miss Beecher," she said, "and she may join us later. Her address just Cook's, Alexandria."

CHAPTER XV
ON THE TRAIL

Breakfasting, a little one-handedly, that Monday morning, Billy was approached by his companion of the night. The young Englishman looked fresh and fit and subtly triumphant.

"Good news—what?" he said with a genial smile.

"If authentic," said the dogged Billy.

"Of all the fanatic f——!" The sandy-haired young man checked his explosiveness in mid-air. He gave a glance at the bulge of bandage beneath Billy's coat sleeve and dropped into a chair beside him. "How's the arm?" he inquired in a tone of restraint.

"Fine," said Billy without enthusiasm.

"Glad of that. Afraid the canal bath wouldn't do it any good. Beastly old place, that." Then the Englishman gave a sudden chuckle. "It's a regular old lark when you come to think of it!"

"Our lack of luck wasn't any great lark." Savagely Bill speared his bacon.

"Luck? Why we—Oh, come now, my dear fellow, you can't pretend to maintain those suspicions now! Of course the letter is authentic!" Falconer spoke between irritation and raillery. "That Turkish fellow could hardly fake that letter to them, could he? No, and we will have to acknowledge ourselves actuated by a too-hasty suspicion—inevitable under the circumstance—and be grateful that the uncertainty is over. That's the only way to look at it."

"We don't know that the Evershams have received a 'letter.' It might be another fraudulent telegram that was sent them from Alexandria."

"That is a bit too thick. You're a Holmes for suspicion!" Falconer laughed. "I believe if Miss Beecher herself walked into this dining room you would question if she were not a deceiving effigy!"

"I might question that anyway." Billy's tone was dry. "And I daresay I am a fool. But that dancer's story is pretty straight if she didn't know the names, and it fits in disastrously well with my limousine story."

"You're not the first man to be staggered by a coincidence," Falconer told him. "And that woman's yarn was convincing enough, though all the time I was dubious, you remember. But now that the Evershams have heard," and the young Englishman's deep note of relief showed how tormenting had been his uncertainty, "why now we have no further right to put Miss Beecher's name into the affair. There is evidently some other girl concerned who may or may not be as guileless as she represented to the Baroff girl, and I shall lay that story before the ambassador and leave her rescue to authentic ways."

He laughed a little shamefacedly at the unauthentic ways of last night, and added, looking off across the room, "My sister and Lady Claire are going to Luxor to-night, and I expect to accompany them. If you should have any word about Miss Beecher's return here I should be glad if you would let me know."

"If she is safe in Alexandria she'd never think of writing me," said Billy bluntly. "Our acquaintance is distinctly one-sided."

"I quite understand. She was your countrywoman in a strange land and all that."

"And all that," Billy echoed. "What time is your train?"

"Six-thirty."

"Then if I don't see you before that here's good luck and good-by."

Billy rose and shook hands and the two young men parted after a few more words.

"You have an *idée-fixe*—beware of it!" was Falconer's caution, serious beneath its air of banter, and on the other hand Billy perceived in the cautioner a latent uneasiness considered so irrational that he was doing his sensible best to disown it.

So Falconer took himself off about the preparations for departure and Billy B. Hill was left to face his problem alone. Black worry plucked at him. He did not know what under the sun he could do next. Already that day he had done what he could. He had been out early and run down the one-eyed factotum loitering about the corner and under cover of a transaction over a scarab he had made a number of plans.

He wanted the Captain followed every instant of the day. There were enough active little Arabs greedy for *piastres* to do that well and send back constant word to him. There was coming that day, he felt, an interview between him and that Captain. Then he wanted the one-eyed man to insinuate himself into the palace. He must find out things. He could use his connection with the eunuch who was uncle of his brother's wife.

So much Billy had already arranged and now after a hasty breakfast he was off to the consul, where he proceeded to unfold his story while the consul drew little circles on his blotter and looked out of the corners of his eyes at this astonishing young man.

He made no comment when Billy paused. Perhaps he could think of none adequate, or perhaps, after all, he had ceased to be amazed. He merely said slowly and thoughtfully, "Of course the dancer's story is all you really have to go upon. You had better bring her here."

"Nothing easier," Billy declared, and thinking a cab as prompt as a telephone he drove briskly off.

The hotel held a shock for him. Fritzi Baroff was gone. She had gone the evening before, the clerk reported, consulting the register, and she had paid her bill. As he had not been the one on duty then he knew nothing more about it. She had left no address.

Ultimately the clerk who had been on duty was unearthed in the labyrinths of the hotel's backgrounds, but he could supply very little further except the certainty that she had paid her bill in person, and the vague belief that she had been accompanied. This belief was companioned by a hazy notion that some one had called on her that evening.

Even Billy's sense of humor was unstirred by the half-cynical sympathy of the night-clerk's gaze; Billy didn't feel a laugh anywhere within him. He was balked. The dancer had vanished with her story, and that story was essential to the consul. Like a fool he must return empty-handed with this yarn of her disappearance and the consul would be justified in declaring that he had no actual proof to act upon. Which was precisely what the consul did, but he offered, impressed with Billy's earnestness, "to take the matter up," with the proper authorities.

It seemed the best that could be done. Billy urged him to prompt action, and to himself he promised some prompt action of a totally unofficial character. He knew now what he was going to do, or rather he thought he did, for the day still held its unsettling surprises for him, and as he set forth on business bent that afternoon he found himself besieged by a skinny little boy in tattered blue robes, who danced around him with a handful of dirty postcards.

"Be off," said Billy, in vigorous Arabic, and the little boy answered proudly, in most excellent English, "I am a messenger, sir. I am the boy who held the canoe that night. Buy a postcard, sir? Only six piastres a dozen, six piastres, Views of Egypt, the Sphinx, the Nile, the——"

Impatiently Billy cut him short.

"Never mind the bluff. No one is listening. What's your message?"

"The streets have ears, sir. Buy a postcard?... I have come from the palace. I brought in the bread. I—*I* got in under their nose while the big Mohammed was turned away without sight of his uncle," bragged the little Imp. "I am a clever boy, I. No one else so clever to find out things. The American man did well to come to me."

"What the devil, then, did you find out?"

"Five piastres a dozen, then, only five.... Go on walking, sir, I will run alongside. Keep shaking your head at me—very good.... I find out where she are."

"Where *who* are?"

The little braggart had roused Billy's suspicions. He determined to be wary.

"The young girl with the very light hair. Mohammed send me to ask of her. You know, sir," the little fellow insisted, hopping up and down beside him. "Only four a dozen—very cheap!" he screeched at him in a tone that must have carried for blocks. "I run in with the bread and take it to the kitchen where women are working. And I pretend make love to one very pretty girl, tell her how I come marry her when I old enough and make enough, and hold up piece money to show how rich I am. And the rest they think I just make game, but I whisper to her quick how much you pay her for news of that lady upstairs with the fair hair, and I give her some money. It are not much, sir. I promise her to come back with more."

"Go on," demanded Billy, stopping short. "What did she tell you?"

"Walk along, sir, walk along. Just half a dozen then—very cheap, very beautiful!" cried the little rascal with deep enjoyment of his rôle. Billy found his hands clenching frenziedly. The Imp proceeded, "She are much afraid, that girl, to say things, but I tell her how safe it is an' I tell her you great big rich man who pay her well. I make her honest promise to come back with money—and she very poor girl. She whisper quick what she know, looking backward over shoulder like this." Turning his face about after this dramatic illustration the Imp caught sight of Billy's countenance, and rolled the rest of his narration into one speedy sentence.

"She are gone," he cried.

"Gone?"

"Took away.... Take these cards, sir, stop and look at them.... Yes, she are took away. It happen very quick; early that morning after the other lady go in the night. Everyone much excited that night, great noise about, and no one know just what happen. But the Captain give orders quick, and early the motor car is ready and the strange girl go away. Old woman go, too. Nobody know where."

"That would be Sunday morning," Billy cried excitedly. "Are you sure there is no mistake? There were lights in that room on Sunday night."

"I tell what the girl tell. She are very honest girl," the Imp insisted. "She say the other lady run away with her lover an' Captain afraid the new lady has a lover so he send her away quick."

"But he didn't go himself?"

"No, he have something with his reg-reglement," gulped the Imp hastily, "that day and he stay and he there now—but now he sick."

"What's the matter?"

"I don't know, sir, but I know the doctor comes because she say to me to come back and say I am boy from doctor with medicine, and if I don't see her I must say I lost that medicine and go away, and come again as I can till I bring that money to her. She are very much afraid, sir."

Billy shuffled the postcards with absent hands and stared down at them with unseeing eyes. She was gone—and the Captain was not with her! That much at least was gain. And the fellow was here sick from his shot hand, apparently. "I hope gangreen sets in," he said between his teeth.

"You are pleased with me, sir?" the Imp was demanding. "You are glad of so much clever boy? And you give me that money now to give that girl? I make her most honest promise—and you see, sir, I am very honest boy, I tell you all I know and I ask nothing of price yet. I know that you are honest American man."

At that Billy came out of his brown study and praised the tattered little Imp with hearty earnestness. He saw no reason to doubt the boy's story. If he had been trying to invent something in order to make capital out of him he would hardly have invented that story of Arlee's departure, for that put an immediate end to further remunerative investigations in the palace. Of course Billy might be mistaken, and the boy might be mistaken, but one had to leave something to probabilities. He was very generous with the boy, and the droll little brown face was lined with grins. Most naïvely he besought that the American would not reveal the extent of his donations to

Mohammed, the one-eyed man, as the boys had promised their employer a just one-half.

It was the first laugh Billy had enjoyed in a long time. His spirits were vastly lightened by the news that Arlee was out of the palace where the Captain was staying. Fritzi had optimistically informed him that the Turk's courtship could be made most lengthy, but that had been a sadly slender hope and the picture of Arlee playing such a fearful game was simply horrible to him. So his relief at her departure was intense, although it complicated more and more the hope of speedy rescue.

For where was she now? In Cairo? In some of the outlying villages? He felt swamped by the number of things were to be found out immediately. He must find where that big gray motor went so early on Sunday—surely there were people who had remarked it if they could only be found and induced to talk! And he must find where the Captain had other homes or palaces where he would be likely to hide a girl. And he must find out where the Captain was every instant of the day and night.

That was the most important thing of all. For the Captain unless delayed by extreme illness, or held back by a caution which Billy judged was foreign to his nature, would not wait long before he joined Arlee. He had evidently stayed behind for some review of his troops and also to be *au courant* of whatever stir would result from Fritzi Baroff's reappearance in the world, and be on hand to disarm whatever further suspicions would result from it. The lights in the rose room that last night and the used look of the room, puzzled Billy, but he concluded that the Captain liked the room and there was a good deal in that palace that had better be left to no imagination whatever.

So back to the hotel went Billy to enter upon a period of waiting that frayed his nerves to an utter frazzle. Inaction was horrible to him, and now it was inevitable. He must wait for word from that agile web of little spies which the one-eyed man was weaving about the Captain's palace, and be ready to start whenever the word came.

He slept with his clothes on that Monday night, but he slept heavily for he was tired and his arm was no longer painful. The tear of wound he called a scratch was healing swiftly.

Tuesday morning passed in the same maddening suspense. Captain Kerissen rode out that morning but only to the parade ground, where he took part in a review with his troops. It was noticed that his right hand was bandaged, but the injury could not have been severe for his thumb was free from the bandage and he occasionally used that hand upon the reins. It was the bright eyes of the Imp that were sure of that.

In the afternoon the Captain went again to the barracks and then to the palace of one of the colonels in his regiment. Then he went home.

Utterly disgusted with this waiting game Billy began to dress for dinner. All lathered for a shave he stood testing his razor on a hair when his unlocked door was violently opened and a panting little figure darted across to him. It was the Imp.

"Sir, he goes, he goes upon the minute," he panted out. "He is in the station. Quick!"

Like a streak of lathered lightening Billy went for his clothes. A centipede could have been no more active. He jerked up his suspenders; he jerked on a shirt; he jerked on a coat; he was wiping his face as he darted through the halls and down the stairs. No lift had speed enough for his descent. At the desk he flung some gold pieces at the clerk, cried something about being called out of the city, and asked to have his room kept; then he was down the steps and into the carriage that the Imp had magically summoned.

The drive to the station was a series of escapes. Between jolts the Imp gasped out the rest of the story. The Captain had ridden out in the automobile. The Imp had given chase and so had the one-eyed man, also on guard, and by dint of running for dear life they had kept the motor in sight until the crowded city streets were reached and a series of delays enabled them to catch up with it. As soon as they saw the motor stop before the station the boy had rushed for Billy while the Arab remained to shadow the Captain and learn his destination.

They themselves were at the station now, and Billy was still tying his cravat. Now they jumped down and pressed through the confusion, dodging dragomans, porters, drivers and hotel runners and making a vigorous way past hurrying travelers and through bewildered blockades of tourist parties. Suddenly over the bobbing heads they saw the face they sought. A single eye glared significance upon them. An uplifted hand beckoned furiously.

"Assiout," whispered the one-eyed man as Billy reached him. "Assiout. That one goes to Assiout on the night express."

"My ticket? Got a ticket for me?"

Upturned palms bespoke the absence of ticket and the Arab's deep regret. "The price was much. I waited — — "

Billy was off. There was no chance of his getting past that stolid guard without a ticket and he charged toward the seller's window, where a line of natives was forming for another train.

"*Siut!*" he shouted over their heads, and scattering silver and smiles and apologies he crowded past the motley line to the window and fairly snatched the miles of green ticket from the Copt's quick fingers.

He was the last man through the gate, and as he darted through the clicking of compartment doors was heard with the parting cries of the guards and the shouts of dragomans and porters. It was a train *de luxe* where the sleeping sections had long been reserved, but to accommodate the crowded travel ordinary compartment cars had been added at the last minute, and it was at one of these that Billy grasped, as the wheels were moving faster and faster. A gold piece caused a guard to unlock the first compartment door, although it said, "*Dames Seules,*" and "Ladies Only" in large letters.

It was not a corridor train and the compartment was already filled, and as Billy wormed his way, not into the nearest corner, for that was not yielded to him, but into the modicum of space accorded between two stout and glaringly grudging matrons, he became aware from the hostile stares that his entrance had not been solitary.

Between his legs the Imp was coiling.

"I made a sneak with you," the boy whispered. "I say I your dragoman, sir. You will be glad. You need such bright boy in Assiout."

Billy thought it highly probable that he would. But the ladies neither needed nor desired him now, and ringed in by feminine disgust the two scorned intruders sat silent hour after hour while the train went rushing south through the increasing darkness of the night.

CHAPTER XVI
THE HIDDEN GIRL

Hour after hour the little boat held its steady course; hour after hour the distant banks flowed past in changing scenes. Forward on the narrow deck a girl sat in a lounge chair beneath a striped awning and gazed out over the water. Squatting in the shade behind her an old woman stared up out of half-closed eyes with pupils as keen and bright under their puckered lids as the eyes of a watching hawk.

No disturbing consciousness of this incessant scrutiny muffled the serenity of the girl's appearance. Her hands lax in her lap, her blue eyes quietly intent upon the view, she lay back in her chair with as much confident unconcern as she might have shown in an opera box. As a matter of incredulous fact she was feeling incredulously at ease.

The terrible tension of those days in the palace was over—for the time, at least. She did not understand this new move, she had been bewildered ever since that early dawn, on Sunday, when the old woman and the eunuch had rushed her into the limousine, driven her swiftly through the empty streets to a landing place on the river beyond the bridge, and hurried her on board this little boat, an old *dahabiyeh* reconstructed and given a new engine.

The Captain had not appeared except for a brief interview in the vestibule where he had told her that the quarantine was prolonged and that he was going to try to escape out of Cairo where the authorities would not be aware, and would first try to smuggle her out of the city, too. She must do exactly as the old woman indicated and everything would be all right.

And she had said, "How exciting!" and "What fun!" with lips that smiled pluckily in apparent acceptance of this flimsy excuse.

She had connected this flight with the pandemonium she had heard in the palace the night before, and she guessed that in some way her presence there had become embarrassing for the Turk. Perhaps her friends had traced her! Perhaps Robert Falconer—for after all it would only be Robert Falconer's flouted devotion, she thought, that would interest itself in her. He mistrusted Kerissen; he would suspect.

So hope rose high in her, and hopeful, too, was this new glimpse of freedom. Somewhere, soon, she thought confidently, the chance to escape would come. The old woman could not watch forever. The big eunuch was occupied with the boat. She could hear him now muttering angrily to the little brown boy at the engines, while over the sound of his muttering rose the rhythmic, unconcerned chant of two other boys marching up and down the narrow passageways of deck outside the little staterooms with a scrubbing brush under each left foot. "*Allah Illeh Lessah*," they chanted monotonously, with a scrub of the brush at each emphasis. "*Allah Illeh Lessah.*"

"Allah help *me*," thought Arlee Beecher.

All day Sunday she had sat there in that chair watching the pyramids, at first so sharp-cut against the cloudless blue, wane imperceptibly and fade from sight, watching the golden Mokattan Hills and the pearly tinted Tura range slip softly from the horizon and all the old landmarks of the Egypt that she knew disappear and be replaced by strange, new sights. Other pyramids showed like child's toys upon the horizon; dense groves of palm trees appeared along the banks, then the banks grew higher and higher and upon them, silhouetted against the bright blue sky, showed a frieze-like procession of country folk driving camels or donkeys or bullocks.

All night long they had steamed, a search-light on the bow, and Arlee had lain in the little stateroom trying to sleep, but continually aware of the breathing of the old woman huddled outside against her door, of the soft thudding of bare feet about the deck, of the pulse of the engine, beating, beating steadily, and of quick, muffled commands, of reversals, grinding of chains as some treacherous shallow appeared ahead, then of the onward drive and the steady rhythmic progress again.

Where were they taking her? South to some haunt where she would be farther than ever from the civilization which had flowed so unheedingly past that old palace of darkened windows, south toward the strange native cities and tiny villages and the grain fields and the deserts. But it was all better than that stifling palace and the absence of the Captain gave her a sense of temporary security.

Sunday had been hot and dry, but this Monday was cooler and the north wind, blowing freshly over the wide Nile, broke the amber-brown of the water into little waves of sparkling blue edged with silver ripples. The river was beautiful to her, even in her sorry plight, and to-day there were little clouds in the sky, furtive, scuddy little clouds with wind-teased edges, and they cast soft shadows over the river and over the tender green of the fields and the flat, mirroring water standing level in the trenches. In the fields brown men and women were working, and on the river banks the half-naked figures of *fellaheen* were ceaselessly bending, ceaselessly straightening, as they dipped up the water from the *shadoufs* to feed the thirsty land. Sometimes in the fields Arlee saw the red rusty bulk of the old engines, which the Mad Khedive had tried to install among his people, to do away with this back-breaking work, now lying useless and ignored. God forbid that we do otherwise than our fathers, said the people.

Across the water came the monotonous chant of their labor song, and sometimes the creak and squeak of some inland well-sweep drawn round and round by some patient camel. She felt herself to be in another world, as she sat in that boat guarded by that old woman and an eunuch, a world strange and remote, yet desperately real as it enmeshed her in its secret motives, its incalculable forces....

As she watched, as the surface of her mind reflected these sights and was caught in the maze of fresh impressions, the back of that mind was forever at work on her own terrifying problem. She thought confidently of escape, not able to plan it but waiting intently upon opportunity, upon the passing of a boat perhaps, or the moment of tying to some bank.

There was in her a high spirit of undaunted pluck and an excitement in adventure, which made her heart quicken instead of flag at the odds before her. Only the thought of the desperate stakes and the reality of her hidden fears would often draw the color from her cheeks and stop an instant the beating of that hurrying heart.... If those hawk-like eyes were watching then they might see the slim hands pressed feverishly together before warning self-control turned them lax again.

So hour after hour the boat went on. On the left now the long mountain of Gebel-el-Tayr stretched golden and tawny like a lion of stone basking in the sun. They passed Beni-Hassan, where a Nile steamer lay staked to the shore, the passengers streaming gaily out and starting off on donkeys for an excursion to the tombs. If only it had been a little nearer, close enough to risk a desperate hail—! But the very sight of it was comforting.

Toward dusk the engine failed. That night the boat lay by the bank, tied to long stakes which the boys had driven in. The big Nubian sat at one end, cross-legged, a rifle on his knees. At the stern sat a brown boy. And so Arlee sank into the tired sleep that claimed her, and did not wake until the warm sunshine in her tiny window and the ripple of water against the sides told her that another morning was at hand and that they were on the move again.

Stepping out on deck for breakfast, she found the boat was sailing. Two *lanteen* sails were hoisted; a great one in the bow, a small one in the stern, and the boat was running swiftly before the north wind that blew fresher than ever. But the course was variable now as the river curved and as sandbanks threatened, and Arlee watched the waters eagerly for a near-passing boat. But when they did draw close to a *dahabiyeh* upon whose deck she saw some white-clad loungers, the Nubian gave a low order to the old woman who rose and gripped Arlee on the wrist and led her to the stateroom, sitting in silence opposite her like a squat gargoyle, till the Nubian's voice permitted them to emerge.

And now they came to a city upon the right bank and the domes and minarets, the crowded building and high flat roofs pierced Arlee with a terrible sense of loneliness. And when her eyes caught the gleam of flags over a building and she saw her own stars and stripes blowing against this Egyptian sky, the tears could not be fought back. With wet eyes and working mouth she stood there and looked and looked. She thought she could endure no more and that her heart was breaking.

Leaden discouragement was upon her as the boat made in toward the shore. It did not approach the city landings; it came in south near a shallow bank, and one of the brown boys jumped overboard and splashed to the shore while the boat went on. But by and by it turned in its course and came beating back against the wind till opposite it was the city; then it tacked in to that same place near the bank, and there the boy was waving at them. Skillfully the *dahabiyeh* was brought about close to the high bank; and ropes thrown from bow and stern were quickly staked and made fast.

A plank was put over the side and with the eunuch ahead and the old woman behind Arlee was taken ashore and mounted on one of the camels the boys had brought, with the old woman behind, gripping her about the waist. The eunuch, on another camel, held the bridle rope, and led them at a terrific pace along the river road and then across the fields, thudding down the narrow, beaten paths, till the lush green was past and the dry desert lands began.

Ahead of them a low, tawny mass of mountain seemed to shimmer and waver in the hot sun, and as they drew nearer and nearer the mass was resolved into many masses broken into small foothills at the base, through which the Nubian threaded a rapid, circuitous way that led out on a rolling ground. A wide detour, still at the same urgent speed which jolted the breath from the girl and made her cling to the carpeted pummel of the saddle with both hands, led them at last within sight of palm trees and mud walls.

Arlee had no means of guessing whether these houses were the outskirts of that city she had glimpsed or whether they were a separate village. She only saw that they were being taken to the largest house of the place, which stood a little apart from the others and was half-surrounded by mud walls.

Into this walled-in court her camel was led and halted and jerkingly it accomplished its collapsing descent, and Arlee found herself on her feet again, quite breathless, but very alert.

Her fleet glance saw a number of black-robed figures about a stair; the next instant a mantle was flung over her head and that compelling hand upon her wrist urged her swiftly forward, and up a flight of steps. Within were more steps and then a door. Thrusting back the mantle she found herself in the sudden twilight of a small, low-ceiled chamber. There was no other door to it but the one she heard bolted behind her; there was one window completely covered with brown *mashrubiyeh*. She flew to it; it looked out over wide sands, with a glimpse, toward the right, of a mud wall and pigeon houses. The room was musty and dusty and dirty; but the rugs in it were beautiful, and a divan was filled with pillows and hung with embroidered cotton hangings. Other pillows were on the floor about the walls. A green silk banner embroidered in gold hung upon one of those walls and a laquered table stood by the divan.

And as Arlee Beecher stood there in that strange, stifling room, the mutterings of foreign voices, the squeals of the camels, the bray of a donkey coming through that screened window, a sudden rage came over her which was too hot to bear. Her heart burned; her hands clenched; she could have beaten upon those walls with her helpless fists and screamed at the top of her unavailing lungs. It was a fury of despair that seized her, a fury that she fought back with every breath of sanity within her. Then suddenly the air was black. The room seemed to swim before her eyes and the ground came swaying dizzily up to meet her, and receive her spent unconsciousness.

Water had been brought; she woke to find herself upon the couch, the old woman woodenly sopping her head and hands. She smiled weakly into that strange dark face; it was as unchanged as if it had been carved from bronze. The business of reviving finished, the old woman left her a handkerchief damp with a keen scent and went about the work of unpacking a hamper that she brought in.

Dully, Arlee saw the preparations for a meal advancing. She shook her head at it; a cup of tea was all that she could touch. A lethargy had seized her; even the anger of revolt was gone. She closed her eyes languidly, grateful when the old woman went away, grateful when the darkness deepened. When it was quite night, she thought, she would break open the wooden screen and fling herself through the wood into the sands. She lay there passively waiting; her heavy eyes closed, and she slept.

CHAPTER XVII
AT BAY

Voices sounded below; footsteps hurried; a door slammed. Then feet upon the stairs, and a hand at the door. Arlee struggled to her feet in sudden terror; the candle was out and the room was in darkness. Outside a gale was blowing. The door opened, but the figure which hurried in was not the one her fright anticipated.

It was the old woman again, bustling with haste. She brought more candles for the table, and then a tray with a bottle and glasses and dishes covered with napkins. Then she bestowed her attention to Arlee, bringing her a mirror and a comb from the hamper she had left upon the floor, and a cloth thick with powder. Then Arlee was sure.

She stood rigid a moment, listening to that low buzz of voices from below, then desperately she shook out her tangled hair and combed it back from her hot face. It was still damp from the water that had been dashed upon her, and as she knotted it swiftly, soft strands of it broke away and hung in wet, childish tendrils. She brushed some powder on her face; she bit her bloodless lips, and stared into the glass, to see a wan and big-eyed girl staring back affrighted.

Then the door opened, and desperately calling on her courage, Arlee heard the Captain speaking her name and saw his smiling face advancing through the shadows.

"A thousand greetings, Mademoiselle. Ah, I am glad to see you." A strained emotion quivered through the false assurance of his tone.

She stood very straight and tense before him, a childishly small figure there in the dusk, the blowing candles making strange play of light and shadow over her. Steadily she answered, "And I am very glad to see you, Captain Kerissen."

"And I am glad that you are glad." But his ear had caught the hardness of her voice, for answering irony was in his. Some devil of delay and disappointment seemed to enter into him, for his face, as she saw it now in his advancing, struck fright into her. The four fingers of his right hand were wrapped in a bandage and he extended his left to her, murmuring an apology. "A slight accident, you see."

"There is so much I do not see that I do not feel like shaking hands," gave back Arlee. "Captain Kerissen, this is too strange a situation to be maintained. You must end it."

"It is a very delightful situation," he returned blandly, looking about with dancing eyes. "To be again your host, even in so poor a place as this old house of the Sheik—and the place has its possibilities, Mademoiselle. It is romantic. Your window overlooks that desert you were so anxious to see. The sunsets——"

"Captain Kerissen, I must say that you use a very strange way to keep me your guest!"

"I might respond that any way was justifiable so that it kept you a guest.... But you wrong me. Did I not bring you safely out from that quarantine, as you besought me?" His smile was mockery itself.

"But you did not bring me to my friends. I do not like your sending me here, without explanation," she returned, trying to be very wise and speak quietly and not rouse him to anger. "We passed a city where the American flags were flying over a house, and I could have gone there."

"I am sorry you do not care for my hospitality. I did not know that I was displeasing to you."

"It is those ways that are displeasing to me. I——"

"Then you shall change them," he laughed. "That will give me pleasure.... But I did not come in the dead of this night, half sick and fatigued, to find such welcome. Come, you must smile a little and sit down at the table with me. Here are delicacies I sent from Cairo."

Smilingly he seated himself at the divan by the table and lifted the covers from the plates, nodded satisfaction at the food, and began to help himself, while she stood there, motionless.

Without looking up, "Will you not help me to the Apollinaris, Mademoiselle?" he suggested. "My right hand, you see, is not as it should be. There is a bottle opener on the tray."

Feeling a fool, but unwilling to provoke a crisis, Arlee tugged at the cork and poured him a glass of the sparkling water and then a glass for herself, which she thirstily drank. "How did you hurt your hand?" it occurred to her to say.

"By playing with fire—the single pastime of entertainment!" He spoke gaily, but his lips twitched. "But will you not sit down and join me? This caviar I recommend."

"I do not care to eat."

"No?" He finished his sandwich and drained his glass, talking banteringly the while to her. She did not answer. Something told her that the time of explanation between them was coming fast; he had ceased to play with his good fortune, ceased to feel he could afford to wait and look and fancy. He had come urgent, in the dead of night. His mood was teasing, mocking, but imperative.... Slowly she moved toward the unlatched door.

Alertly he was before her; the bolts shot home. "Ah, pardon, but I was negligent! We might be interrupted—and also," he laughed, as if deprecatingly, "I have foolish fears that you are so dream-like that you will vanish like a dream without those earthly bars. Locks are for treasures.... And now where is that welcome for me? I came in that door on fire to see you, and your eyes froze me. I came to love—you made me mock. Shall we begin again? Will you be nice now, little one, be kind and sweet——"

"Captain Kerissen, you make it impossible for me to like you at all! Why do you treat me like this? You shut me in this house like a prisoner. If you— if you care for me at all," stammered Arlee, "you would not treat me so!"

"And how, then, would I treat you?" he inquired slowly.

"You would—you would take me to my own people and give me back my independence, my dignity. Then there would be honor in your—your courtship. I——"

"Would you come back to me?"

"I——"

The lie choked her. And the passion of anger which had flared in her that afternoon sprang up in flame again; the candlelight showed the hot blood in her cheeks. "I shall not come to you if you keep me here!" she gave back fearlessly.

"But here I can come to you. And the preliminaries are always stupid—I have no desire to reënact them. I am well content with where we have arrived. Be content, also."

She stared back at his smiling face. And all she thought was, "Shall I defy him now, or try to hold him off a little longer?" She had ceased to feel afraid; her blood was on fire; it was battle now between them; perhaps a battle of the wits a little longer, then——

"In America men do not make love by force," she flung at him. "You are mad, Captain Kerissen! You will be sorry if you go on like this. If you wish to marry me you must give me the freedom of choice. You must give me time. I must have a minister of my own faith. Do you think I will submit to this? You make me hate you!"

"Hate is often love with a mask," he laughed, his eyes fixed on the spirited, flushed face, the flashing eyes, the defiant mouth. "And do not quote your America to me. You are done with America."

"You say that? You forget who I am! My brother—I tell you my brother will— —"

"Do I not know the risks?" His eyes narrowed. "But your brother will ask in vain. He will not see you—until we reappear as husband and wife. I will take you to the Continent, then I will give you everything a woman wants, luxury and jewels—the pearls of my ancestors I will hang on you. These have no woman of mine worn. You shall be my adored, my dearest— — Oh, you must not turn from me," he pleaded, his voice sinking softer and softer as he stole closer to her. "You know that I am mad for you. You have bewitched me, little Rose, you have made me strong and weak in a breath. I am clay in your hands. Be sweet, be kind, be wife to me— —" His hot hand gripped her arm. He bent over her, and she sprang back, her hands flung out before her.

"Oh, wait!" she cried beseechingly. "Wait—please wait."

"Wait? I have waited too long!" His voice was a snarl now. The mask of indolent mockery was gone; his face was stamped with cruelty and greed. "*Nom d'un nom*, I am through with this waiting!"

She sprang back before his approach, then whirled about to face him, trying to beat him back with words, with reason, with appeal. Insanely he laughed and clutched at her as she flew past his outstretched arms; in the corner he pinioned her against the wall and gripped her to him.

Terror gave her the strength of two—and his hand was bandaged. Desperately she attacked it, and as his laughter changed to curses, she wrenched free once more and flew across the room. With both hands she seized the candles and flung them into the pillowed divan; holding the last two to the draperies. Like magic the little flames zigzagged up the cotton hangings.

He threw himself upon the fire, dragging down the hangings, beating on the cushions, but the corner was ablaze. Overhead the flames seized cracklingly on the dry wood and darted little red tongues over the dry surface and a scarlet snake ran out over the carved ceiling.

In utter wildness Arlee had carried the last candle to the open hamper and the garments there caught instant fire. She was oblivious of the sparks falling about her, oblivious of the increasing peril. When Kerissen ran to the door, tearing open the bolts, furiously cursing her, she gave him back the ghost of his earlier mocking laughter and threatened him with a blazing cloth as he turned to drag her from the room.

But the fire reached her fingers and she flung the cloth at him, to have him trample it under foot as he sprang toward her again.

"Would you be burned—be marred?" he shouted at her. "You are mad, you— —"

Behind him the door opened. Behind him a tall figure appeared through the thickening smoke. She saw a face she knew; a voice she knew cried out her name:

"Arlee!"

"Oh, here!" she cried and flung herself toward him.

"Not unless you want another?" said Billy B. Hill to the Captain, turning his gun suggestively.

One tense instant the three faced each other in that flaming room, then with a sound of impotent fury, Kerissen turned and darted out the door. But as Billy turned to follow, his hand on Arlee's, there was a sound of sliding bolts.

"Burn, burn, then! Burn together!" called a hoarse voice through the wood.

Hill flung himself against the door; it was unyielding. On the other side the taunts continued. He ran to the window, catching up the little table as he ran, and rained a fury of blows with the table against the close-carved screen. The wood splintered and broke; he wrenched a side away, and dropping his gun in his pocket he crashed through the hole and hung on the outside by his hands.

"Climb out on my shoulders," he commanded, and Arlee climbed—how, she never knew. For one instant she had an impression of hanging out over an abyss with fire crackling in her face; the next instant the soles of her feet were smarting and her eyes still seemed to see stars.

There was a run, stumbling, with Billy's hand sustaining her, and then she was on a camel, clutching the saddle as the beast rose swiftly in response to urgent whacks, and beside her Billy was on another. Some one on foot goaded the beasts into a startled run, and behind them yells and screeches were growing louder and louder.

Over her lurching shoulder she had one last glimpse of a burning building and saw flames pouring from the roof, and the room where she had been an open furnace, and then she turned her face toward the dark ahead.

"Hang tight," Billy was calling to her, and she saw him lean over and lash both camels into furious speed. "Some one is riding after," and then he turned and shot his gun warningly into the air.

The yells behind them stopped. But after some moments they heard a camel snarl, and knew that some one was still back there in the darkness, hanging on their trail. So they rode hard ahead, into the enveloping night, over the rolling dunes, with the wind leaping and tearing and hurling the sand in their faces, as if the very elements were fighting against them.

It was a strange chase and a hot one, pounding on and on, racked with the wild, lurching flight, deeper and deeper into the yellow-gray night that welcomed them with more strident blasts and more stinging particles of sand.

"It's a storm," Billy shouted at her, raising his voice above the wind. "It's been blowing up this way for an hour now—they won't follow long in the face of it. Can you hang on a little longer?"

"Forever," she cried back, gripping the pommel tight and bending her head before the whirling particles. There was sand in her hair, sand on her lashes and in her eyes, sand on her face and down her neck, and sand in her mouth when she wet her lips, but she heard herself laughing in the night.

"By and by we'll get off," he called back, and by and by when the hot, stifling, stinging, choking, whirling gale was too blinding to be borne, he checked the camels in one of the hollows of the desert dunes from which the wind was skimming ammunition for its peppery assaults, and the beasts knelt with a haste that spoke of gladness.

"It's the backbone of it now; cover your head and lie down," Billy commanded, and Arlee covered it with what he thrust into her hands—his overcoat, she found—and tucked herself down against him as he crouched beside the camels.

"I should think—it was—the backbone," she gasped, unheard, into her muffling coat. For the wind howled now like a rampaging demon; it tore at them in hot anger; it dragged at the coat about her head, and when her clutch resisted, it flung the sand over and over her till she lay half buried and choking. And then, very slowly and sulkily, it retreated, blowing fainter and fainter, but slipping back for a last spiteful gust whenever she thought it finally gone, but at last her head came out from its burrow, and she began cautiously to wipe the sand crust off her face and lashes.

"In your eyes?" said a sympathetic voice.

In the darkness beside her Billy Hill was sitting up, digging at his countenance.

"Not now—I've cried—that all gone," she panted back.

He chuckled. "I'll try it—swearing's no use."

She sat up suddenly. "Are they coming?"

"Not a bit. No use, if they did. You're safe now."

"Oh, my *soul*!" She drew a long, long breath. "I can't believe it." Then she whirled about on him. "How—why—why is it *you*?"

He looked suddenly embarrassed, but the darkness hid it from her. He became oddly intent on brushing his clothes. "Oh, I guessed," he said in a casual tone.

"You guessed? Don't they know? What did they think? Oh, where did everyone think I was?"

He told her, dwelling upon the misleading details; the hasty message of farewell from the station, the directions about luggage, the money to pay the hotel bill. "You see, his wits and luck were just playing together," he said.

"Then the Evershams *are* up the Nile?"

"Of course. They never dreamed — "

"They wouldn't." Arlee was silent. She wondered confusedly—she wanted to ask a question—she wanted to ask two questions.

"But—but—no one else— —?" she stammered.

There was a particularly large lump of sand in Billy B. Hill's throat just then; he cleared it heavily. "Oh, yes, some one else guessed, too," he said then. "That English friend of yours, Robert Falconer, he and I had a regular old shooting party in the palace last Sunday evening. If you'd been there then he would certainly have had you out."

"So he knows." She said it a little faintly, Billy thought, as if she was disappointed and troubled. She would know, of course, by intuition, how the Englishman would think about a scrape of that sort.

"But he doesn't know now," he said eagerly. "He is sure you are all right in Alexandria, because the Evershams received another fake telegram from you from Alexandria. The Captain was stalling them along, apparently, keeping everything under cover as long as possible. And when Falconer heard about that, his suspicions were over. He thought we'd made fools of ourselves in going to the palace."

She was silent. Looking at her, after a while, Billy saw her staring out obliviously into the darkness; her hair was hanging all about her.

His glance seemed to recall her thoughts. She started and then brushed back her hair; the sand fell from it and she took hold of one soft strand. "Look out, I'm going to shake this!" she warned, and he half shut his eyes and underneath the lids he saw her shaking her head as vigorously as a little terrier after a bath.

"Isn't it awful?" she appealed.

"I could scratch a match on my face," he confirmed.

"But tell me," she began again, "how did you know I was in that palace? And I must tell you how I happened to go and how I was kept there."

"You were told there was a quarantine, weren't you?" Billy supplied, as she hesitated.

Her astonishment found quick speech. "Why, how did you know *that*?"

"The Baroff told me—that Viennese girl who came into your room."

"Why, you know *everything*! How did you?"

"Oh, I carried her over a wall, thinking it was you."

"But how could you think it was *I*? And what were you doing at the wall? I don't see how——"

"Oh, one of the palace maids gave me a message in Arabic and I thought it was from you. You see, I suspected—I had seen you drive off in that motor——"

"But how could the maid bring you a message? Where were you? Where did she see you?"

"I was painting out in front of the palace." Billy sounded more and more casual.

"You said you were an engineer," said Arlee. His heart jumped. At least she had remembered that!

"So I am—the painting was just a joke."

"And you happened there," she began, wondering, and after he had opened his mouth to correct her, he closed it silently again. Gratitude was an unwieldy bond. He did not want to burden her with obligation. And he suspected, with a rankling sort of pang, that he was not the rescuer she had expected. So he made as light as possible of his entrance into the affair, telling her nothing at all of his first uneasiness and his interview with the one-eyed man which had confirmed his suspicions against the Captain's character, and the masquerade he had adopted so he could hang about the palace. Instead he let her think him there by chance; he ascribed the delivery of Fritzi's message to sheer miracle, and his presence under the walls that night to wanton adventure, with only a half-thought that she was involved.

Stoutly he dwelt upon Falconer's part in the attack the next night, and upon the entire reasonableness of his abandonment of the trail. He put it down to his own mulishness that he had hung on and had learned through the little boy of her removal from the palace.

He interrupted himself then with questions, and she told him of her strange trip down the Nile in the *dahabiyeh*, under guard of the old woman and the Nubian. "But how did you come?" she demanded.

"Well, I just swung on to the same train he was in," said Billy. "And I got out at Assiout because he'd bought a ticket there, but I couldn't see a thing of him in the darkness and confusion of the station, and I had a horrid feeling that he'd gone somewhere else, the Lord knew where, to you. But the Imp—that's the little Arab boy who adopted me and my cause—went racing up and down, and he got a glimpse of the Captain tearing off on a horse and behind him a man loping along with a bundle on a donkey, and the Imp raced behind him and yelled he'd dropped something. The man went back to look, and the Imp ran alongside him, asking him for work as a donkey boy. The fellow shook him off, but that had delayed him, and though we lost the horseman we kept the donkey-man in sight and followed him on to the village. I reconnoitered while the Imp stole these two camels—jolly good ones they are—and while I was trying to make out where you were, for there were lights in several windows, I suddenly heard your voice and then I saw a glare of fire. Well, my revolver was a passport.... Now, how about that fire? What started it?"

"I did; he—he was trying to make love to me," she answered breathlessly, "and I just got to the candles."

"Are you burned at all? Truthfully now? I never stopped to ask."

"If I am, I don't know it," she laughed tremulously. Then, "Isn't this *crazy*!" she burst forth with.

"It's—it's off the beaten track," Billy B. Hill admitted. "It's a jump back into the Middle Ages." His note of laughter joined hers as they sat staring owlishly at each other through the dark of the after-storm.

A little longer they talked, their questions and answers flitting back and forth over those six strange days; then, as the excitement waned, Billy heard a sleepy little sigh and saw a small hand covering a yawn. The girl's slender shoulders were wilting with incalculable fatigue.

Instantly he commanded sleep, and obediently she curled down into the little nest he prepared, pillowing her head upon his coat, and almost instantly he heard her rhythmic breathing, slow and unhurried as a little child. His heart swelled with a feeling for which he had no name, as he sat there, his back against a camel, staring out into the night, an unknown feeling in which joy was very deep and triumph was merged into a holy thankfulness.

CHAPTER XVIII
DESERT MAGIC

He had meant but forty winks, but it had been dark when his eyes closed and he opened them to the unreal half-lights of early dawn. The sky was pearl; the sands were fawn-colored; the crest of a low hill to the east shone as if it were living gold, and the next instant it seemed as if a fire were kindled upon it. It was the sun surging up into the heavens, and great waves of color, like a sea of flame, mounted higher and higher with it.

Impulsively Billy bent over the little figure sleeping so soundly at his side, speaking her name gently. And Arlee, waking with a start and a catch of her breath that went to his heart, opened her eyes on a wild splendor of morning that seemed the outer aspect of the radiant joy within her.

They looked and looked while the east flamed like a burning Rome, and then the glow softened and paled and dissolved in mysteries and miracles of color, in tender rose and exquisite shell pinks, in amethysts and violets and limpid, delicate, fair greens. All about them the sands were turning to gold, and the rim of the distant horizon grew clearer and clearer against the brightening blue of the sky, like a great circling tawny sea lapping on every side the arch of the heavens.

As they looked their hearts stirred and quickened with that incommunicable thrill of the desert, and their eyes turned and sought each other in silence. The gold of the sun was on Arlee's hanging hair and the morning-blue of the sky in her eyes; her face was flushed from sleep and a tiny tendril still clung to the pink cheek on which she had been sleeping. Somehow that inconsequent small tendril roused in Billy a thrill of absurd tenderness and delight.... She was so very small and childish, sitting there in the Libyan desert with him, looking up at him with such adorable simplicity.... In her eyes he seemed to see something of the wonder and the joy in his. It was a moment of magic. It brought a lump into his throat.... He wanted to bend over her reverently, to lift a strand of that shining hair to his lips, to touch the sandy little hands....

Somehow he managed not to. The moment of longing and of glamor passed.

"It's exactly as if we'd been shipwrecked!" said Arlee, looking about with an air of childish delight.

"On a very large island," he smiled back, and felt a furtive pain mingling with his joy. He was just her rescuer to her, of course; she accepted him simply as a heaven-dropped deliverer; her thoughts had not been going out to him in those long days as his had gone to her.... Decisively he jumped to his feet and said breakfast. Where was it? What was to be done?

Directions were vague. They had come south on the edge of the desert, and the Nile lay somewhere to the east of them, and to the east, therefore lay breakfast and trains and telegraph lines and all the outposts of civilization.

To the east they rode then, straight toward the tinted dawn, and as they went they laughed out at each other on their strange mounts like two children on a holiday. Their spirits lifted with the beauty of the morning, and with that strange primitive exhilaration of the desert, that wild joy in vast, lonely reaches, in far horizons and illimitable space. The air intoxicated them; the leaping light and the free winds fired them, and with laughing shouts and challenges they urged their camels forward in a wild race that sent the desert hares scattering to right and left. Like runaways they tore over the level wastes and through the rolling dunes, and at last, spent and breathless, they pulled back into a walk their excited beasts that squealed and tossed their tasseled heads.

Their eyes met in a gaiety of the spirit that no words could express. When Arlee spoke she merely cried out, "I've read the camel had four paces, but mine has forty-four," and Billy gave back, "And forty-three are sudden death!" and their ringing laughter made a worried little jackal draw back his cautious nose into his rocky lair.

They were in broken ground now, more and more rocky, leading through the low hills ahead of them, and great clumps of grayish *mit minan* and bright green hyssop dotted the amber of the sands. Here and there the fork-like helga showed its purple blossom, and sometimes a scarlet ice-plant gleamed at them from a rocky crack. Across their path two great butterflies strayed, as gold and jeweled as the day. High overhead, black against the stainless blue, hung a far hawk.

At last the way entered a narrow defile among the rocky hills, and a sharp curve led them finally out upon the other side, looking down into green fields, as straight and trim as a checker board in their varying tints, and off over the far Nile. The fertile lands were wide here, and fed with broad canals that offered the surprise of boats' white wings between the fields of grain. Not far ahead, before the desert sands reached that magic green rose a group of palms, and near them some mud houses and a pigeon tower.

"Breakfast," said Billy triumphantly, and gaily they rode down on the sleeping village.

Back toward the Libyan hills runs the canal El-Souhagich, and as it curves to the north a reach of sand sweeps down from the higher ground, interrupting the succession of green fields. Several jagged rocks have tumbled from the limestone plateaus above and increased the grateful bit of shade which the half dozen picturesque palms do not sufficiently bestow.

Here the runaways breakfasted upon the roast pigeon, dates and tangerines they had bought from the curious villagers, and here Billy, his back against a rock, was smoking a meditative cigar over the situation. Beside him, tied to a palm, knelt the camels, and before him, nibbling a last tangerine, Arlee was sitting.

"We have to rest the beasts a bit." This from Billy, suggestive of a conscience pricking at this holiday delay. "And then——"

"Then—?" echoed Arlee cheerfully.

"Then, what in the world am I going to do with you?"

"With me?"

"Yes. It's simple enough, I suppose, getting back to the city—-but if you don't want your friends to know——"

The quick shadow in her eyes distressed him. "I *don't*," she cried sharply. "At first—I might have made a lark out of it—but afterwards.... No, I don't want to go explaining and explaining forever and ever. Can't I just reappear?"

"You can reappear from Alexandria," he said. "He, himself," his tone changed as he reluctantly brought Kerissen into the beauty of that morning, "has arranged it very neatly for you. You can just have been camping in the desert—and true enough that is!—with those friends of yours whom the Evershams don't know. Only your reappearance has to be—managed a bit."

Very carefully she tore the tangerine skin into very little bits, her head bent over it. Then she flung the fragments far from her with a gesture of rebellion. "I hate fibs," she said explosively. And then, "But I hate explanations more!" She hesitated, stealing a quick glance under her lashes at his frowning face.

"And some people," she stammered, "might—might not—understand—they would feel that—some people would——"

The Palace Of Darkened Windows

"Some people are great fools, undoubtedly," Billy promptly agreed. But back of the some people he saw Falconer in her mind, and Falconer's instinctive distaste of all strangeness and sensation.

"I have a perfect right to keep it from—them," she went on argumentatively, and then with an upward glance, "Haven't I?"

"Good Lord, yes! It was your adventure; it doesn't concern another soul in this wide world."

"You know," said Arlee, locking and unlocking her fingers, "you know, some people wouldn't take it all for granted the way—you do.... And it was very horrid."

"It's over," said he crisply, "except I'd like to pound him to a jelly."

"I couldn't bear to *speak* of him before," said the girl, "but now it seems all far away and nightmarish.... And I'd like to tell you how it was—a little."

"You needn't."

"I know I needn't." Arlee's tone was suddenly proud. Then she melted again. "But I want you to know. He was—he was trying to make me care for him.... He wasn't really as dreadful as you might think him, only just insane—about me—and utterly unscrupulous. But he did want me to like him and so, when I found out, when Fritzi told me I was in a trap, I tried to play his game. I *flirted* one day in the garden, at lunch, and made him think— — You see, I *had* to gain time and try to get word to people. But I hated him so I— —" She broke off, the pupils of her fixed eyes big and black with the memory.

"You know I can't—I can't think of you—alone there," came huskily from the young man.

"He never *dared* to touch me—really—till last night," she said fiercely. "He tried, but I—I held him off. Only he talked to me—Oh, how he talked. Like a river of words.... I hate all those words.... If ever again a man asks me to marry him I don't ever want him to *talk* about it. I want him just to say two words, *Will you?*" Her laugh caught quiveringly in her throat.

It taxed all the young man's control to keep his tongue off the echo.

"He just raved," she went on after a pause, "and I had to listen—but last night he was horrible. I could never have got to the candles if his hand hadn't been hurt."

"I wish I'd shot his hand off," said Billy bitterly.

"Oh! Was it you who— —?"

"When we were in the palace." He told her again about the raid and she nodded delightedly over it.

"It's so wonderful for you to have done all this," she said with sudden shyness. "You had just met me——"

The things on Billy's tongue wouldn't do at all. None of them. What he did say was absurdly stiff and constrained. "You were my countrywoman—and alone."

"So are the Evershams," said Arlee, with sudden bubbling laughter, and then as suddenly checked herself. Her fleet glance at him was half-scared. "You—you are very good to your countrywomen in distress," she got out stammeringly.

Billy contemplated his cigar. It was safer.

Presently she reverted to the topic of discovery. "But about Mr. Falconer? Are you sure his suspicions are over now?"

"Perfectly sure. Or they will be the moment he sees you. You'll have to laugh at him if he mentions them, of course;" Billy spoke with heartiness.

"He'd hate it," the girl said musingly. "The talk and all—about me—Oh, after being such a fool *I'd never be the same to them!*" she broke out passionately.

The furtive pain was bolder now; Billy felt it worming deeper and deeper into his sorry consciousness. It mattered so much to her what Falconer thought—so much....

"But I'll do anything you say," she said meekly, looking up at her rescuer with those big eyes whose blueness always startled him like unsuspected lakes. He saw then that she meant to be very grateful to him. Somehow that deepened the pang. He didn't want that kind of bond....

"Then you will bury even the memory of this time and never whisper a word of it," he told her stoutly. "The talk and explanation will be over five minutes after your return. The thing is, to manage that return. Now the Evershams left Friday and this is Wednesday—six days."

"Only six days," she echoed with a ghost of a sigh.

"Now let me see where were we on the sixth day? When I was on the Nile?" He knitted his brows over it. "Why, the steamer leaves Assiout at noon of the fifth day—that was yesterday."

"Oh! I must have passed them on the Nile," cried Arlee.

"Maragha is where they stopped last night. To-day they'll be steaming along steadily and stop to-night at Desneh. To-morrow night they'll be at Luxor."

"And they stay three days at Luxor?"

"The steamer does, I believe. I left the steamer there and went to the hotel for a while and spent another while at Thebes with a friend of mine."

"The excavator!" cried Arlee quickly.

"Then you do remember," said Billy with a direct look, "that dance and——"

"And our talk," she finished gaily. "And your being Phi Beta Kappa. Oh, I was properly impressed! And I didn't know then that you were a regular Sherlock Holmes as well."

"I didn't know it either," said Billy grinning. But he knew that she didn't know now how much of a Sherlock Holmes he had managed to be for her.

"That seems ages ago," she declared, "and in an altogether different world. The only real world seems to be this desert——"

"Bedouin breakfast and camel races," finished Billy. "And it's so much of a lark for me that I can't keep my mind on the problem of the future. But I have to get you to Luxor by to-morrow night——"

"And I can't arrive in the rags and tatters of a white silk calling gown," mentioned Arlee cheerfully, surveying her disreputable and most delightful disarray. "I must have trunks and a respectable air—and a chaperon, I suppose."

"And I won't do at that. But if you get to Luxor you'll be all right. You can go to the hotel and to-morrow night the Evershams' boat will get in about seven in the evening."

"Did you say my trunks were sent to Cook's?"

He repeated the story of the telegram to the Evershams. Over the arrival of the boy with money for her hotel bill she wrinkled her brows in perplexity. "I suppose he thought there would be less discussion about me if my bills were paid," she said finally. "But I'd like to get that money back to him."

"I'll see he gets it—with interest," responded Billy.

"And you——?" She looked up at him with a startled, vivid blush that stained her soft skin from throat to brow. "You must have been to a great deal of expense——"

"Not a bit. Please don't——"

"But I must. When I get to a bank. I still have my letter of credit with me," she said thankfully, "but it didn't do me any good in that wretched palace. It was just paper to them. I showed it to the girl once and tried to make her understand."

"The first station we find we'd better wire for your trunks to be sent by express to Cook's at Luxor—or to the Grand Hotel. And then you can take the train straight to Luxor and buy some clothes there."

"But the train—I can't travel in this! And there would be people on it who would talk——"

"Had we better make it to Assiout then?" said Billy doubtfully. "Once in the city, of course, you'd be safe——"

"How far is Assiout from Luxor? Where are we now?"

"We're Alice in Wonderland about that. Somewhere about twenty-five or thirty miles south of Assiout, I should say. It must be nearly a hundred and twenty, as the crow flies, from Assiout to Thebes—that's right across from Luxor, you know."

Arlee was silent a moment. She lifted a handful of shining sands and let them run down from her fingers in fine dust. "It's such a pity," she mused, "when we've such a good start——"

Billy stared.

"And I never rode a camel," she went on. "I may never have such a chance again."

"You don't mean——?"

"It would make my story a little truer, too.... And wouldn't it be quicker?"

"Quicker? The quickest way is to go back to Assiout and catch the middle-of-the-night express there and get to Luxor to-morrow morning."

Arlee sighed. "I always wanted to be a gypsy," she murmured regretfully, "and now I've begun it's such a pity to stop.... And I'm *afraid* to go back!" she cried, "They will be out looking for us—they are probably now on the way. And they'll shoot at you and carry me off—Oh, do let's go on! Don't go back to that city! We can catch the train another place. Oh, it's so much more *sensible*!"

"Sensible?" Billy repeated as if hypnotized.

"Why, of course it is. And safer. For all those people back there must be in that tribe of the sheik whose house I was in, and they are dangerous,

dangerous. I want to get as far away from them as possible. I'd rather ride all the way to Thebes than run the risk of falling in their traps."

Billy was silent.

"And I'm sure the camels could make the trip in a couple of days," she continued, sounding assured now, and pleasantly argumentative. "I used to read about their speed in my First Reader.... That is, if you don't mind the trouble," she added apologetically, "and being with me that day more?"

Billy choked. She looked entirely unconscious, and his dumfounded gaze fell blankly away. "There isn't anything in the world I'd like better," he said slowly, sounding reluctance in the effort not to sound anything else, "but from your point of view—if we should meet——"

"Only *fellaheen* on the banks," she returned unconcernedly. "Not half as awkward as people on trains."

"But the—the chaperonless aspect of this picnic——?"

"Oh, *that*!" She was mildly scornful. Then she giggled. "I think a chaperon would look very silly tagging along behind on a camel.... Besides we've gone so far already. You took the liberty of rescuing me, you know, and then the sand storm and this breakfast *à deux*—What's a few meals more?"

There was truth in that—and truth in what she said about the danger of returning to the city. They were already lingering overlong and Billy jumped up and packed their supply of food in sudden haste. It was folly, of course, to dream of the entire trip to Thebes on camelback, but Girgeh was about fifty miles south, and it would be safer and almost as near to push on there or to the next town, wherever that was, and there get the train as to return to Assiout....

Oh, Billy, Billy! What specious argument! And why must every bright delightful fruit be forbidden by dull care or justified by flagrantly untenable artifice? Who but a fool would boggle over this chance, this gloriously deserved crown of the adventure, this gay, random ride over the deserts with Arlee?... To her it was nothing but a prolonging of the lark into which the affair had miraculously been turned. Billy was Big Brother—the American Big Brother with whom one might go safely adventuring for a day or a year.... And suddenly Billy felt a warm gladness within him. Not even her escapade with the unspeakable Turk had been able to shake her dear faith in her own countrymen.... He was not man to her; he was American. Billy waved the flag loyally in his grateful thoughts.

Aloud he said, "There's risk in trying to go back, of course. That's what they're expecting of us. But there will be uncertainty in going on— —"

"I rather like it. It's the certainty that frightens," she gave back eagerly. "I want the way that puts the greatest distance between me and that man.... I don't care what else happens so he doesn't find us."

It is utterly astonishing how unastonishing the most astonishing situations become at the slightest wont.

Nothing on the face of it could have been more preposterous to Billy B. Hill's imagination than trotting along the banks of the Nile on a camel with a gossamer-haired girl trotting beside him, two lone strays in a dark-skinned land, and yet after a few hours of it, it was the most natural thing in the world!

It was all color and light and vivid, unforgettable impressions. It was all sparkle and gaiety and charm. They were two children in a world of enchantment. Nothing could have been more fantastic than that day.

Sometimes they rode low on paths between green *dhurra* fields, sometimes they rode high along the Nile embankment, watching the blue waters alive with winged fleet, black buffaloes splashing in shallows under charge of little bronze babies of boys, watching all the scenes about them shift and change with magic mutability.

They lunched beside an old well, they dined by the river bank, and then as the velvet shadows deepened in the folds of the Arabian mountains across the river and the first stars pricked through the lilac sky above them, they pressed on hurriedly into the southwest that glowed like molten gold behind the black bars of the palms.... And by and by when even the after-glow had ceased to incarnadine the far horizon and the path was too black and strange for them, they turned off across the fertile valley into the edging desert again and saw the new moon rise like an arrow of fire over the rim of the world and pour forth a golden flood that lightened the way yet farther south for their tired beasts.

Arlee rode like a fairy princess of mystery, the silver shawl which they had bought at a village to shield her from the sun, drooping in heavy folds from her head, its metal threads glimmering in the moon rays.... Her eyes were solemn with the beauty and the wonder, of the night, and the strange solitude and isolation; her look was ethereal to Billy and mystically lovely.

But Girgeh seemed to retreat farther and farther into the unknown south, and at last it was no fairy princess but only a very tired girl who slid stiffly down from the saddle, and pillowed a heavy head on Billy's coat. And it was a very tired young man who lay beside her, listening to the deep breathing of the beasts and the faint breath that rose rhythmically beside him. Yet for a time he did not sleep. His heart was full of the awe and mystery of the moonlit world about him—and the awe and mystery of that little bit of the living world curled there so intimately in the dark....

With a reverent hand he drew the wraps he had purchased closer over her. The night was growing cold. Far off the jackals howled.... With his gun at hand he slept at last, and slept sound, though sand is the hardest mattress in the world and a camel's back not the softest pillow....

CHAPTER XIX
THE PURSUIT

"But I shall die," said Arlee. "I shall simply die if I have to go another step upon that creature."

She said it cheerfully, but firmly, a sleepy, sunburned little nomad, sitting cross-legged in the sands, slowly plaiting her honey-colored hair. "Even this," she announced, indicating the slight gesture of braiding, "is agony."

"It's the morning after," said Billy, testing his shoulder with wry grimaces. "It's yesterday's speed—and then this infernally cold night. No wonder we're lame. Why, I have one universal crick wherever I used to have muscles. But let me call your attention to the fact that we are in the wilds of Egypt and that tangerines are hardly a lasting breakfast. Something has to be done."

"Not upon camels," said Arlee fixedly.

"They say it doesn't hurt after an hour or so more."

"I shouldn't live to find out."

"A walk," he suggested, "a slow, swaying, gently undulating walk——?"

"A long, lingering, agonizing death," the young lady translated. She tossed the curly end of her braid over her shoulder and rose, with sounds of lamentation. "I ought to have known better than to sit down again when I was once up," she confided sadly.

"Just what," inquired her companion, "is your idea for the day? How do you expect to reach Girgeh? It can't be very far away now——"

"Then we'll walk—*we'll* walk," she emphasized, "and tow those ships of the desert after us. That will be bad enough, but better—*what's that?*"

Like a top, for all his stiffness, Billy spun about to stare where her finger pointed. Over the crest of a hillock, far to the north—yes, something was hurrying their way.

"A man on horseback," said Arlee anxiously. "They can't have traced us, can they, all this way——?"

"Of course not—but we'll take no chances," returned Billy briskly; "no more talk of pedestrian tours now!" and promptly he helped the girl, no longer demurring, into the saddle, and thwacked her camel into arising, just dodging the long, yellow teeth that the resentful beast tried to fasten upon his shoulder.

They started at no soothing walk, but at a hurrying trot.

Worriedly, her delicate brows knitting, "It's absurd, but," said Arlee, "they could have traced us, I suppose, from my telegraphing at that little native station for my trunks to be sent."

"And mine," said Billy. "And from my trying to get my letter of credit cashed."

"That Captain could have telegraphed to all the places down the line to know if we'd been seen——"

"Even if we hadn't wired or tried to get money, our presence alone and our buying food would have aroused talk. I told everybody," the young man continued, "that I was an artist and you were my sister, and that passed all right—but if Kerissen has been making inquiries——"

"I'm desperately glad we didn't go back toward Assiout," she thrust in. "We'd have walked right into some trap of his!"

"Lord knows what we ought to have done! Lord knows what we ought to do now!"

"Just keep on going," she encouraged. "We can't be very far from Girgeh, can we?"

"I don't know," said Billy soberly. "It may be half a day or a whole day more—you remember how vague that old woman was last night...!" Bitterly he added, "And I'm afraid you've got a chump of a guide."

"I've the best one in the world!" she flashed indignantly.

But her assurance brought no solace to the young man's troubled soul. He reflected that they could have taken a train the day before. To be sure, he had not money enough for tickets to Luxor, yet he had enough for two to Girgeh. But Arlee had shrunk from entering a train in her dishevelled costume, fearful of watching eyes and gossiping tongues, and had advised riding on to Girgeh, where shops and banks would help them, and he had yielded apparently to her desires, but in reality to his own secret self that clung to every joyful contraband moment of this magic time with her. Sincerely he had thought their danger ended.... But those trailing horsemen—"*Brute!*" he raged dumbly at himself. "Dolt! Idiot!"

Anxiously Billy looked at Arlee. It was an ordeal of a ride.

They had ridden on in silence, occasionally glancing back over their shoulders. At last Arlee said, quietly, "Do you see anything—over there—to the left?"

Billy had been seeing it for fifteen minutes.

"Another horseman, isn't it?" he carelessly suggested.

"He seems to be riding the same way we are."

"Well, we've no monopoly of travel in this region."

She answered, after a moment, "There's another close behind him. I just saw him on top of a little hill. I suppose they can see us?"

"Probably." Billy's face was grave. If they continued their winding path in from the desert to the intervening hills that shut them from the Nile valley, and the horsemen continued their course along the base of those hills, they would soon meet.

"Do you mind speeding up a little?" he asked. "I'd rather like to cross to the Nile ahead of that gentry."

But as they speeded up the pursuers did the same, and from mere dots they grew to tiny figures, clearly discernible, furiously galloping over the sands.

Billy thought hard about his cartridges, wishing he had more in his clothes. When he had left the hotel that Tuesday evening he had thrust the loaded revolver in his pocket, but he had already discharged it twice at the beginning of their flight.... And then he startlingly reflected that the Captain could easily cause their arrest for stealing those camels, and wild and dreadful thoughts of native jails and mixed tribunals darted into his harassed and anxious mind. As a long ridge of sand intervened between them and their pursuers he made a sudden decision.

"Let's turn off," he said quickly, and from the little winding path, edging southeast, they struck directly south over the trackless sand.

"You see, they'll expect us to make a railroad station as soon as possible," he explained, "and they are probably trying to nab us on the way to it—if those men have anything to do with us at all." He said nothing about his vivid fear of arrest for the camels and the tool such an arrest would be for Kerissen's designs. He merely added, "I think we'd better try to give them the slip and steer clear of all the little native joints until we get to Girgeh, which is big enough to give us some protection. There must be an English something-or-other there.... I really think we ought to go as fast as we can now, and when the way is clear, hurry across the hills into the Nile valley."

But the way did not become clear. Disconcerted by that unexpected dash off the path, and reduced for a time to mere dots again, the horsemen, three in a row now, hung persistently upon their left flank, keeping a parallel course between them and the hills.

The day had dawned with a promise of sultry heat, and as the sun rose higher and higher in the heavens the heat grew more and more intolerable to their ill-protected heads and thirsty tongues. The gaiety of yesterday was gone; the enchantment had vanished from the waste spaces, and the desert was less a friend now than an enemy. Chokingly the dust rose about them, and glaringly the gold of the burning sands beat back the glare of the downpouring sun. From such a heat the landscape seemed to shrink and veiled itself with a faint and swimming haze.

By noon the flask of water in Billy's pocket was empty. By noon their mouths were parched and their skins burning. And still on their left there hung the hounding dots, like prowling jackals.

Anxiously Billy looked at Arlee. This was an ordeal of a ride that tried the stuff the girl was made of. She was no princess of mystery now, crossing the moonlit sands; she was no gossamer wraith of a girl miraculously with him for a time; she was a very hot and human companion, worried and tired, shutting her dry mouth over any word of complaint, smiling pluckily at him with dusty lips from the shrouding hood of her veil. She was completely and thoroughly a brick.

And Billy's heart ached for her, even while his spirit exulted in her spirit.

"Beastly hot, isn't it?" he gasped, pulling his insufficient cap down over his bloodshot eyes.

Valiantly she smiled. "What's a little—heat?" came joltingly back.

"And rough going."

"What's a little—roughness?"

There wasn't any word good enough for her. There wasn't any word good enough to describe such superhuman courage and sweetness. Billy had credited all beauties with being spoiled. All he had known had been distinctly spoiled, even the near-beauties, and the not-so-near ones, yet here was the most radiantly lovely girl he had ever seen behaving like an angel of grit.

He didn't quite know what else he expected her to do—have hysterics, perhaps, or weep, or reproach him for having taken a wrong way and elected a rash course. He had known that this girl could be a very minx when piqued. But in the graver crises of life she proved herself a thoroughbred. She would go till she dropped and never whimper.

He thought of all she must have been through in that horrible palace, and he marvelled at the swiftness with which her spirit had reverted to blitheness again. The disaster, that might have been so stunning, so irremediable, had passed over her head like lightning that had not struck.... Even the horror of it had seemed yesterday to fade in her like the horror of an evil dream. That was what it had been to her—an evil dream. She was so young, so much of her was still a child, that the full terror had not touched her.

They had come to a road at last, a road which seemed to be leading in from the desert very gradually to the hills upon their left, and it seemed to Billy that it must be a caravan road to Girgeh, and he felt themselves upon the right track. They must keep their lead, and when that lead seemed sufficient, they must put on all possible speed to make the crossing through the hills into the Nile valley ahead of their pursuers. Once more he stirred their lagging camels into a jogging trot....

It was around the middle of the afternoon now, and it had been noon since their tongues had tasted water. Arlee felt her mouth parched and her tongue dry and curling; her skin was feverishly hot; her whole body burned and ached, and her head was giddy with the heat and the hunger. But she thought how little a thing it was to be hot and hungry and tired—when one was free. And she drew the silver shawl closer over her head and wrapped the silken tunic of her frock about her scorching shoulders, and clung tight to the pommel of her big saddle as her beast pounded on and on in his lurching stride.

It had been some time since they had seen the dots, and now the road ahead of them, like the former path they had abandoned, was turning more and more to the left, winding in and out the low and broken foothills, and as they followed its course with increasing security, Billy began to tell himself that their fears had been unfounded and the alarming horsemen were merely following their own route south.

And then he heard a whistle.

A prescience of danger shot through him. His fears returned a hundredfold. Sharply he scanned the way about them, but nothing was in sight. The whistle was not repeated; he could have imagined that he dreamed it. An utter stillness possessed the wilderness.

And then around the corner of a jutting rock ahead of them a horseman trotted, a big black man on a gray horse, and reined in, waiting, facing them. Arlee gave a choking cry.

"The eunuch!" she gasped out.

Behind them Billy flung a lightning glance, and over the heads of the dunes two more riders appeared, converging down upon them from the rear. Three in sight—how many more behind the rocks?

Desperately Billy gripped his bridle rope, and with a wrenching pull and a whack of his guiding stick he turned his camel sharply to the left, snatching at Arlee's bridle rope as the beasts bumped against each other in their surprise.

"Quick—this way," Billy commanded, and with the left hand clutching the girl's rope, with the right he wielded the stick furiously. Out over the sand both camels plunged, goaded into wild speed by such violent measures, and a cheated yell broke from the horsemen and the outcries of pursuit.

While rage at such unreason lasted the camels went like mad, but such speed could not be for long. They had been hard ridden for two days and they were nearly spent. The horsemen behind had drawn together and hung on their trail like three hounds, riding cautiously in the rear, but easily keeping the distance. It occurred to Billy that these pursuers could have changed horses on the way, and must inevitably tire them out. And then?

On and on he beat his poor beasts, racing toward the hills that, just ahead of them, rose sharply from the broken ground, seeking among them some fortress of rocks for a defiant stand.

A tug on the bridle rope nearly jerked it from his hand. Arlee's camel had stumbled; the poor thing was lurching wearily.

"He can't go—any more," the girl cried out pitifully. "He—he's sobbing. Don't beat him—I won't have him beaten!"

"We must get there," he called back, waving at the cliff-like rocks.

"Then go—on foot. I could—run faster."

"No, you couldn't," he shouted fiercely back.

She flared. "Don't you hit him again!"

The maddening absurdity of the quarrel in the face of hostile Africa filled Billy with the futile fury of exasperation. He ground his teeth, glowering at her, and wound her halter rope about his smarting hand. All his hope was concentrated upon the necessity of winning to that rocky shelter before their pursuers overtook them. To him the camels were nothing in the face of such necessity.

They were going slower and slower; his blows had no avail now on either beast. They plodded on. He turned suddenly in his saddle and saw the three riders spreading fan-shape around them, the one in the center nearest. He whipped out his gun and fired at the horse.

His own motion made the ball fly wild, but the horseman drew up instantly, and the other edged discreetly away. And in the ensuing moments the two fugitives gained the base of those cliff-like hills and perceived the dark oblong of a cave mouth.

Down from their exhausted camels they flung themselves, and hand in hand raced to the entrance of the cave. Coolness and blackness received them. Their eyes discovered nothing of the tunnel-like interior.

Putting Arlee some distance within, Billy went to the mouth and stood, his gun in his hand, peering watchfully out. He saw the horsemen draw together for a parley, then one remained on guard while the others circled on separate ways beyond his range of sight. His fear was that one of them might steal alongside the cave and leap unexpectedly into its very mouth upon him, so with taut nerves he crouched expectant.

Behind him Arlee gave a sudden shriek.

"Billy went to the mouth, peering watchfully out"

CHAPTER XX
A FRIEND IN NEED

He whirled. "I'll fire!" he warned, staring into the dark, but his eyes, dazed with the sun, discerned nothing, and in utter ignorance he faced the black possibilities.

"A man—a hand——" Arlee gasped incoherently.

"Good Lord, what is it?" said a voice so near at hand that both were startled.

"Burroughs!" ejaculated Billy. "Is it you—Burroughs?"

"Yes, it's I, Burroughs," the owner of the voice retorted irritably. "And who the deuce are you?"

"Hill—Billy B. Hill," came the jubilant answer, and "Billy be damned!" said the astonished voice, with sudden joviality, and a dark shape strode up to them. "What on earth are you doing here? And what about that firing? Think I was a robber bold?"

"Well, there are three robber sneaks outside that we are hiding from, so I wasn't sure.... Great Cæsar, old scout, but I'm glad to see you! That puts us out of the woods at last.... It's the excavator friend," he added, turning to Arlee. "Burroughs, I present you to Miss Beecher. She and I have been having a thoroughly impossible adventure."

"Let's have a little light upon these introductions," returned the excavator, and a click was heard, and a light jumped out overhead, flooding the tunnel-like place with brightness. In its beams the three stood staring queerly at each other.

Arlee saw a slim, wiry young American, in rough khaki clothes stained with work, a browned, unshaven young man with sleepy looking eyes and a mouth like a steel trap.

What the excavator saw was more surprising. There was his friend Billy, whom two weeks before he had seen off on a Nile steamer returning to Cairo, in tropic splendor of white serge and Panama hat, now a scarlet spectacle of sunburn and dirt, in most disgraceful tweeds, and beside him what Burroughs took to be a child in tatterdemalion white, a silky, fluttering white, which even his untrained observation knew was hardly elected for desert wear. The little girl's hair was hanging tangled over her shoulders, and was much the color of the sand with which her face was coated, and underneath that coating he saw that she was red as a peony with sun and wind. They were a startling pair.

Gravely, with unchanging eyes, he acknowledged the introduction, and then, "What's this about robbers?" he went on. "What kind of a yarn are you putting over?"

"Nothing I want put over on the general public." Billy was thinking very hard. "You're going to be our salvation, Burroughs, but even to you—well, I'll put it briefly. We were having a desert ride and some Turkish fellows who have annoyed her before chased us. There are our camels, just outside. And you can see one of the fellows on horseback keeping watch. The others are somewhere about.... And now, for heaven's sake, get us a drink of water."

Burroughs walked to the door of the tomb and looked out an instant, then he turned and went toward the back, returning with a small native jar full of water.

"I've no glass, but if you can manage this——?" he said to Arlee, and she clutched the cool pottery with two hot little hands and, murmuring a quick affirmative, she put it to her lips.

Then she held it out to Billy.

"I suppose—we mustn't—-drink as much as we want."

"I couldn't," said Billy, after a grateful swallowing. "I'd drain the Nile.... Got a camp here?"

"Yes. You'd have seen my men any other time of day, but we knocked off a while out of the sun," Burroughs explained. "I've rigged up this tomb as living quarters while I'm here. Now what do you want me to do? Would you like a guard?"

"We'd like a guard and a bath and cold cream," said Billy joyfully. "And then we'd like dinner and donkeys."

Burroughs grunted.

"Umph—I should say you'd one donkey already in your party—careering around the desert with a little girl like this," he vouchsafed, and Arlee's eyes widened at his brusque nod at her. She was staring about her now with a curious interest, for all her aching tiredness, gazing wonderingly at the dazzling white walls with their strange and brilliant paintings. She saw they were in a long, deep chamber, from which other openings led to unimagined deeps.

"I guess you never were in a place like this before?" Burroughs inquired, and she shook her head dumbly, feeling suddenly too spent for words.

"Can she get a rest here?" said Billy anxiously. "We've had the devil of a ride."

"The place is all hers," returned Burroughs. "I'll send you some food and cold cream—you mustn't wash that sunburn, you know, or you'll be a sorry girl to-morrow—and then you can rest as long as you like. How much of a hurry are you in?" he added to Billy.

"Well, we want to take a train to Luxor to-night. I suppose Girgeh's the next station?"

"You suppose? You *are* at sea—where did you start from, anyway?" But hastily Burroughs sped from that inquisitive question. "Balliana is your next station," he reported. "You've all the time you want, and I'll take you over myself. Now make yourself as comfortable as you can," he added to Arlee, handing her a big jar of cold cream and lugging forward an armful of rugs. "I'll be back with some food in a jiffy."

"You're very kind," Arlee spoke stanchly, but as soon as the two men stepped from the tomb, she seemed to wilt down into the rugs and lay there, too tired to stir.

Outside Burroughs blew sharply on a whistle, and from the mouth of another cave a file of black boys in ragged robes made a straggling appearance. Burroughs gave orders which resulted in a kindling of fire and the opening of boxes, and then he walked back to where Billy was surveying the weary camels. At a distance, like an equestrian statue, the watching horseman was standing. Burroughs stared hard at the distant Nubian, then stared harder at Billy.

"This is wonderful luck," Billy said to him, very soberly. "I didn't think of you as nearer than Thebes."

"We just heard of some fresh finds here, so I'm combing over the tombs.... But you—it's none of my business, Billy, but what in hell are you doing racing over Egypt with a ten-year old kid?"

"Ten-year-old—Great Cæsar, man, that's a *real girl*! She's *grown up*! She's old enough to vote—or nearly."

Burroughs stared harder than ever.

Then, "I shouldn't call that an extenuating circumstance," he mentioned wryly.

"Extenuating nothing! Look here, let me— —"

"You needn't tell me anything, you know," Burroughs suggested in great indifference.

"Oh, shut up!" Billy spoke with deep disgust. "You've got to help us out of this and then forget the whole business." He paused a moment; then, "Miss Beecher made the mistake of taking a rash ride with me. She was traveling alone, to meet some friends, to Luxor—and the indiscretion is entirely mine, you understand. I got her into it. And then, as I said, a Turkish fellow, that had been making himself objectionable by following her, got his men out after us and chased us down here. Her trunks have gone on to Luxor where those friends are, and we have to find some presentable wraps for her and get her to the first train. *Verstehen?*"

"Grasped—and forgotten," said his friend laconically. Just for an instant his sleepy gaze touched Billy's rugged face, then fell casually away. "I suppose any comments that occur to me are superfluous?" he pleasantly observed.

"Completely.... And, Lord Harry, but I'm glad to see you!"

"Same here." Burroughs gave Billy's arm a friendly grip and Billy spun fiercely about on him. "Don't you do that again!" he warned. "Take the other one. That's got a—a scratch."

"A scratch? One of those fellows wing you out there? Let me have a look— —"

"No, it's all right—it's nothing— —"

"Let me see, you old chump— —"

"It's all right, I tell you. It's been taken care of—it's just a relic of Cairo."

"Cairo!" Slowly Burroughs let fall the hand he had laid upon Billy's arm. "You do seem to be having a lively trip," he commented, grinning. "Here, hurry up, you rascals, hurry up with that big jug."

Taking the large jar from them, he returned to the tomb, stopping abruptly at sight of Arlee's weary abandon. She half sat up, a frail, exhausted little figure, whose grace was strangely appealing through all her sandy dishevelment.

"Some water—for washing," he stammered.

"You're very thoughtful."

"I'll have to beg your pardon," he blurted, for Burroughs was no squire of dames. "I thought you were a little girl and spoke to you as if— —"

"It's just the hairpins that make the difference, isn't it?" said Arlee, with a whimsical smile. "I don't suppose you have any of those in camp that I could borrow?"

He shook his head regretfully. Then his brain seized upon the problem. "Bent wires?" he suggested. "I might try——"

"Do," she besought. "I'll be grateful forever."

He withdrew to make the attempt, and in his place came Billy with a tray of luncheon.

"Just—put it down," Arlee said faintly. "I'll eat—by and by."

Worriedly Billy looked down on the girl. Her eyes closed. Excitement had ebbed, leaving her like some spent castaway on the shores. He dropped on his knees beside her, dipping a clean handkerchief in the jar of cold cream.

"Just let me get this off," he said quietly. "You'll feel better."

Like a child she submitted, lying with closed eyes while with anxious care he took the sand from her delicate, burning skin. He did the same for her listless hands; he brushed back her hair and put water on her temples; he dabbed more cold cream tenderly on the pathetic little blisters on her lips.

"I'm—all right." The blue eyes looked suddenly up at him with a clear smile. "I'm—just resting."

"And now you'll eat a bit?"

Obediently she took the sandwich he made for her, and lifted her head to drink the cup of tea.

"I'm a—nuisance," she murmured.

"You're a *brick*!" he gave back, with muffled intensity. "You're a perfect brick!"

Then he backed hastily out of her presence, for fear his stumbling tongue would betray him—or his clumsy, longing hands—or his foolish eyes. He felt choking with the tenderness he must not express. He ached with his Big Brother pity for her, and with his longing for her, which wasn't in the least Big Brotherly, and with all the queer, bewildering jumble of emotion that she had power to wake in him.

Very silently he returned to Burroughs, and when he had made a trifle of a toilet and eaten far from a trifle of lunch, the two young men stretched themselves out in the shade, just beyond the entrance of the tomb, conversing in low tones, while around them the labor song of Burroughs' workmen rose and fell in unvarying monotony, as from a nearby hole they carried out baskets of sand upon their heads and poured the contents upon the heap where the patient sifters were at work.

Burroughs talked of his work, the only subject of which he was capable of long and sustained conversation. He dilated upon a rare find of some blue-green tiles of the time of King Tjeser, a third dynasty monarch, and a mummy case of one of the court of King Pepi, of the sixth dynasty, "about 3300 b.c.," he translated for Billy, and then suddenly he saw that Billy's eyes were absent and Billy's pipe was out.

In sudden silence he knocked out the ashes from his own pipe and slowly refilled it. "Congratulations," he ejaculated, and at Billy's slow stare he jerked his head back toward the tomb. "I say, congratulations, old man."

"Oh!" Billy became ludicrously occupied with the dead pipe.

"Nothing doing," he returned decidedly.

"No? ... I thought ——"

"You sounded as if you had been thinking. Don't do it again."

"And also I had been remembering," said Burroughs, with caustic emphasis, "knowing that in the past wherever youth and beauty was concerned ——"

So successfully had that past been sponged from Billy's concentrated heart, so utterly had other youth and beauty ceased to exist for him, that he greeted the reminder with belligerent unwelcome.

"I tell you it was all an accident," he retorted irritably. "There's nothing more to it.... Hello, our horseman is coming this way again!"

Grateful for the interruption to this ticklish excursion into his sacred emotions, he jumped to his feet and went out to meet the man who was riding slowly toward them, the two others in his train. Burroughs went with him, and a brief parley followed.

"He says," Burroughs translated, "that these are his camels and he is going to take them away. He says you stole them from him at Assiout."

"That's right," Billy confirmed easily. "He can have 'em," and Burroughs, vouchsafing no comment on this curious development, gave the message to the Nubian. Then he turned again to Billy. "He wants: the money for their hire."

"For their——! Of all the dad-blasted, iron-clad cheek! You just tell him for me that he'll get his 'hire' all right if he hangs around me. Tell him I'll have him arrested for molesting and robbing travelers; and tell him to tell his master that if he shows his head near an English girl again I'll have him hanged as high as Haman—and shot to pieces while he swings! The infernal scoundrel——"

Whatever work Burroughs made of this translation it sent the sullen, inscrutable-looking fellow off in silence, his followers leading the recovered camels.

"And may that be the last of them," said Billy B. Hill, in fervent thanksgiving. "Except Kerissen. I've got to meet him again—just once."

Perhaps it was the hairpins. Perhaps it was the bathed face and the sleep-brightened eyes and the rearranged gown. But certainly Burroughs stared in amazement at the slim little figure that issued from the entrance, and a queer, a very queer confusion seized upon him. Not even outrageous sunburn and pathetic blisters could hide Arlee's young loveliness. They only added an utterly upsetting tenderness to the beholder, and a most dangerous compassion.

And just as each man is smitten with madness after the manner of his kind, so Burroughs, the taciturn, was struck into amazing volubility. As they sat about a cracker box of a table at an early supper, he became a perfect fount of information, pouring out to this girl an account of his diggings that would have astounded any of his intimates, and would surely have amazed Billy B. Hill if that young man had been in a condition to notice his friend's performances. But he was wrapped in a personal gloom that had descended on him like a cloud of unreason. The escapade was nearly over. The little girl comrade was gone, the little girl whose face he had so tenderly scrubbed of its grimy sand. A very self-possessed young lady was sitting beside him, drinking her coffee, an utterly lovely and gracious young lady—but unfathomably remote—elusive....

Perhaps, again, it was the hairpins.

Off to town on donkey back the three Americans rode slowly, a native escort filing after, and there in town the bazaars yielded a long pongee dust coat and a straw hat and a white veil, "to escape detection," Arlee gaily said, and a satchel which she filled with mysterious purchases, and then, clad once more in the semblance of her traveling world, safe and sound and undiscovered, she stood upon the station platform, awaiting the train to Luxor.

Beside her, two very quiet young men responded but feebly to the flow of spirits that had amazingly succeeded her exhaustion. Burroughs was suddenly suffering from a depression most unfamiliar to his practical mind, which caused him to moon about his work for days and made his depleted jar of cold cream a wincing memory, and Billy was increasingly glum.

It was all over now. The girl, who for two winged days had been so magically his gypsy comrade, was returning to her own world, the world in which he played so infinitesimal a part. For very pride's sake now he could never force himself upon her ... as he might before ...

He stared down at her eagerly, hopefully, for a sign of regret at the ending of this strange companionship, much as a big Newfoundland might watch for a caress from a cherished but tyrannic hand, but not a scrap of regret was evidenced. She was as blithe as a cricket. Her only pang was for discovery.

"You're sure," she murmured as Burroughs left them to interview the station clerk, "you're sure they'll never know?"

"I'm positive," he stolidly responded. "Just stick to your story."

"The Evershams won't question—they are never interested in other people," she mused, with thankfulness. "But Mr. Falconer——"

"Won't have a doubt," said Billy firmly. His gloom closed in thickly about him.

It was a local, a train of corridor compartments. In one, marked "Ladies Alone," Arlee was ensconced, with an Englishwoman and her maid, and two pleasant German women, and in another Billy B. Hill sat opposite some young Copts and lighted pipe after pipe. When the train started out on the High Bridge across the Nile to the eastern bank, he came out in the corridor to look out the wide glass windows there, and found Arlee beside him.

"How do you do?" she said brightly. "How nice to meet accidentally like this—you see, I'm rehearsing my story," she added under her breath.

"Let's see if you have it straight," he told her.

"I arrive on a local which left Cairo this morning.... Did I come alone?"

"You'd better invent some nice traveling friend——"

She shook her head in flat refusal. "I won't. I'm not equal to inventing anything. It's bad enough now to—to tell the *necessary* lies I have to." The brightness left her face looking suddenly wan and sorry. "I suppose it's part of my—punishment—for my dreadful folly," she said in a low tone.

"It's just part of the coin the world has to be paid in for its conventions," Billy quickly retorted. "*Don't* let it worry you like that—in a day no one will think to question you."

"I know—but—it's having the memory always there. Always knowing that there is something I can't be honest about—something secret and dreadful— —"

She was staring unseeingly out the window, her soft lips twitching.

"The Egyptians were a most sensible people," said Billy. "They drew up a list of commandments against the forty-two cardinal sins, and one of them was this, 'Thou shalt not consume thy heart.' That is a religious law against regret—vain, unprofitable, morbid, devastating regret. And you must take that law for your own."

"Th—thank you." The low voice was suspiciously wavery. "I—you see, I haven't had time to think about it till just now—we've been going so fast— —"

"And the best thing that could have happened. And now that you have the time to think, you mustn't think *weakly*. It was just a nightmare. And it's over."

"Just a nightmare.... And it's over," she repeated. Her eyes lifted to Billy's in a look of ineffable softness and wonder. "It's over—because *you* came."

"I want you to forget that." The young man spoke with cold curtness in his effort to combat the wild temptation of that moment. "I only did what anyone else in my place would have done—to have accomplished it is all the gratitude I want. Please don't speak of it to me again. You must forget about it."

"Forget—as if I could help being grateful as long as I live!"

"But I don't *want* you to be grateful. It—it's obnoxious to me!"

She was as blankly hurt as a slapped child. Then she looked away, a little pulse in her throat beating fast. "Then I won't—try to thank you," she answered in a very small voice, and stared harder and harder out the window.

Billy felt that he had accomplished a tremendous stride. "A feeling of obligation kills a friendship," he told her didactically, "and I want you to be really my friend."

"I am." Her voice was distinct, though queerly lack-luster. And she did not look at him again.

He went on: "The Evershams will be in on the boat about seven. From the station I'll take you straight to the boat, where your stateroom is surely being kept for you. Then to-morrow your trunks will arrive from Cook's, and by the time you are through resting, you will be ready to sally out and meet the world.... I hope my own trunk will make its appearance, too," he added. "I telegraphed the hotel to pack my things and send them on."

She made no comment on the obvious haste with which he had left Cairo. She said slowly, "I want to do a little mathematics now. What is the shocking sum I owe you?"

He shut his lips in an obstinate line. After a moment she added, "I can't take *that*, you know."

It struck him as a trifle ludicrous that dollars were so important among all the rest, but unwillingly enough he understood.

"Won't you just let it stand as it is?" he said under his breath. "Let me have the whole thing—please."

"I can't."

"You mean you won't?"

"I can't," she repeated inflexibly, and then, with a childish flash, "Since you dislike me to feel grateful—I should think you would be glad to let me reduce the debt."

"All right." He spoke gruffly. "Then you owe me what you spent just now and what your railroad ticket cost. Not a cent more. For what went before I am absolutely responsible, and I decline to let you pay *my* debts."

This time he was inflexible. She repeated, with a spark of resentment, "It's not fair to let you pay so much——"

"It was *my* adventure," said Billy firmly.

She said, "Very well," in a voice that puzzled him. He felt she was annoyed. And he realized more than ever that he could never take advantage of her indebtedness to make her pay with her companionship. It was becoming a queer tangle.... He felt they had suddenly slipped out of tune.... She seemed to be escaping him—withdrawing ...

He wondered, very unhappily, with no fine glow of altruism at all, if he had rescued her for another man. Those things happened, they happened with dismal frequency. Billy distinctly recalled the experience of a college friend who had carried a girl out of a burning hotel, to have her wildly embrace an unstirring youth below. Yes, such things happened. But he had never contemplated having anything like that happen to him.

He contemplated it now, however, contemplated it long and bitterly, when Arlee had gone back to her compartment and he sat silent in his beside the chattering Copts while the train rattled on and on. There would be three days at Luxor before the boat proceeded upon its southern journey. And then——

Three days.... Three miserable, paltry, insufficient days, blighted by the chaperoning Evershams.... Frantically he hoped against his dark foreboding that one menace at least might be averted—that by now Luxor would have ceased to shelter a certain sandy-haired young Englishman.

CHAPTER XXI
CROSS PURPOSES

Luxor was warm and drowsy with afternoon sun. Motionless the fronds of the tall palms along the water front; motionless the columns of the temple reflected in the blue Nile. Even the almost continuous commotion of the landing stage was stilled.

The two big Nile steamers, of rival lines, lay quietly at rest, emptied of their tourists, and on the embankment the dragomans, the donkey boys, the innumerable venders, were lounging in the shade at dominoes or dice.

In the big white hotels facing the river many drawn blinds spoke of napping travelers, and in the shade of the garden of the Grand other travelers were whiling away the listless inertia of the hour before tea.

"I suppose it's *quite* too early?" murmured a girl at one of the tables, in the shade of a big acacia. Her companion, fussing with a pastel sketch, answered absently, without looking up, "Oh, quite," and then with a note of brisker attention, "I thought we were waiting for Robert?"

"Do you think he'll be back? It's *such* a trip to the Tombs of the Kings, you know!"

"To be sure he'll be back!" Miss Falconer spoke with asperity. "And why he wanted to go over it again—it's odd you didn't care to go, too, Claire," she added, most inconsequently. "It was such an excellent opportunity—and you had already spoken of wishing to go again."

"But not so exhaustively. They are doing the entire programme. I only wanted some particular things."

"You could have done them."

"And it was hot."

"It must have been just as hot in the bazaars with Mr. Hill."

"Was it?"

This was purposeful vagueness and Miss Falconer's crayon snapped. She made a sound of annoyance, then began gathering her sketching things tidily together. Presently, "He's rather an agreeable person, that young American, after all," she cannily observed.

"Why, after all?" Lady Claire was implacably aloof.

"Well, first impressions, you know— —"

"*My* first impressions of Mr. Hill were very delightful." The English girl laughed softly, her eyes full of reminiscent amusement. "He was a *deus ex machina* to me—I quite jumped at him, I assure you!"

"You don't have to assure me!" was the elder lady's unspoken comment. She had been in a state of chronic irritation, ever since that Friday noon when Billy B. Hill's tall figure had appeared in the hotel dining room. And hurrying Claire away from the conversation he was promptly evoking, she had encountered Arlee Beecher and the Evershams streaming with the other passengers from their boat to see the temple of Luxor, a wonderfully gay and excited Arlee, so radiant in the happiness of her own safe world again that she was bright gladness incarnate.... Instantly Robert had reverted to his alarming infatuation ... and Lady Claire had most shamelessly welcomed the American. It was all unspeakably annoying....

Aloud Miss Falconer observed, "I wonder what brought Mr. Hill back to the Nile."

"I wonder," said Lady Claire pleasantly. "But it makes it very nice for us, doesn't it?" she continued amiably. "He knows quite *everything* about temples."

"And particularly nice for Miss Beecher—though I can't say she is treating him very well. However, that may be their way. 'Romance apart from results,' was, I believe, his phrase."

Lady Claire was silent. But not overlong. "You really think— —?" she suggested tranquilly.

"He came on the same train."

"Coincidence. He mentioned he did not see her in the train till Balliana."

"Umph!" Miss Falconer drew out of her bag the especial knitting which she reserved for the Sabbath, and her fingers flew with expressive spirit. "It's scandalous," she said at length. "Girls gadding about the face of the earth—picking up chaperons when they remember them."

"It's their way, you know."

"Oh, yes, it's their way. And their men seem to like it. Mr. Hill didn't seem to consider it even *unusual*.... But as I said, he's hardly a judge," Miss Falconer went on unsparingly. "The man's bewitched. He never takes his eyes off her."

"I'm sure I don't blame him." Lady Claire's tone was most successfully admiring. "She's too *wonderful*, isn't she, with those great blue eyes and that astonishing hair! I'm sure Robert is bewitched, too!"

"Nonsense!" But Miss Falconer's tone was too vigorous, betraying the effort to rout a palpable enemy. "What nonsense!" she repeated. "He's civil—naturally—when *you* haven't a moment for him. The boy has pride. Too much." The knitting needles clicked warningly.

"Civil!" The girl's low laughter was mocking. "Dear Miss Falconer, you are such an *euphuist*!"

Miss Falconer looked up, a trifle startled. Her young charge was more than a match for her in irony, but the elder lady did not lack for solid perseverance, and she charged on undeterred.

"Of course the girl's pretty—too pretty. And Robert's a man—he has eyes in his head and likes to please them. And she knows who he is and draws him on."

"I don't think Miss Beecher cares a twopence who Robert is," said Lady Claire honestly. "When I told her he was going to stand for Roxham she answered that she had a very poor opinion of M.P.s—from reading Mrs. Ward. I can't *quite* see what she meant—but as for her drawing him on, a moment ago, dear, you were accusing her of luring Mr. Hill back from Cairo."

"I said he followed. I daresay she lured, too. The second string——"

"Then it's quite *nice* of me, isn't it, to carry off her second string to the bazaars and prevent her playing him against Robert!"

Lady Claire laughed mischievously, in a flight of daring so foreign to her usual reticence that Miss Falconer grimly perceived that she was changed indeed. She thought helplessly that it was a great pity that young people couldn't be treated as the children they were—smacked and made to do what was best for them.

"And after all this dreadful gossiping how can we face our guests at tea?" the girl continued in mock chiding.

"If they are much later we shall not be facing them at all," the older woman declared. "I shall certainly have my tea at the proper time."

The sight of an Arab servant with a tray of dishes had stirred her to this declaration, and promptly she gave her order. In the middle of it, "I'm always late!" said a merry voice, and little Miss Beecher and Falconer were standing on the grass beside them.

"This time we had no following engagement," said Miss Falconer, unpleasantly reminiscent of another tea time in Cairo, ten days before, but even with her resentment of this American girl's intrusion into her long-cherished plans, she could not prevent the softening of her regard as she gazed upon her.

"You don't look as if you had been riding very hard at the Tombs of the Kings," she observed, in reluctant admiration.

"Oh, but we have! We did quite a lot of Tombs—not anything like thoroughly, of course!—and then we rode back early and made ourselves tidy for your tea party," Arlee blithely explained, and Miss Falconer perceived that her brother Robert had returned to the hotel without seeking them out, had arrayed himself in fresh white flannels and returned to the boat to escort Miss Beecher across the road into the hotel garden.

Absently she sighed. Her eyes fell away from the peach-blossom prettiness of Arlee's lovely face to the subtle simplicity of her white frock of loosely woven silk, and she wondered if that heavy embroidery meant money—or merely spending money. And then she looked across at Lady Claire, and sighed again for her dream of an aristocratic alliance.

"Mrs. Eversham—?" she thought to inquire.

"They're having the vicar—or is it the rector?—to tea. They asked him this morning before your message came," Arlee explained. She did not explain that the vicar, or the rector, had imagined, in accepting, that she, too, was to be of that tea party on the boat and was even now inquiring zealously of her of the Evershams.

"Here's Mr. Hill," said Lady Claire.

Miss Falconer stirred; there was room for the fifth chair between her and Arlee. Lady Claire also stirred; there was room between her and Robert Falconer. And there Billy B. Hill seated himself after a general exchange of greetings.

"How were the bazaars?" said Arlee gaily across the table.

"You mean the department store of Mr. Isaac Cohen," Billy laughed back. "They are all under him, you know."

"Not *really*!" Falconer exclaimed, in disillusionment. "It rather takes it out, doesn't it, to know it is so commercialized."

"What did you expect—it is the twentieth century," Miss Falconer retorted, putting aside her knitting as the tea things arrived.

"Sometimes it is," said Arlee.

"I think it's more so than ever, here," declared Lady Claire. "Egypt's so *frightfully* civilized——"

"Not when you're camping in the desert."

Again that funny little smile flitted over Arlee's face; not once did she glance at Billy, but for all her air of unconsciousness he felt that she was subtly sharing her thoughts with him and a quick spark of gladness flashed in him.

Those had been three horrible days for Billy B. Hill.

Friday morning he had been practically a prisoner until his trunks had arrived. He had emerged upon a spectacle of England triumphant—Robert Falconer escorting Arlee to the temple of Luxor. Later that afternoon he had called upon Arlee upon the boat to find Falconer still there, and the Evershams very much so.

Robert Falconer had accompanied him back to the hotel. There was something that he wanted to ask, and he asked it bluntly, but with embarrassment. Had Billy said anything at all to Arlee of that nonsense at the palace?

Here was a contingency for which Billy was not provided. He made no provisions for this with Arlee.

"Have you?" he parried.

"Not a word," said the young Englishman. "We've not mentioned the fellow's filthy name. But I wondered——"

"I did tell her we got worried one night, and tried to get into his palace like a pair of brigands," Billy answered slowly.

"She must have thought us great fools," the sandy-haired young man replied disgustedly. Clearly he felt that Billy had flourished this story before Arlee to appear romantic, and he winced at its absurdity.

"Oh, no—she just thought of it as a lark on our part," Billy went on. "I didn't let her in for the horrible details—I don't think she's likely to mention it to you. Or you to her," he added.

"Rather not." The young Englishman was emphatic. "I'm sorry you said anything about it." Then he looked at Billy, a crinkle of amusement in his eyes. "Rather a sell, you know—what?"

"I should say so!" returned Billy, with a hearty appearance of chagrin, and a laugh cemented the understanding.

That was all between them concerning the escapade.

Billy had raced back to the boat, and secured an earnest fifteen minutes with Arlee, who promised unlimited care, and then forced upon him the wretched sovereigns that she owed. She was feeling desperately spent and tired after her day of excitement, and declared herself unequal to the dance upon the boat that evening. Anxiously Billy had urged her to rest, and he spent a drifting and distracted evening roaming alone in the temple of Luxor listening to the distant music from the boat—thinking of Arlee.... Later he had learned that she remained up for at least two dances with Falconer.

So much for Friday. Saturday had been worse. Arlee had said on Friday night that she would join the passengers in the all-day excursion to the Tombs of the Kings, and Billy had somehow found himself in an arrangement with Lady Claire and Falconer to go with them. Then Arlee had not gone. Mrs. Eversham reported that she had a headache, and Falconer had very promptly dropped out of the party, leaving Billy with Lady Claire upon his hands, and so he went, and he and Lady Claire and the Evershams and about sixty other passengers had a brisk and busy day of it. When he returned just before dinner he saw Arlee, apparently headacheless, upon the deck of the steamer, chatting to Falconer.

That night she had attended the dance at the hotel under Miss Falconer's wing. Billy had danced with her twice, and between times his pride had kept him aloof—she might just have made one sign! But though her bright friendliness was ever responsive; though she was instantly, submissively, ready to accept his invitations or fulfill his requests, he felt that there was something strangely lacking.

The gay spark of her coquetry was gone; she did not tease or play with him; animated as she was in company, when they were alone together a constraint fell upon her.

Miserably he felt that he reminded her of unhappy scenes and that she would be secretly relieved when he was gone.

So now he was absurdly glad to hear her declare, in answer to Lady Claire's questionings, "Oh, but the desert is wonderful! I loved it in spite of——"

"In spite of—?" Lady Claire echoed.

"The sand," said Arlee promptly. But under her lashes, her eyes came, at last, half-scared, to Billy's face.

"But the sand *is* the desert," Lady Claire was murmuring.

"It's only part of it," Billy took it upon himself to answer. "Space is the biggest part—and then color. And sometimes—heat."

"You spent quite a time on the desert edge with some excavators, didn't you?" said the English girl, and Billy fell into talk with her about his friend's work, and Falconer and his sister engrossed Arlee.

And to-night was the very last night of her stay at Luxor. To-morrow the boat would take her on out of his life—unless he pursued her along the Nile, a foolish, unwanted intruder.... The three days here had all slipped from his clumsy grasp—they seemed to have put a widening distance between them.... He heard Falconer calculating that the boat would touch again at Luxor for the next Friday night. There seemed to be talk of a masked ball....

Billy leaned suddenly across the table.

"You have forgotten it's the best of the moon to-night?" he asked. "You must let me take you to see it on Karnak."

Falconer gave him a very blank look.

"We've already planned for that," said he.

"We'll all go," cried Arlee, with instant pleasantness. "We mustn't miss it for anything."

"You haven't seen the moon on the temple yet?" Billy inquired of Lady Claire in the pause that ensued.

"Only once—four nights ago. But it wasn't full then."

Billy remembered that moon acutely. It had lighted two fugitives across a waste of sand. He saw a little figure swaying rhythmically high upon a camel, a quaint, old-world figure in misty white, with a shimmering silver veil—like Rebecca coming across the desert, he thought oddly. Then he looked up and saw a most modern figure in white across the table, nibbling a cress sandwich, and laughing at some jest of the Englishman's....

With a start he realized that Lady Claire was waiting for an answer.

"I beg your pardon. You asked——?"

"If *you* had seen the temple in moonlight, Mr. Hill."

"Not Karnak—only Luxor—night before last."

"Only Luxor!" The girl beside him laughed. "How spoiled you are, Mr. Hill! *Only* Luxor!"

It came to Billy, with the force of revelation, that it was going to be *only* a great many things for him after this.... Those wild days in the desert had seen to that, with devastating completeness.... Girls were only other girls—and delight in them a lost word. This charming one beside him, with the friendly eyes where a faint shadow of wistfulness underlay the surface brightness, was only Lady Claire....

He wondered if he was going on like this forever. He wondered if he was everlastingly to carry this memory about with him, like a bullet.... Suddenly he felt enraged at himself, at his dumb pain and useless longings, and with a stanch semblance of animation he flung himself into the flow of talk which this pretty English girl was so ready to offer him.

CHAPTER XXII
UPON THE PYLON

Two miles of Sphinxes in the moonlight—a double row of them on each side of the way from the temple of Luxor—and then a towering pylon overhead. Karnak was reached.

Out of the victoria jumped two young men in evening clothes, one sandy-haired with a slight moustache, the other black-haired and clean shaven, and handed out three ladies. The first lady was middle-aged and haughty featured, in a black evening gown overhung with a black and gold Assiout shawl; the second was a tall girl in a rose cloak, the third was a small girl, and her cloak was a delicate blue.

There was a pause at the pylon for the presentation of the little red entrance books, and then the gate closed behind them, and the five moved cautiously forward into the shadowy dark of the confusion of the ruins. Beside the blue-cloaked girl bent the sandy-haired young man; the black-haired young man was between the rose-cloaked girl and the lady with the Roman nose.

"You must be our dragoman, Mr. Hill; I understand you are up on all this," said the lady, adhering closely to his side. "Where are we now?"

"Temple of Khonsu," said Billy with bitter brevity. Ahead of them Arlee's blonde head was uptilted toward Falconer's remarks.

"Khonsu? I never heard of him! Or is it her?" Lady Claire laughingly demanded.

"Khonsu is the son of the god, Amon, or Amon-Ra, and the goddess, Mut, and so is the third person of the trinity of Thebes," Billy pedagogically recited, his eyes on the little white shoes ahead picking their delicate way over the fallen stones. "This temple at Karnak is the temple of the god Amon, and so it was natural for old Rameses the third to put the temple to Khonsu under the father's wing like this—but it spoils the effect of the entrance from this pylon. You don't get Karnak's bigness at a burst—but wait till you reach the court ahead. Then you'll see Karnak."

And then they did see it—as much as one view can give of that vast desolation. Ahead of them, shadowy and mysterious in the velvet dark and silver pallor of the stars, loomed the columns of the great court, huge monoliths that dwarfed to pigmies the tiny groups of people dotting the ground about them, trying to say something appropriate.

The place had been made for dead and gone gods, giants of gods, and their spirits stalked now through its waste spaces, dominating and ironic. There was an air about the place that seemed to scorn the facile awe it woke in the breasts of the beholders and that fleered at the human banalities upon their lips.

"There are no words for a spot like this," said a voice near them.

"Silence is fittest," corroborated a second voice.

"Thomas Hardy once said, speaking of the heavens," said the first voice again, "'There is a size at which dignity begins; farther on there is a size at which grandeur begins; farther on there is a size at which solemnity begins; farther on a size at which awfulness begins; farther on a size at which ghastliness begins.' Surely that was written unknowingly for this temple of Karnak?"

A fluttering murmur from the group confirmed this thought.

"Nice little speech," said Falconer in an undertone.

The second voice was raised a trifle resentfully. "Yet was not the very pith of it spoken by Ruskin when he stood upon this identical spot? His words were these, 'At last size tells!'"

Another murmur agreed that it was indeed the pith.

"That's Clara Eversham," said Arlee under her breath. "They came over early with some people from the boat."

"She must be frightfully up on the guide books," muttered Falconer.

"She's a *miner* in them," Arlee laughed, as they made their way over the rubbishy ground where great beams of stone and fallen statues lay half-buried in the sands.

"They must be very glad to have you back again with them," Falconer told her, trying hard to keep their progress ahead of the others.

"Oh, I don't know!" Honest dubiety spoke in Arlee's tone. "They have mentioned twice how convenient it was to use my stateroom!"

"They felt very badly when you ran away from them in Cairo."

"I was shockingly sudden about that," owned the girl lightly, "but the chance came—Are we going to climb the great pylon now?"

"It will be a jolly high place to see the moon rise."

It *was* a jolly high place to see the moon rise, and to see all Karnak, and all Luxor, with its high Moslem minaret towering over its crumbling columns, and to see the dark and distant country with its tiny hamlets crouching under humbler mosques and lonely palms, and on the other side the wide and winding Nile with the shadowy cliffs of Thebes beyond. It gave Arlee the dizzying sensation of being suspended between heaven and earth, so high was she above those far-reaching plains, so high above the giant columns beneath her, the vast beamed roofs, the pointing obelisks. It made her breath quicken and her pulses beat.

"Watch the moon," said Falconer in a low tone.

Blood-red it rose behind the dark pile, throwing into sinister relief a gallows-like angle of stone beams, then higher and higher it soared till its resplendent light poured unchecked into the wide courts and broken temples, the unroofed altars and the empty shrines.

"A dead world lighting a dead world," said Arlee under her breath.

"I could read by it," stated Miss Falconer impressively.

Lady Claire glanced up at Billy with a touch of mischief. "Would you like to paint it?" she suggested.

"Heaven forbid!" said Billy soberly.

Falconer said nothing at all, except to Arlee. He was very shrewdly drawing her to the other end of the pylon, seeing that the time of descent was nearly upon them. And when the time arrived, and the English ladies and their stoic escort started down the steep steps, Falconer made no motion of following them. He stood still, his hands in his pockets, and chuckled softly at the sound of his sister's voice, floating lesseningly up to them.

"How Emma is dragoning that William Whatdycallit Hill," he said appreciatively.

"Why do you call him that?" questioned Arlee.

"Oh, that chap is so deuced odd about that name of his. I asked him what the B. stood for, and he looked me in the eye like a fighting cock and said for his middle name.... Queer chap—" Suddenly Falconer looked sidewise at Arlee and stopped.

"He is—unusual," she agreed, moving toward the steps.

The curious expression upon Falconer's face deepened. "Let 'em go on," he said jerkily. "I don't want to leave this yet, do you?"

Arlee glanced about hesitantly, without answering, and slowly she let fall the white froth of skirt she had been gathering for the descent.

In silence she looked out over the temple. The moon had paled from fire to molten silver now, and like scattered sparks of it burned the thousand circling stars. She felt very strange and unreal—a tiny figure topping this great gate in the face of the ancient silence....

"We never have a chance for a word together," Falconer was mumbling, with a nervous hand at his mustache.

Her thoughts came fleetly back from the ancient worlds.... Her own was upon her. She turned and laughed at him. "We've talked for three whole days!"

"Have we? But always in some group.... I understand that Hill told you what a couple of donkeys we made of ourselves on your account?" Anxiously he scanned her face, silver-clear in the moonlight, for signs of ridicule.

But Arlee's smile was very sweet. It made the sandy-haired young man's heart quicken mysteriously. "He told me," she said. "I think it was fine of you."

"Fine? It was lunacy.... He'd got worked up over some horrible story he'd heard," went on the young man in the mingling humor and embarrassment, "and nothing for it but that you'd gone the same way. And if you'll believe it, he had us prowling around that old palace like a pair of jolly idiots primed to get their heads blown off—and served us jolly well right! He was in luck to get off with nothing but a scratch."

"A scratch—? You mean—you *don't* mean——?"

"He didn't tell you that?" Falconer was surprised; he had imagined that Billy's narration had led romantically to Billy's wound. He made the American a silent apology. "He was shot in the arm."

"Badly?"

"Of course not badly—he's all right now, isn't he? He said it was a scratch."

Arlee was silent. He had been hurt all the time that he had been riding with her over the desert ... he had been hurt all through those horrible hot hours. And he had said nothing....

"When I think of what that chap got me in for—scaling a man's walls, smashing in his locks, letting myself down the front of his house like a monkey on a rope! I might have been a dashed school kid again." Resentment and reluctant humor struggled in the young man's speech. "Why, the fellow has the imagination of a detective ... and of course he had some reason." Falconer's thoughts touched on the fair-haired girl of Fritzi's report. "I'll admit he had me worried—until I heard from the Evershams that you were all O.K. You see what bally nonsense you put into young men's heads," he added with a look of meaning.

"He's a very—chivalrous—young man," said Arlee.

"He's a very unbalanced young idiot," contradicted Falconer. "I rather like the chap, himself, you know; he has nerve to spare—but no ballast. He might have set all Cairo talking of you." His voice hardened; "I told him that. I told him you wouldn't thank him for it."

"I do thank him. I thank him with all my heart."

"Well, you've no reason to," Falconer returned in blunt belief. "Linking your name with that Turk fellow; hinting you were in the palace—he might have started a lot of rotten rumor!"

"What's—rumor?" said the girl in a breathless voice. "He was thinking of—my safety!"

"Well, your safety didn't depend on him, did it?" Sharp jealousy of her defense of the American intruder drove Falconer to unseemly curtness. He gave a short laugh. "You and I," he said, "seem to be always tilting over some chap or other."

A faint smile touched the girl's lips, a sorry little smile, edged with rueful reminiscence ... and strange comparisons. In silence she looked down into the shadowy temple courts where absurdly small-looking people were strolling to and fro, while Falconer stood looking down at her, with something akin to angry wonder in his adoring eyes.

"Why didn't you write to a chap?" he abruptly demanded.

"Why should I?"

"Then you meant to let it go at that?" He drew a sharp breath. "Just the way you flared off from that table—not a word more?"

"Why didn't you write?" the girl parried.

"I did," indignantly. "Twice—to Alexandria."

"Oh.... I didn't get them."

"I wrote, all right. I was so stirred up over that alarm of Hill's that I urged you to answer me at once. And when you didn't, and when I heard you *had* written the Evershams, well, I thought I knew what I had to think.... When I met you here Friday I half expected you to cut me, upon my word!"

"But I didn't!" She laughed softly. "I remembered you—perfectly."

"Oh, you did, did you?... You've acted as if that was about all you did remember."

"I've been very, *very* nice to you!"

"But with a difference," he insisted resentfully. "Didn't you know I must have written? You didn't think I wanted to let it stop there, did you? You didn't think I meant that nonsense at tea — —"

"Please don't go back to that," said the girl hurriedly. "We've been good friends these three days without bringing it up — don't let us do it now."

"Well, I don't enjoy thinking about it." His voice was sharp with feeling. "You gave me the most miserable time of my life."

"I was very horrid."

"You told me you didn't give a *piastre* for what I thought!"

"I said I didn't give half a *piastre*!" murmured Arlee irrepressibly, with a wicked dimple.

Reluctantly he grinned. "Well?" he put to her questioningly.

"Well?"

Their eyes met, sparkling, combative.

"You do, don't you?"

"What?"

"You do give a *piastre* for what I — —"

"I'm afraid I do. I'm afraid I give a good many *piastres* for what everyone thinks." The girl's smile had suddenly faded; her eyes lowered and sought the far horizons.

In the silence he came a little closer to her. "Then Arlee — Arlee, dear — —"

She started, and turned hurriedly. "We must go down — —"

"Why must we?"

"They'll be waiting."

"Let 'em. They'll be glad of the chance if they can get away from Emma.... I want to talk to you."

"I think Mr. Hill is quite as nice as Lady Claire," flashed Arlee in a childish voice.

"Claire seems to agree with you." Falconer spoke lightly, but underneath sounded the note of the disgruntled male ... resentful of the defection of even the girls he left behind him. He added, with his fatal gift of truculent expression, "But that's perfectly absurd."

"Why absurd?" Arlee's voice held careful calm. The flash in her eyes was hidden.

Falconer made a gesture of extreme exasperation. To waste these precious moonlight moments in trifling debate was the very height of maddening futility.

"Oh, the chap's a feather-headed adventurer. What's the use of talking about him?... But that's aside the mark. I want— —"

"You mustn't call him an adventurer!" The flash was far from hidden now. Her wide eyes blazed challenge at the disconcerted young man. "It's not fair. It's not true."

"Oh, I don't mean it in any—any *financial* sense," the harassed Falconer gave back. "But you can't expect me to take him seriously after his exploits in Cairo? He's flighty. He goes off like a rocket. He has illusions—but— —"

"If you are going to slander him because of what he did for me—" Arlee's voice was shaking.

"Oh, can't you see that's the key to his character!"

"Yes, I do see it." She sounded triumphant now. For a moment her eyes met his full of bright defiance; she hung fire, half scared, then blazed into her revelation.

"For I was in that palace."

"What? What?" Falconer questioned in sheer vacancy of shock.

"I said—I was in that palace, Kerissen's palace."

"*What!*" came from him again, but now in twenty different intonations, with absolute incredulity struggling for dominance.

Desperately she rushed on, her voice shaken but passionate.

"I tell you it is so. He got me there by a trick, a call upon his sister. And he kept me by another trick, pretending a quarantine. I was trapped there. The messages and all the Alexandria story were Kerissen's frauds. He wanted to marry me. I'd have been there to-night if it hadn't been for Billy Hill—that adventurer, as you call him!"

It was impossible. It was unthinkable. Falconer stood staring down at this girl whose white, upturned face, so amazingly ethereal and childish, met his astounded gaze with unfaltering fixity, and from his stiff lips dropped disjointed words and phrases, ejaculations of denial, of disbelief.

She swept them utterly aside in her complete affirmation. "It's all true—every bit."

"You—in that man's palace!" He was very pale, but into her white face there surged a sudden flood of color, crimsoning it from brow to throat.

"He didn't—hurt me," she stammered. "He was—quite mad—but he didn't—hurt me."

She heard Falconer draw his breath with a queer, whistling sound. He pushed back his hat and drew his hand over his forehead.

"It's—impossible," he persisted thickly, but there was bitter relief in his voice. "The blackguard—the filthy blackguard!"

"Don't, don't, please don't! I can't bear to think of him. I've done with even the thought of him.... He was trying to make me marry him. I told you he was quite mad."

Sharply Falconer pulled himself together, in the tense effort to meet this horrible astonishment like a man.

"And Hill got you out?"

"Yes.... He got me out."

"But the Evershams—they don't know——?"

"No, no, I've told no one. I'm not going to tell anyone. No one knows of it but you and me—and Billy Hill."

"That's right." He drew another long breath, this time in sharp relief. The color was coming back to his face, splotching it unevenly. "You mustn't tell anyone. You don't know how a beastly thing like that would spread. You mustn't let anyone have a hint. Not even my sister."

Arlee's eyes were in shadow. Her voice came slowly. "They would think so badly of me?"

"No—not of you—but it's the kind of thing, the impossible things—A girl simply can't afford——"

"She can't afford to have even speculation against her," Arlee finished quietly, but a little pulse in her throat was beating away like mad. She knew he spoke the simple truth, but the taste of it was bitter as gall to her mouth. However she had humbled herself in secret self-communion, she had known no such shame as this.... She felt cheapened ... tarnished....

"It's beastly—but she can't," he jerkily agreed, but with evident relief at her sensible understanding. Perhaps he had remembered Billy's fearful prophecy of the conversation with which the adventure would supply her. "But of course nobody has a notion——"

"Not a notion. And I shan't give them any—not till I'm a white-haired old lady in Mechlin caps, and *then* I shall make up for lost time by boring all my world with the story of my romantic youth and the wild deeds done for me!" She laughed airily, pride high in her face, hiding her secret hurts.

"And Hill got you out," Falconer repeated, with a sudden twinge of jealous envy in his young voice. "He—he's a lucky one."

"*I'm* the lucky one," Arlee flashed. "Think of the glorious luck for me that sent him to paint there, outside the palace, where a maid mistook him, and so gave a message. Why, it was a chance in a million, in ten million—and it happened!"

"Happened?" Falconer looked at her a minute before continuing. Then he asked quietly, "He told you that he just—happened—there?"

"Yes, he said by accident. He was painting——"

Now Falconer was an honest young man—and a gentleman. Deliberately he brushed away his rival's generous subterfuge. "He doesn't paint," he told her. "He did that for an excuse—for a reason to stay outside the palace. No chance directed it."

"Why, how—how did he know? Before——"

"He guessed. He was uneasy from the beginning—he made conjectures and set himself to verify them."

After a moment, "I never knew—*that*!" said Arlee in slow wonder.

"Well, you know now," returned Falconer with a sense of grim justice to the man he had belittled.

In the silence the girl moved toward the steps. He made a gesture to stay her.

"You're not going—yet?"

"Yet?" she echoed, faintly mocking. "It's *hours*."

"But—but we can never see this again," he argued, weakly, parrying with himself.

"We won't—forget it."

The words held a too-keen prophecy for him. He looked at her in heart-beating uncertainty, and it seemed to him that all his future was waiting on that moment. Should he speak? Should he utter that which had been so near utterance when her astounding revelation had stopped him?... After all, he knew nothing of her—but that she was lovely and wilful and enchanting—with a capacity for risk—and a dire disregard of consequences.... She was volatile, unstable, bewildering—so he thought stiffeningly as he looked at her, but he looked too long.

She was the very spirit of loveliness in the silver moon, her hair a crown of light, her eyes deep with shadowy wistfulness, her lips half sad, half tender.... He felt the blood burn hot in his face, and took a quick step to bar the way.

"You must wait to hear what I was saying," he said, with a ring of new command.

She gave him a sudden, startled look, and moved as if to pass him.

"You were saying—nothing," she answered proudly.

"I was saying—everything," he gave back incoherently. "Oh, Arlee, do you think that story stops me! Don't you know—how much I want you?" and with sudden vehemence he bent to clasp her in his arms.

CHAPTER XXIII
THE BETTER MAN

Down in the court of Rameses, Lady Claire and Hill were straying. A most opportune old bachelor, passing with a party of acquaintances, had diverted even Emma Falconer from her dragoning, and the young English girl and her American escort were left for the time to their own devices.

Not much was said. Claire, who had been fitfully gay all afternoon, grew still as a church mouse now as they paced back and forth in the shadows, stealing a slant glance from time to time at Billy's set and silent face. She wondered a little at his absorption. But chiefly she was thinking that she had never seen him look so handsome ... with his brows knitted and his clear-cut lips pressed sharply together ... but the boy of him somehow kept by that wilful lock of black hair over his forehead.

To Billy it seemed that the bitterest drop of the cup was at his lips. Those two—upon the pylon—were they never coming down? He was waiting for them in every nerve, and yet he shrank from the look he might read upon their faces. He thought, very grimly, that this could mean but one thing, and that thing was the end forever and ever, for him.... His heart was sick in him and he longed most desperately to break away from these other women and the sham of talk and dash off to dark solitude where the primitive man could have his way, could tramp and fight and curse and sob and break his heart in decent privacy. He faced with loathing the refinements of torture which civilization imposes.

But the game had to be played. He was no quitter, he told himself fiercely; he could stand up and take his punishment like a man. She was not for him. He had loved her from the first, he had loved her so that he had been clairvoyant to her peril, he had risked his neck for her a dozen times and snatched her from a life that was a death-in-life—and yet she was not for him. She was for a man who had not believed in her danger, had not bestirred himself.... Black, seething bitterness was boiling in Billy B. Hill. Darkly, through a fog, he heard the outer man replying to some speech from the girl beside him.

He understood, he told himself in a burst of despairing anguish, how Kerissen could have plotted for her. Almost he longed to be a scrupleless

Oriental and carry her off across his saddle bow.... And then he brought himself up short.

Was that all she meant to him, he asked himself with the sweat of pain on his forehead beneath that black lock which was finding such favor in Lady Claire's eyes—was that all she meant to him?—a prize to be won? One man had tried to steal her; he had wished to *earn* her—but she was a gift beyond all price and the giving lay in her own heart alone.... And if Falconer was the man for her, then at least he, Billy B. Hill, was man enough to stand up and be glad for her and be humbly grateful to the end of his days that he had been able to save her ... and give her her happiness. For it was really he who had given it to her. And in that thought Billy Hill's young heart expanded, and his soul stretched itself to such unwonted heights that it seemed to push among the stars.

"It is an unforgettable night," said the girl in the rose cloak.

He thought that was just the word for it, and a wryly humorous glint was in the look he gave her. And he thought that she, too, was playing the game mighty stanchly, and had been playing it bravely these three days, since her conquering little rival had made her reappearance. His heart warmed toward her in understanding and compassion. They were comrades in affliction. He was not the only one in the world who was not getting the heart's desire.

Aloud he answered, "And the last night for me."

Lady Claire looked up quickly. Her voice showed her struck with sudden surprise. "You are going—so soon?"

"To-morrow."

"To Assouan?" Odd sharpness edged the question.

He waited a perceptible moment, though his resolution had been taken. "Back to Cairo."

"Oh ... How long shall you be there?"

"Just till I get sailings. It's time for me to be off. I'm really a working person, you know, not a playing one."

"You make bridges—and dams—and things, don't you?" she questioned vaguely.

"Bridges—and dams—and things."

"Why don't you wait here for your sailings?" she asked impersonally after another pause. "It's so *much* more attractive here than Cairo."

"I'd like to." He thought of next Friday—and Arlee's return—and the masked ball. For a moment temptation urged. Then he threw back his head with a gesture of decision. "But I can't. It's impossible."

Now Lady Claire did not know that he was thinking of next Friday—and Arlee's return—and the masked ball. She only knew that he spoke with a curious fierceness, and that his eyes were very bright. And something in the girl, something strange and acknowledged that had been so fitfully gay and light these three days, quickened in mysterious excitement.

"Nothing is impossible," she gave back, "to a *man!*"

Billy thought she was resenting the conventions of the restricted sex. She could not make any open advance toward Falconer while he, as man, could make all the open advances to Arlee he was willing to—but in this case his hands were tied. A man cannot inflict himself upon a girl who may not feel herself free to reject him. He laughed, with sorry ruefulness.

"There's a whole lot," he observed, "that is impossible to a man who tries to be one," and then, oblivious of any construction she might choose to put upon this cryptic utterance, he strolled moodily on, in brooding silence.

After a pause, "Of course," said Lady Claire in so gentle a little voice that it seemed to glide undisturbingly among his silent meditations, "of course, a man has his—pride."

"I hope so," said the young man briefly. He understood her to be probing for his reason for abandoning the chase; he understood that for her sake she would like to see him successful with Arlee, and he was queerly sorry to be failing to help her there. But he had done all that he could....

The girl spoke again, her face straight ahead, her shadowy eyes staring out into the moonlight. "Is it—money?" she said in the same little breath of a voice.

"Money!" Billy threw back the words in surprise, half contemptuous, "Oh, Lord, no, it's not *money*! I haven't much of it *now*, but I'm going to make a bunch of the stuff—if I want to." He spoke with naïve and amazing confidence which somehow struck astounded belief into the listener. "There's enough of it there, waiting to be made—no, it's not money—though perhaps one might well think it ought to be. I suppose my work might strike a girl as hard for her," he went on, considering aloud these problems of existence, "for it's here to-day and there to-morrow—now doing a building in a roaring city and now damming up some reservoir deep in the mountains—but it always seemed to me that the girl who would like me would like that, too. It's seeing so much of life—and such real life!

Oh, no," he said, and though a trace of doubt had struck into his voice, "that in itself wouldn't be what I'd call impossible—not for the right girl."

"But your work—would it always be in America?" said Lady Claire.

"Oh, always. It has to be, of course."

"Oh.... And—and—you—have to have—that work?"

"Why, of course, I have to have it!" Billy was bewildered, but entirely positive. "That's *my* work—the thing I'm made to do. *I* couldn't earn my salt selling apartment houses."

"Oh, no, no," the girl hurriedly agreed.

A long, long silence followed, a silence in which he was entirely oblivious to her imaginings. The moonlight lay heavy as dreams about them; her thoughts went darting to and fro like fluttering swallows.... She felt herself a stranger to herself.... She looked up at him with a sudden deer-like lift of her head, and then looked swiftly away.

"Don't go," she said in a quick, low voice. "Don't go—yet. Even things that look impossible—can be made to come right."

He understood that she was pleading with him, partly for the sake of her own chance with Falconer, but the sympathy flicked him on the raw. He was sorry for her, sorry for the queer, strained look in her face, sorry for the voice so full of feeling, but he couldn't do anything to help her.

In silence he shook his head and was astounded at the look of sudden proud anger she darted at him.

"You're a mighty real friend to take such an interest in my luck," he said quickly, with warm liking in his voice, "and I only wish you could play fairy godmother and give me my wish—but you can't, Lady Claire, and apparently *she* won't, and that is the end of the matter. I have to take off my hat to the Better Man."

Lady Claire did not gasp or stammer or question. She did none of the dismayedly enlightening things into which a lesser poise might have tottered. After an inconsiderable moment of silence she merely uttered her familiar, "Oh!" and uttered it in a voice in which so many things were blended that their elements could hardly be perceived.

She added hurriedly, "I'm sorry if I've seemed to—to intrude into your affairs."

"My affairs are on my sleeve," answered Billy and wondered at the quick look she gave him.

"Oh, no—not at all," she answered a little breathlessly. "I'm sure they haven't seemed so to me—but then I'm stupid." She stopped for a moment of hot wonder at that stupidity. She had not believed Miss Falconer—had thought her prejudiced ... maneuvering.... Like lightning she reviewed the baffling interchange of sentences, then glanced up at Billy's silent absorption. She felt queerly grateful for his innocent density. "And perhaps *she's* stupid, too," she told him. "You'd better make sure. You'd better make absolutely *sure*."

He looked down on her with sorry humor in his face. "Do I need to make *surer*?" He nodded in the direction of the giant gateway. "They've had time to settle the divisions of the Balkans up there."

"Oh, yes, they've had time!" She seemed speaking at sudden laughing random. "But *we've* had the same time and you see we haven't settled anything with it—not even that you're to stay. Yes, you'd better make *sure*, Mr. Hill."

Billy was hardly heeding. A laugh had caught his ears, a light high laugh like the tinkle of a little silver bell through the darkness. In the shadows behind them he made out a man and a woman arm in arm.

"Just a moment," he begged of Lady Claire. "May I leave you here a moment? I must see those—I think I know——" Without listening to her automatic permission he was gone.

The next moment he had laid his hand on the arm of the man with the woman. Both spun quickly about. A babble of explanation broke out.

"*Ach, mein freund, mein freund——*"

"Oh, it is Billy——"

"How *gut* to find you here——"

"Our American Billy."

The last voice, piquantly foreign, was the voice of Fritzi Baroff. And the first voice gutterally foreign was the voice of Frederick von Deigen. Arm in arm, flushed, happy, sentimental, the two began talking in a breath, thanking Billy for the letter he had sent von Deigen which had brought them together, and apologizing for their hasty flight—"a honeymoon upon the Nile," the German joyfully explained.

Discreetly Billy forbore to make any discoveries as to the exact status of their "honeymoon." The German's face was very honestly happy, and the little dancer was brimming with restless life and vivacity.

"It was the picture in my watch—*hein*? The picture I carry night and day," Frederick repeated in needless explanation, and was about to draw out the picture when Billy restrained him.

He had a favor to ask. The American girl of Kerissen's palace had escaped unharmed and returned to her friends who were ignorant of all. She was this moment in the ruins. It would be a great shock to her to meet Fritzi, to have Fritzi recognize her. On the morning she would be gone. Would Fritzi——"

"Fritzi must disappear—for the night?" said the little Viennese smiling wisely, but with a trace of cynicism. "The little American must not be reminded—h'm? We will go.... For you have done so much for me, you big, strange, platonic Mr. Billy!" Dazzlingly she smiled on him, her dark eyes quizzically provocative.

"You're not at the Grand?"

"No, not that." She named another. "You come see me, when that girl goes—h'm?"

Billy caught the German's eyes upon him, in their depths a faint trouble, a vague appeal. He comprehended that the infatuated young man had engaged in the tortuous business of keeping sparks from tinder.

"I'm gone to-morrow," he replied.

"Maybe in Vienna?" went on the dancer. "We go soon—another day or so maybe—and then back over the water to that life I left! Oh, my God, how happy I am to go back to it all—to dance, to sing—Oh, I could kiss you, Mr. Billy, if it would not make you so shock!" she added with a malicious little laugh. "You know the news—about *him*—h'm?"

"Him?"

"Kerissen—that devil fellow. He is in Cairo with a fever—in the hospital there. A man who come from that hospital just tells us—just by accident he tell us. A *bad* fever, too!" She laughed in satisfaction. "I hope he burn good and hard up," she added, with energetic spite, "and teach him not to act like a wild man. That man say he got a bad hand," she added, with a shrewd glance at Billy.

The young man merely grunted. "I hope he has," he replied. "It matches the rest of him. Good night."

"Good night—for the now—h'm, Mr. Billy?" and with a quick little clasp of his big hand and a gay little backward look the girl was gone into the shadows upon the arm of her jealous cavalier.

Three people were waiting at the statue foot where he had left the English girl.

"They've come at last, Mr. Hill," Lady Claire's voice struck very gaily upon him, "and Miss Falconer has just come to tell us we must see the colored lights in the great court—and then go home. So hurry!"

She turned as she spoke and put her arm suddenly through Falconer's who was standing next her. "Come on," she lightly commanded, and promptly led the way.

That was something like a fairy godmother! Into Billy's eyes flashed a warm light of gladness. Some moments out of that wretched evening should yet be his own, bitter-sweet as they were in their sharp finality.

He turned to the blue-cloaked figure at his side. "Do you like colored fire?" he demanded. "Won't you come and see something else—something I've wanted to see and to have you see with me? It's near the way out. We can meet them at the pylon."

Of course she acquiesced. That was part of the cursed restraint between them, he was reminded, to have her accept so obediently any point-blank request of his. But for the nonce he was glad. He wanted those few minutes desperately.

"What is it?" she murmured.

"I'll show you," and then, as he turned from the way they had come and followed a winding path that dipped lower and lower between the dune-like piles of sand, "It's the Sacred Lake," he explained. "Perhaps you've seen it in the daytime—but I've been wanting to see it at night."

"I think I just caught the glint of it from the pylon," she observed.

"You had time to," said Billy, trying to twinkle down at her in friendly fashion.

She did not twinkle back. She looked as suddenly guilty as a kitten in the cream, and Billy's heart smote him heavily. He did not speak again till they had rounded a corner and their path had brought them out upon the shore of the Sacred Lake.

Like a little horseshoe it circled about three sides of the ruined temple of the goddess Mut, inky-black and motionless with the stars looking up uncannily like drowned lights from its still waters, and inky-black and motionless, like guardian spirits about it, sat a hundred cat-headed women of grim granite. It was a spot of stark loneliness and utter silence, of ancient terror and desolate abandonment; the solitude and the blackness and the aching age smote upon the imagination like a heavy hand upon harp strings.

"Who are—they?" Arlee spoke in a hushed voice, as if the cat-headed women were straining their ears.

"They're mysteries," said Billy, speaking in the same low tone. "Generally they're said to be statues of the Goddess Pasht or Sehket—but it's a riddle why the Amen-hotep person who built this temple to the goddess Mut should have put Sehket here. Sehket is in the trinity of Memphis—and Mut in that of Thebes. And so some people say that this is not Pasht at all, but Mut herself, who was sometimes represented as lion-headed. Between a giant cat and a lion, you know, there's not much of difference."

"I like Pasht better than Mut," said Arlee decidedly.

"There you agree with Baedecker."

"What did Pasht do?"

"She was goddess of girls," said Billy, "and young wives. She got the girls husbands and the wives—er—their requests. Girls used to come down here at night and make a prayer to her and cast an offering into the waters."

"And then they had their prayer?"

"Infallibly."

"I'd like a guardian like that," said Arlee, with a sudden mischievous wistfulness that played the dickens with Billy's forces of reserve. "Do you think she'd grant *my* prayer?"

"Have you one to make?" said Billy, staring very hard for safety at the monstrous images.

"They look as if they were coming alive," he added.

The moon had come up over an obstructing roof and now flashed down upon them; a ripple of light began to swim across the star-eyes in the inky waters; a finger of quicksilver seemed to be playing over the scarred faces of the granite goddesses.

"They never died," said Arlee positively. "They're just waiting their time. Can't you see they know all about us?... They particularly know that you are the most deceiving young man they ever saw! Why didn't you tell me you were shot in the arm?" she finished rapidly.

"What?... Where did you hear that?"

"Mr. Falconer enlightened me."

"I wish Falconer would keep his stories to himself," said Billy ungratefully. "It's just a——"

"Scratch," said Arlee promptly. "That's always a hero's word for it."

Billy turned scarlet. He felt hot back to his ears.

"And why did you tell me that you *happened* to be painting outside the palace?" went on the unsparing voice. "You let me think it was all accident—and it was all you, just *you!*"

"Good Lord," groaned Billy, effecting merriment over his discomfiture, "Is there anything else he told you?... Look here, you shouldn't have been talking about it," he said with sudden anxiety.

Arlee smiled. "It's all over," she said. "I told him everything."

Billy's heart missed a beat, and then hurried painfully to make up for it. He felt a curious constriction in his throat. He tried to think of something congratulatory to say and was lamentably silent.

"Why did you deceive me so?" she continued mercilessly. "Because my gratitude was so *obnoxious* to you? Were you so afraid I would insist upon flinging more upon you?"

"That's a horrid word, obnoxious," said Billy painfully.

"I thought so," thrust in a pointed voice.

"I only meant," he slowly made out, "that a sense of—of obligation is a stupid burden—and I didn't want you to feel you had to be any more friendly to me than your heart dictated. That is all. It was enough for me to remember that I had once been privileged to help you."

"You—funny—Billy B. Hill person," said the voice in a very serious tone. Billy continued staring at the unwinking old goddess ahead of him. "You take it all so for granted," laughed Arlee softly, "As if it were part of any day's work! I go about like a girl in a dream—or a girl *with* a dream ... a dream of fear, of old palaces and painted women and darkened windows. It comes over me at night sometimes. And then I wake and could go down on my knees to you.... I suppose there isn't any more danger from him?" she broke off to half-whisper quickly.

"He's sick in the Cairo hospital," Billy made haste to inform her. "I found out by accident. I understand he has a bad fever. So I think he'll be up to no more tricks—and I'm out the satisfaction of a little heart-to-heart talk."

"Oh, I told you you couldn't," she cried quickly. "You would make him too angry. He isn't just—sane."

"Then all I have to do in Egypt is to hunt up my little Imp," said Billy. "I must see the little chap again—before I go."

He waited—uselessly as he had foretold. She said nothing, and if the glance he felt upon him was of inquiry he did not look about to meet it. He was still staring a saturnine Pasht out of countenance. There was a pause.

Then, "However were you able to think of it all?" said Arlee in slow wonder. "However were you able to think such an impossible thought as my imprisonment?"

"Because I was thinking about you," said Billy. Suddenly his tongue ran away with him. "Incessantly," he added.

She looked up at him. Unguardedly he looked down at her. No one but a blind girl or a goose could have mistaken that look upon Billy B. Hill's young face, the frustrate longing of it, the deep desire. The heart beneath the sky-blue cloak cast off a most monstrous accumulation of doubts and fears and began suddenly to beat like mad.

Totally unexpectedly, startlingly amazing, she flung out at him, "Then what made you stop?"

"Stop?" he echoed. "Stop? I've never stopped! There hasn't been a moment——"

"There have been three days. Three—horrible—days!"

"Arlee!"

"Do you think I *like* being snubbed and ignored and—and—obliterated?" she brought indignantly out. "Do you think I call that—being friends?"

"I—I wanted to leave you free—not to force your friendship——" he stammered wildly.

"You couldn't force *mine*," said Arlee Beecher.

"But—but there was Falconer," he protested. "You had to be free to—to have a choice——"

"A choice? Do you call that a *choice*?"

"I thought you were making it. That first night——"

"I stayed up to dance with *you*," she cried hotly. "You never came back!"

"But the next day——"

"I *wanted* to go. But I couldn't keep up any more. I *had* to rest.... And you went with Lady Claire!"

"Why, I had to! We'd planned. But when we came back, he was on deck with you——"

"Yes, and I was waiting up—to see *you*. And you only took two dances that night——"

"You didn't seem to want me to——"

"I never guessed you wanted them! *I* had my pride, too. I wasn't going to be in the way—because you'd rescued me. I thought you didn't want me in the way!"

"Arlee—my girl—my precious girl——"

"No, I'm not. I'm not."

"Yes, you are," he said fiercely. "I don't care if you are engaged to Falconer or not, I'm going to tell you so."

"I'm not engaged to Falconer," she protested.

He blurted in bewilderment. "Then what in the world were you doing up there on that pylon?"

Her elfish laughter disconcerted him. "Do you think one has to get engaged if she stays on a pylon?... We were getting *not* engaged."

"I thought—I thought you liked him," he said bewilderedly.

"I did. I do, I mean—but not that way. He—he—Oh, I really *like* him," she cried tremulously, "but not—we've had it all out and everything's all over. I'm sorry—sorry—but he'll be really glad bye and bye. For my story shocked him terribly.... And then there's Lady Claire. He didn't like to have her down with you even when he was up with me." She laughed softly. "Oh, I shouldn't have let him be so friendly here but I did like him and you—you were so—so hateful."

The moon and stars whirled giddily around him as he put his arms about her. Like a man in a dream he drew her to him.

"I love you—love you," he said huskily over the bright maze of hair.

"You don't!" came with muffled intensity from the hidden lips. "You said to that man—when I was in that cave—'Nothing doing!'"

"It wasn't his affair—I hadn't a hope.... Oh, my dear, my dear, I've been breaking my heart——"

"And I've had such a perfectly h-hateful three days," sobbed the voice.

His arms closed tighter about her, incredible of their happiness.

"Oh, Arlee, I can't tell you—I haven't words——"

"I've had *deeds!*" she whispered.

Through his rocking mind darted a memory of her earlier speech to him. "You said you didn't want words. Arlee—*will you?*"

She flung back her head and looked up at him, her face a flower, her eyes like stars tangled in the bright mist of her hair.

"Billy, what's your middle name?"

"Bunker.... I can't help it, dear. They wished it on me and asked me not to let it go. But *Bunker Hill*— —!"

"It's a wonderful name, Billy! A perfectly irresistible name!" Her eyes laughed up at him through a dazzle of tears, and prankishly over her curving lips hovered a mischievous dimple. "It's a name—that—I—simply—can't—do—without—Billy Bunker Hill!"

The dimple deepened then fled before its just deserts. For if ever a dimple deserved to be caught and kissed that was the one.